ESSAYS IN LABOUR HISTORY 1918 — 1939

Essays in Labour History 1918 - 1939

Edited by

ASA BRIGGS
Provost of Worcester College, Oxford

JOHN SAVILLE
Professor of Economic and Social History University of Hull

CROOM HELM   LONDON

ARCHON BOOKS, HAMDEN, CONNECTICUT

© 1977 Asa Briggs and John Saville
© 1977 *The Striker Stricken* Margaret Cole

Croom Helm Ltd, 2-10 St John's Road, London SW11

ISBN 0-85664-239-9

First published in the United States of America 1977
as an ARCHON BOOK, an imprint of
The Shoe String Press, Inc., Hamden, Ct.

Library of Congress Cataloging in Publication Data
Main entry under title:
Essays in labour history, 1918-1939.

    Includes bibliographical references and index.
    1. Labor and laboring classes — Great Britain —
Addresses, essays, lectures. 2. Trade-unions —
Great Britain — Addresses, essays, lectures.
I. Briggs, Asa. II. Saville, John.
HD8290.E78   331'.0941   76-30487
ISBN 0-208-01641-4

Printed in Great Britain
by Redwood Burn Ltd, Trowbridge and Esher

CONTENTS

FOREWORD

This is the third collection of essays we have edited under the same title. The first, published in 1960, was a memorial volume to GDH Cole who had died in the previous year. The essays spanned the whole of the nineteenth century. The second volume, published in 1971, covered the closing years of the nineteenth century to the period immediately after the first world war. We promised a third volume dealing with the years between the wars, and this we have now produced.

We wish especially to thank Dame Margaret Cole. She has been associated with these volumes from the beginning, and we are particularly glad to be able to publish again one of her own essays. We are further grateful to her for allowing us to publish the famous operetta, *The Striker Stricken*, which Douglas Cole wrote very soon after the 1926 General Strike was called off. It has been talked about for many years, but very few have seen the script, and now we are able to present it with editorial notes by Margaret Cole herself.

Among others who have helped with this volume, we offer our thanks to Dr Joyce Bellamy, whose expert editorial abilities have always been available to us; to our publishers, David Croom and Judy Bennett; and to Dr Marion Kozak, who compiled the Index. To our contributors we owe much and we must record our thanks for their individual essays as well as their collective patience.

AB
JS

1 CONCESSION AND COERCION: THE POLITICS OF UNEMPLOYMENT INSURANCE IN THE TWENTIES

Alan Deacon

The existence of a potentially revolutionary situation in Britain in the years immediately after the First World War is uncertain. That the period saw widespread industrial unrest, together with disaffection in the army, navy, and even the police, is clear, but whether or not such events constituted 'elements of real danger to the social order'[1] is a matter of interpretation. As Adams notes, 'no accurate historical apparatus exists for such assessments.'[2] None the less, there can be little doubt of the concern with which contemporary politicians viewed the situation, or that the need to avert political disorder became a dominant influence upon them. This is especially true of the 1918-22 Coalition and Lloyd George's role is often seen as crucial. Morgan refers to his 'skilful delaying tactics'; Saville — more bluntly — to the 'judicious mixture of lies, half-truths, evasion and deceit' with which he saw 1919 'through to tame conclusions'.[3]

There remains, however, a surprising neglect in the literature of the role played by social policy in this context. This stems from a general preoccupation with industrial relations, and a consequent failure to appreciate both the militancy of the unemployed and the anxiety it generated in Whitehall. The release of the Cabinet and Departmental papers, however, has done much to redress the balance, and here the work of Bentley Gilbert has been particularly influential. In Gilbert's view the 1920s were years when successive governments were faced:

> not with the request for charity for the helpless, but with an intract-able demand for work or maintenance from society's most dangerous and volatile element, the unemployed adult male. Beside the threat of revolution, nothing else was important.[4]

The increase in public expenditure upon unemployment relief in the decade appears to provide a striking vindication of Gilbert's assertion, all the more so when it is compared with spending on health or education. Between 1920 and 1930, for example, the state contribution to the Unemployment Insurance Fund rose from £3,100,000 to £37,000,000, or from 3.4 per cent of expenditure on the social services (excluding war pensions) to 37 per cent.[5] Although part of this increase was simply a reflection of the large numbers who were unemployed — over a million throughout the decade — the real value of benefits also rose substantially, and that this was due to something more than the kind hearts of Ministers is indisputable. Even so, to present the expansion of relief as simply a series of concessions to working-class militancy is an over-simplification. This is not because unrest was unimportant, but because the concessions were not as great as Gilbert maintains. In particular his statement that the 'safeguards to the unemployment fund virtually were forgotten'[6] ignores a series of regulations governing eligibility for insurance benefits which were introduced in 1921 and 1922 and extended thereafter. These were of the greatest significance and were to result in nearly 20 per cent of applicants being refused benefit by the end of 1927. Thus, at the same time as benefits were becoming more generous, administrative changes were reducing the impact of those concessions.

The nature and operation of the new regulations are examined below. Such an examination, however, itself raises a further question; how did they come to operate with such effect in the political circumstances of the twenties? If, in other words, it was politically impossible for governments to cut the rates of benefit, why were they able to tighten their administration so dramatically? The answers, of course, must be sought in the attitudes towards administration held within the Labour Party and the extra-Parliamentary groups which claimed to represent the unemployed. That these were both complex and changing is indicated by the fact that the most important regulation — the genuinely seeking work test — was extended by the first Labour government only to be abolished by the second. The extension aroused virtually no opposition in the labour movement as a whole, while its later abolition split the movement down the middle.

The purpose of the present essay is consequently twofold. First, to examine the policies of the Coalition and following Conservative administrations in the field of unemployment insurance, and second, to explain both the response of the labour movement towards these and the measures of the first two Labour governments.

I

It is argued below that the unemployment insurance scheme was extended in the early 1920s because Ministers were convinced that such a concession was essential if a serious threat to political stability was to be avoided. Several reasons for this belief can be located, most obviously the extent and violence of the unrest and the manner in which information upon it was transmitted to the Cabinet. The perceptions of Ministers of the events in Continental Europe after the Armistice, however, were also important, and it is impossible to appreciate the apprehension with which British Cabinets viewed domestic unrest unless the lessons which they drew from those events are understood.

The deepest impression had been made by the troubles in Germany, where the naval mutiny of November 1918 had been followed by the proclamation of a Republic and, later, the declaration of Soviet Bavaria. Before 1911 Germany's social services had been the model for many British social reformers, and Lloyd George was quick to note the implications of her apparent collapse. He told the Cabinet in March 1919:

> Russia had gone over almost completely to Bolshevism and we had consoled ourselves with the thought that they were only a half civilised race; but now even in Germany, whose people were without exception the best educated in Europe, prospects are very black . . . Great Britain would hold out, but only if the people were given a sense of confidence — only if they were made to believe that things were being done for them.[7]

Above all, events in Europe were believed to have shown the dangers that could arise from the activities of small well-organised groups even when the bulk of the population remained docile. These would be particularly acute in the case of the unemployed where the political repercussions of unrest would be formidable, even if no general uprising occurred. Lloyd George in 1921:

> No Government could hope to face the opprobrium which would fall upon it if extreme measures had to be taken against starving men who had fought for their country and were driven to violent courses by the desperation of their position.[8]

Trouble first arose in London towards the end of 1920. In October there was a violent clash between police and over 20,000 demonstrators, and by early December three town halls, five libraries and numerous other buildings were occupied by the unemployed. Following a series of street battles in Whitehall, the government announced that it was considering the erection of permanent iron gates to guard the approaches to public buildings. These would be 'more effective, more dignified, and in the long run, considerably cheaper than a continual series of wooden barricades.'[9]

Similar events spread rapidly across the country in the wake of rising unemployment. By January 1921 the rate amongst insured persons had risen from 3.7 per cent in the previous November, to 8.2 per cent. By March it stood at 11.3 per cent and in June reached 18 per cent with a further 10 per cent on short time. In April 1921 the National Unemployed Workers Movement was formed to channel the resulting disaffection into a national campaign for 'work or maintenance'. The obvious first targets for the Movement's National Organiser, Wal Hannington, were the local Boards of Guardians. In areas where the Poor Law was still being strictly administered, his tactic was to combine mass applications to the workhouses with demonstrations in support of higher scales of relief, leading if possible to spectacular occupations of the Guardians' offices.[10] Although it never included more than a tenth of the unemployed in its membership, and propagated little in the way of a revolutionary theory, the Movement's activities seemed to Whitehall to epitomise the minority action which foreign events had taught them to expect and to fear.

Almost as significant as the unrest itself, however, was the often alarmist manner in which it was reported to the Cabinet by the Home Office Directorate of Intelligence.[11] This supplied weekly reports on 'Revolutionary Organisations in the United Kingdom', containing surveys of all the demonstrations and meetings of the unemployed together with dire warnings of impending doom if their sufferings were not relieved. On 8 September 1921, for example, a report claimed:

> The organisation of the unemployed is proceeding feverishly, the outstanding feature being the demands made on the Guardians in every English county. The Labour Party appears likely to be hoist with its own petard for the demand for full maintenance has been adopted by the extremists to an extent which has alarmed even the Woolwich Labour Councillors . . . the tendency to demonstrate is spreading with lightning rapidity.[12]

There followed a seventeen-page summary of the disturbances which had occurred in different parts of the country, the largest number being inspired by the NUWM. In Woolwich some 10,000 marchers had barricaded the Guardians in their offices after they had refused to increase the rate of relief, in Hackney the workhouse was occupied, in Bristol the offices of the Guardians were stormed, and in the subsequent riot 'the police were pelted with stones and wood paving blocks and struck with the banner poles of the demonstrators, who carried red flags.'

It was this report which lay behind the warning given to the Cabinet by the Minister of Labour, Thomas Macnamara, on 17 September:

> Hopelessly embarrassed though our finances may be, the situation is one which has got to be faced if grave civil disorder is to be avoided. The Communists have, I think, failed this time just as they failed in connection with the dispute in the Mining Industry. But the winter will give them an opportunity the like of which they have not yet had.[13]

Nor was the alarm confined to Whitehall. On 1 September, Lloyd George had received a letter from the King expressing the latter's fears with stark clarity: 'The people grow discontented and agitators seize their opportunities: marches are organised; the police interfere; resistance ensues; troops are called out and riot begets revolt and possibly revolution.'[14]

In the short run the only alternative to the insurance scheme as an agency of relief was the locally financed Poor Law. The prospect of sending the unemployed to the Guardians *en masse*, however, was daunting. Quite apart from the political consequences, it was extremely doubtful if the Guardians in the poorer areas would be able to cope, since the areas of highest unemployment were also those with the lowest rateable values. The only solution would have been an equalisation of the costs of relief, either through the subsidisation of the poorer Guardians by the richer, or by direct Exchequer help to the poorer. Any such scheme, however, would only encourage the small but growing number of Boards who were paying generous relief in open defiance of the Ministry of Health. As the Minister, Alfred Mond, admitted: 'There is no machinery in existence which could be utilised to prevent the extravagant authorities from exploiting the rest of the community.'[15] Faced with the unemployed on the one hand, and the equally angry poor law authorities on the other,[16] successive governments were forced to make drastic changes in the insurance scheme. These changes took two forms, substantial increases in the real value of benefits and, most important, continual extensions of the length of time for which they could be drawn.

Compulsory unemployment insurance was introduced in 1911 and extended to cover some twelve million workers in 1920. Under the Act of 1920, no claimant could draw benefit for more than 26 weeks in any year and, within this limit, the benefit he could receive was directly related to the contributions he had previously paid in the ratio of one week's benefit for six weeks' contributions. This ratio, the 'one-in-six' rule, was regarded as the chief safeguard against abuse of the scheme, since it was assumed that anyone who really wanted to work would soon find a job and only the malingerer would exhaust his right to benefit. Moreover, the fear of being without benefit in times of real need was believed to discourage those tempted to remain voluntarily idle when jobs were available. Thus, Winston Churchill had assured the Commons when first introducing the scheme in 1911:

> . . . a workman who will malinger in unemployment insurance . . .
> is only drawing his benefit out at a time when he does not want it
> instead of keeping it for a period when he really will be unemployed.
> If he malingers he malingers against himself. I hope I have convinced
> the House that the danger is not a serious one.[17]

Similarly, Sir Alfred Watson declared in February 1921 that the rule was 'equitable', since it 'imposes an automatic check upon the benefit claims of a somewhat shiftless class of the community'.[18] The continued operation of this 'automatic check', however, was impossible at a time of mass unemployment. The Acts assumed that the vast proportion of the unemployed would find another job within weeks and that only a malingerer would be affected by the one-in-six rule. By early 1921 that assumption was demonstrably invalid and with 800,000 about to run out of benefit a panicking Cabinet authorised the introduction of *uncovenanted* benefit; benefit payable over and above that to which an individual was already entitled by virtue of his contributions. The Act of March 1921 abandoned the one-in-six rule just twelve weeks after the 1920 scheme had gone into operation. Nor was it quickly restored. The wilder fears of a general insurrection had abated by 1923, but with over a million unemployed throughout the decade, the political — and practical — obstacles to throwing the burden on to the Poor Law remained. In such a situation few politicians were prepared to face the consequence of abolishing benefit in advance of contributions,[19] and in practice this was paid almost continuously after April 1922. As Bakke noted, the total effect of the one-in-six rule was to make 'necessary the writing of an extra clause in every Act to make the provisions of that Act apply in spite of the rule.'[20]

Similarly, the real value of benefits rose substantially during the decade, particularly those paid to men with families after the introduction of dependants' allowances in November 1921. No attempt had been made to present the 15s. (75p) provided by the 1920 Act as sufficient for maintenance, and the argument that its role was merely to supplement the worker's own savings was destroyed by the suddenness and scale of the unemployment. Compared with November 1920, the amount drawn by a man with a dependent wife and two children had risen 155 per cent in real terms by the end of 1924 and 240 per cent by May 1931. The corresponding figures for single men were 70 per cent and 92 per cent.[21]

In all, more than twenty Acts relating to unemployment insurance were passed during the twenties as successive governments sought to adapt the scheme to political and economic conditions very different from those envisaged by its authors.

II

The onset of mass unemployment and consequent threat of unrest had thus resulted in a major extension of unemployment insurance. This extension, however, was not accompanied by any reconsideration of the nature of insurance within Whitehall, and a return to the principles of 1920 remained the major aim of policy. Nor is this surprising, since the contributory basis of the original scheme had embodied a careful balance between the conflicting aims of maintaining political stability on the one hand, and the pursuit of economy in public expenditure on the other. Throughout the twenties the former was to prove more expensive than had been anticipated, but the goal of economy was never abandoned. Indeed, the reverse was true: the higher the level of benefit and the longer the period for which it was paid, the more earnest was the search for ways of reducing the cost. Similarly, the removal of the 'automatic check' which had been imposed upon claimants by the one-in-six rule, meant that abuse was believed to be a serious problem once more. 'The fear of running through benefits', Churchill had told his colleagues in 1911, 'must be constantly operative.'[22] Now that 'fear' was lifted and something had to be found to replace it.

The most obvious result of the search for economy was the means test. The formal position was that *uncovenanted* benefit was paid at the discretion of the Minister, and claimants who lacked the requisite contributions for the normal — or *covenanted* — benefit had to appear before a Local Employment Committee. These Committees, the composition of which is discussed below, submitted recommendations to the Minister as to whether benefit should or should not be granted in each case. In February 1922 they were told to withhold benefit from certain categories of claimants unless to do so would cause hardship. Those affected were: married persons whose partners were in full-time work, single persons resident with relatives, short-time workers, and aliens. Clearly the Minister's instruction meant that a household means test would have to be applied and Investigating Officers were attached to each Committee for this purpose.[23] Ministers constantly denied that any scale had been laid down, but the Divisional Controllers who were responsible for the initial vetting of the Committees' recommendations, were told that benefit should be allowed where the total income was below 10s. (50p) per head per week, refused where it exceeded 13s. (65p), and that between these limits the Committees were to be given full discretion.[24] This instruction was issued in May 1922 but was not publicly admitted until March 1926.[25]

The means test was bitterly opposed by all sections of the labour movement since its operation required the introduction into insurance of methods hitherto confined to the Poor Law. The 'inquisitorial investigations now taking place into home income'[26] aroused intense anger and one of the first measures of the Labour government of 1924 was the withdrawal of the means test. The Conservatives, however, reintroduced it in a more stringent form in August 1925, and henceforth some 3 per cent of all applications for benefit by men, and 15 per cent of those made by women, were refused on income grounds.[27]

The impact of the means test, however, was considerably less than that of the 'genuinely seeking work' condition. This was first introduced into insurance by the Act of March 1921, clause 3(b) of which required all applicants for *uncovenanted* benefit to prove that they were 'genuinely seeking whole-time employment but unable to obtain such employment.' The crucial difference between this and the existing condition that claimants be 'capable and available' for work but unable to obtain it, was that the onus of proof now lay on the applicant. For benefit to be refused under the 'capable and available' clause, the Employment Exchanges had to prove that work was available in the area and that the claimant had failed to take reasonable steps to obtain it. The problem here was the failure of the Exchanges to win the confidence of either the workers or employers, and only a fifth of all vacancies were actually notified to them.[28] The problem was not serious in times of good trade because malingerers would soon become conspicuous by virtue of the length of the time they remained out of work. In periods of high unemployment, however, the clause was useless and the one-in-six rule was being withdrawn at the very time it appeared in Whitehall to be most necessary to protect the fund.

It was this gap that the 'seeking work' test was designed to fill. All claimants were now to appear before a Local Employment Committee and satisfy its members of their eagerness to work. This usually involved supplying a list of firms visited and giving satisfactory answers to the Committee's questions; why had he or she been to one factory and not another? What was the name of the public house opposite that works? What number bus route was it on? The Committees were told to pay particular attention to the individual's work record, the initiative shown in seeking work and the household income where this might be high enough to cause 'a relaxation of efforts'.[29] The crucial point is that the Committees could recommend that benefit be refused without having to show that the applicant could have found a job had he genuinely sought one. As an additional safeguard it was stipulated in February 1922 that applicants were to accept any job which they were capable of performing, and the right to demand wages and conditions comparable to their previous employment was withdrawn.[30]

Since the essence of the test was that each claimant was presumed to be a malingerer until he or she had produced evidence to the contrary, the attitude of those who conducted the interviews was crucial. There was a Committee based at every Employment Exchange, usually with about thirty members drawn equally from local employers and trade unionists and a Chairman appointed by the Minister. In practice the task of interviewing claimants was delegated to 'rota' committees, consisting of a Chairman and two other members drawn in rotation from locally nominated panels of workers and employers. The Chairmen of these 'rota' committees were chosen in various ways, sometimes by the Minister.

These Committees were not independent of the Minister in any formal sense since all their decisions were technically recommendations to him. In fact, of course, the 'rotas' possessed a wide discretion in the handling of individual cases, and the small number of their decisions which were overruled reflected the careful control the Ministry exercised over their membership rather than its formal powers. The manner of this control has been described elsewhere.[31] Its importance for the present essay is that the Ministry was able to ensure that discretion was exercised at the local level only by those who could be trusted to share its attitudes towards the need for economy and the dangers of abuse. This in turn meant that a Minister of Labour could safely assume that the great proportion of committees would follow the advice or instructions he issued in his circulars. In short, the manner in which the 'seeking work' test operated was a *policy* decision, and its operation could easily be made more severe if the Minister wished. As Thomas Shaw, Minister in the first Labour government, noted, 'It is perfectly easy for the Minister, by a word here and there, by a hint here and there from his staff, to tighten up the administration.'[32] This is precisely what happened after the return of the second Baldwin government in November 1924.

Earlier in the same year the Labour government had extended the 'seeking work' test to all applicants, including those who were qualified for benefit under the one-in-six rule and had hitherto been exempt At the same time, further conditions were imposed upon those who had exhausted their contributory credits. To satisfy these conditions claimants had to prove, among other things, that they had been employed for a 'reasonable' period in the past two years, and that they were making 'all reasonable efforts' to secure employment 'suited to their capacities'.[33] These new conditions were to be administered by the Local Employment Committees, and were intended to be considerably tougher than the original test. As Margaret Bondfield, Parliamentary Secretary at the Ministry of Labour, succinctly put it, 'The person in receipt of benefit after twenty-six weeks has to come under the microscope.'[34] Whatever the intentions of Labour Ministers, there is little doubt as to the use made of this 'microscope' by their successors. In May 1925 Arthur Steel-Maitland, Baldwin's Minister of Labour, opposed any reduction in the level of benefit and suggested to the Cabinet that economies could be realised in other ways: 'The object of good administration should be to exclude the undeserving altogether, not to cut down the rate to the deserving.'[35] The Labour Government's new conditions had already increased the proportion of applicants who were refused Extended Benefit to nearly 10 per cent by the time Steel-Maitland took office, and his 'good administration' was to push that figure to nearly 18 per cent by the end of 1927.[36] One in ten of all claims made in 1927 were disallowed on the grounds that the claimant had either not done enough work in the past two years, or was not making a sufficient effort at the time of the claim. Individual Committees, moreover, produced much higher figures, the most savage being in London. In one twelve-month period, for example, Stepney refused benefit to 36.7 per cent of claimants, over a quarter failing to prove that they were seeking work. The corresponding figures for Walworth Road were 32.7 per cent and 23 per cent, while the highest proportion recorded by the Ministry was the 43.5 per cent of claims refused by the Hackney Committee in the month ending 11 January 1926.[37]

These bare figures, however, understated the severity of the new administration. This was because a successful claimant had now to reappear before the Committee within a maximum of twelve weeks, whereas one refused benefit could not try again for six months. Anyone hanging on to his benefit for a year thus appeared in the statistics as four successful claims with a corresponding reduction in the proportion recorded as disallowed. All told, just short of a million claims were rejected by the Committees as having failed to meet the 'seeking work' conditions in the first three years of the Baldwin Government.

This total resulted from a deliberate campaign to 'tighten up' the administration of insurance conducted by the Ministry through its circulars and other less formal contacts with the Employment Exchanges and Employment Committees. The manner in which the latter had been selected ensured that there was little opposition and, indeed, the tougher response in some areas alarmed even the Ministry. Following a sudden increase in the numbers struck off benefit in Sunderland, for example, the Divisional Controller concerned was warned that 'we do not wish to proceed too rapidly.' At the same time the Controllers for the North-East generally were told: 'That in their dealings the general rule should be "nil per saltum": wholesale disallowances should be avoided.'[38]

The removal of the Committees by the Unemployment Insurance Act of 1927 did little to reduce the impact of the campaign. Under the Act, which was based upon the compromise proposed by the Blanesburgh Committee,[39] *standard* and *extended* benefit were merged in a single benefit with a uniform administration. Henceforth all claims were first considered by the Insurance Officer at the Exchange and disallowed claimants had a right of appeal to a local Court of Referees.[40] The merger also involved the removal of the means test and it was this which caused the fall in the total numbers disallowed after the Act became operative in April 1928. There was no reduction, however, in the numbers refused on 'seeking work' grounds, and by the fall of the Baldwin Government they accounted for nearly two-thirds of all disallowances.[41]

By 1929 all pretence that the test was concerned with anything but personal character had been dropped. Since it was deemed possible for claimants to be 'capable and available' for work but to have no intention of doing any, their attitude towards work became the key issue. The task of the Exchange staff and the Courts of Referees was simply to ascertain 'the state of the applicant's mind'.[42] Neither, however, was exactly skilled in psychoanalysis and the criteria upon which they based their decisions had to be the claimant's performance at the interview and the evidence he or she could produce of personal efforts to find work. Hence the need for the unemployed to make constant visits to factories in search of non-existent work and for the procedures of cross-examination and visits to their homes — and neighbours — to ensure that they did so.[43] The point was made with brutal candour by the Chairman of the Court of Referees for the Rhymney Valley in evidence to the Morris Committee in 1929:

> We expect him to do something more than stay at home, we lead
> him to believe that staying at home doing nothing is not going to
> continue his benefit. We do not ask him where he has been to satisfy
> ourselves that he has been substantial distances, but for the purpose
> of satisfying ourselves that he has been out of the house. We do not
> impose it as a condition. It is not a condition, but more to convey to
> his mind that sitting at home is not to be tolerated.[44]

He went on to complain that the unemployed miners regarded applications at the neighbouring pit as a search for work: 'It is a genuine effort but it is not a sufficient one. That is the thing we cannot drive into them.' In short, the 'seeking work' test was a futile and brutal ritual, through which the unemployed 'earned' their benefit and reassured Whitehall that the incentive to seek work, any work, was being maintained.

III

If the manner in which the 'seeking work' test operated is clear, the reaction of the labour movement towards it is more puzzling. Indeed, the severity of its administration and the huge numbers involved makes the lack of effective opposition before 1930 quite remarkable.

In contrast to the bitter hostility aroused by the means test, the 'seeking work' condition was ignored by virtually all sections of the labour movement before 1924. Its operation was scarcely mentioned in Parliament, attracted no criticism in the *Daily Herald* or official Labour Party publications, was mentioned in only one resolution submitted to the party conference, and was not raised by any of the deputations organised by the NUWM.[45] Thus, in the period when opposition would have had most impact in Whitehall, the labour movement in general failed utterly to appreciate the importance of the new condition. This failure culminated in the decision of the Labour Government both to extend its coverage and stiffen its administration in 1924.

There were several reasons for the indifference shown towards the 'seeking work' condition. In the case of the majority of the Parliamentary Labour Party, a major factor was its own belief in the need for

specific measures to combat malingering. Clynes told the House of
Commons in March 1921:

> We must strengthen the regulations and there must be closer atten-
> tion to the administration of the payment of benefit on lines which
> make it impossible to encourage idleness. Organised labour, I am cer-
> tain, together with the employers, if both were called more in touch
> with the administration of the payment of benefit, could be of very
> great assistance in locating the shirker and in making it impossible
> to get money when work could have been got.[46]

The support of the Labour leadership for the principle of the 'seeking
work' test was to persist throughout the decade and to prove crucial in
1930. Its significance in the early years was that, having accepted the
need for such regulations, the Labour Party could hardly be surprised
if these excluded some claimants from benefit. With the exception of
the means test, therefore, there did not seem to be any cause for concern and the operation of the 'seeking work' test was not seen as
warranting close attention.[47]

This attitude was reinforced by the widespread belief that the test
was primarily directed at married women. There had always been fears
that such women would be able to draw benefit on the strength of the
contributions they had paid when single, even if they were no longer
interested in working. The potential for abuse, however, had been
limited by the ability of the Employment Exchanges to offer them
work, and to withdraw benefit if it was refused, and the fact that in
any case they would quickly exhaust their entitlement under the one-
in-six rule. The removal of the latter at a time when the Exchanges
were not able to offer jobs would thus have created a serious loophole.
Certainly the case for the 'seeking work' test was presented to both the
Cabinet and the House of Commons as a means of forestalling this kind
of abuse.[48] How far the initial operation of the test was in fact restricted to married women is unknown, since the statistics do not differen-
tiate between men and women before 1925. The fact remains, however,
that this was how it was believed to operate and consequently the
Committees' decisions appeared to be based upon clear and concrete
criteria, the applicant's marital status, number of dependants and past
industrial experience. In short, the fate of an applicant seemed to
depend upon the actual facts of the case, rather than upon the Committees' assessment of his or her mental state.

The confusion as to the real nature of the 'seeking work' test which resulted from its association with married women, was further increased by a series of highly misleading statements made by Macnamara in 1921. These gave the impression that the onus of proof remained on the Exchange,[49] and few on the Labour side knew enough about the test to dispute this. Finally, it should be remembered that the manner in which the Local Employment Committees had been chosen was scarcely public knowledge. Indeed, the Parliamentary air fairly echoed with praise of their impartiality, and similar conclusions were drawn by academic commentators. The following statement by Morley — a protégé of Beveridge — is typical of the nonsense published at the time: 'Experience has taught these Committees to pass the bona fide claimant with a minimum of delay, but to check and catch the industrial slackers almost unerringly.'[50] It was against this background that Thomas Shaw decided to extend the test in 1924. Shaw's action was a deliberate political manoeuvre; he believed that without such changes the rest of his proposals — which included higher rates of benefit and the permanent abolition of the means test — would not get through Parliament. Improvements in the scheme had to be accompanied by measures designed to reassure the Opposition and the public that no money would be wasted on the 'undeserving'. He had confided to a deputation of trade unionists in April 1924:

> If that scheme was to work, abuses must be ruthlessly checked. It must be seen that those claiming benefit were genuinely entitled, or, if the scheme was brought into disrepute, away went the Act, and probably they would get a worse one than the present.[51]

To Shaw, the 'seeking work' test was a reasonable price to pay for his other measures, because he sincerely believed that it would be little more than a nuisance to the genuinely unemployed. He was not alone in this belief; neither the *Daily Herald* nor the *New Leader* criticised this aspect of the Bill, there was no hostile resolution at the following Labour Party Conference or Trade Union Congress, and Wal Hannington expressed no disagreement on this issue when he addressed the Labour Conference.[52]

In fact, the only group to oppose Shaw over the 'seeking work' test was the Clydesiders. They had become highly critical of the test's operation in the previous year, and Neil Maclean left no doubt as to their feelings during the Second Reading of Shaw's Bill: 'It is a tragedy. It is worse — it is a crime upon these men and it is disgusting that the Labour Government is going to continue this clause.'[53]

The Clydeside MPs, and in particular George Buchanan, James Maxton and Campbell Stephen, were to remain the most consistent critics of the administration of insurance throughout the period.[54] By the end of 1925, however, their position had begun to attract wider support, notably from the Trade Union Group of MPs and their 'leader', Arthur Hayday. Over the next two years the 'seeking work' test became an issue of major importance and Steel-Maitland faced a succession of angry Adjournment debates and a constant stream of Parliamentary Questions relating to individual cases and details of administration. The opposition in the Commons reached its peak in the bitter struggle surrounding the Unemployment Insurance Bill of 1927. When Baldwin finally moved the guillotine on 1 December, the Committee had already sat for the equivalent of seven and a half days, while Clause 5, which retained the 'seeking work' test, had been under 'consideration' for 29 hours.[55] None the less, the intensity of the feelings which were aroused by this time should not disguise the gradual way in which they had emerged. For example, the joint evidence submitted by the Labour Party and the TUC to the Blanesburgh Committee in April 1926 argued that only those who had definitely refused a suitable job should be disallowed benefit as not seeking work, but did so in the mildest of terms. They went on to praise 'the remarkable efficiency and consideration' of the staff of the Employment Exchanges and recommended the establishment of a Central Advisory Committee, composed of employers and trade unionists, to advise the Minister on the framing of regulations. This, they felt, would remove a 'great deal of unnecessary friction'.[56] It is true, of course, that the subsequent Report of the Committee aroused tremendous anger in the labour movement not least because it was signed by Margaret Bondfield. As noted earlier, the Report recommended the removal of both the Local Employment Committees and the means test, but also proposed reductions in the rates of benefit paid to young persons, the re-introduction of a contributory qualification for benefit and the retention of the 'seeking work' test. Bondfield considered the Report to be a fair compromise but found little support within her party.[57] Although a resolution attacking her personally was ruled out of order at a special Labour Party Conference in April 1927, one condemning her action was passed at the Trades Union Congress in September.[58] It must be emphasised, however, that this hostility to the Report centred around the proposed cuts in benefit, and that the retention of the 'seeking work' test attracted considerably less criticism either in the Labour press, at the party conference or Trades Union Congress, or from the NUWM.[59]

The NUWM itself was slower to recognise the importance of the 'seeking work' test than many in Parliament. It is clear from *Unemployed Struggles*, for example, that Hannington did not regard the administration of the test as a serious problem until after 1928.[60] This surprising failure to recognise what was happening in the earlier years meant that the NUWM took no action before its national hunger march against the test in January 1929, by which time its activities were no longer regarded in Whitehall with anything like the alarmism of 1921.

By the end of 1928, then, a substantial number of Labour MPs, the TUC, and the NUWM had joined the Clydesiders in calling for the outright abolition of the 'seeking work' test. The leadership of the Parliamentary Party had not moved to this position. Of course, neither Shaw nor Bondfield could ignore the manner in which the conditions they had introduced were operating. Indeed, as early as July 1925 Shaw claimed, 'These people are being refused benefits on grounds which certainly the originator of the Act of 1924 never dreamt would be used. That is the essential fact.'[61] In subsequent debates Bondfield and Shaw frequently condemned the way in which their conditions were being applied. At no time, however, did they — or anyone else on Labour's front bench — deny the need for some measure to deter malingering and the leadership remained convinced that the complete withdrawal of the 'seeking work' test was politically impossible. This belief was reinforced by their steadily worsening relationship with those who campaigned against the test. The vehement language used by the Clydesiders, for example, constantly embarrassed and occasionally disgusted them. The chief offender was George Buchanan, whose evidence to the Morris Committee had to be heavily edited to remove the threat of libel actions before HMSO would even agree to publish it.[62] In 1927 MacDonald accused him and Maxton of 'dragging the Party' down to public house levels, after they had been suspended during the Committee stage of the Unemployment Insurance Bill, and the conflict over the 'seeking work' test was an important element in the mutual hostility and mistrust between MacDonald and the Clydesiders at this time.[63] Although Arthur Hayday was not regarded in this light, his attitude on the issue of the test was considered impractical. Under the 'Hayday formula', as it was known, a claimant would only be struck off benefit if the Exchange could prove that he or she had refused a definite offer of a job. While four-fifths of vacancies were unreported to the Exchange, however, neither Shaw nor Bondfield could accept such a complete shift in the onus of proof and both regarded some kind of 'seeking work' test as inevitable.

The Blanesburgh episode had left many in the party deeply suspicious of Bondfield, and her attitude towards the 'seeking work' test made conflict inevitable after she had become Minister of Labour with the return of the second Labour Government. Within weeks of taking office she had not only reaffirmed her opposition to the Hayday 'formula', but had joined Arthur Greenwood and Sydney Webb in recommending that both the means test and scrutiny by local Committees should be re-introduced for the long-term unemployed:

> as the new payment is not a right but a privilege it should clearly be limited to applicants who can satisfy an appropriate needs test . . . The final decision on an application must rest with the Minister, who would have power to refer applications for advice to local persons or committees so far as necessary.[64]

This proposal was promptly rejected by the Cabinet, but Bondfield and Greenwood constantly raised the question of a means test in the following months.[65] Indeed, it may be noted in passing that the establishment of a Royal Commission on Unemployment Insurance was originally suggested by Greenwood specifically as a means of educating the public on the need for such a measure.[66] In an attempt to avoid an open conflict over the 'seeking work' test, Bondfield had appointed a Committee to review its operation headed by the President of the Industrial Court, Sir Harold Morris. This was in July 1929, and pending the Committee's report, all cases in which doubt arose over the genuineness of the search for work were to be referred by the Employment Exchange to Boards of Assessors. These consisted solely of a local employer and trade union representative and their introduction did in fact reduce the proportion of claimants who were disallowed by nearly one-third.[67] This was not enough, however, to avert a major demonstration of grass-roots disaffection at the following party conference in October 1929. Despite appeals from Lansbury and Clynes, a motion to refer back the relevant section of the Parliamentary Report because of the failure to abolish the 'seeking work' test was pressed to a vote and defeated by only 1,100,100 to 1,027,000.[68]

The members of the Morris Committee failed to agree on the crucial issues and produced three separate reports in October 1929, the most significant of which was signed by the Chairman and one other member.[69] This suggested that the Exchange should first have to prove that work suitable for the claimant was available in the area, usually by pointing to cases where such work had recently been obtained by others. Only when this had been established would the applicant be required to prove that he or she had made 'reasonable efforts by the usual means' to secure such work. The new wording differed from the 'Hayday formula' in that the Exchange did not have to offer a specific job, but would still remove the objection that claimants were expected to seek non-existent work. Similarly, the phrases 'reasonable efforts' and 'usual means' were intended to provide a clearer basis for decisions than assessments of the claimant's state of mind.[70]

Not surprisingly, this compromise was seen by Bondfield as providing a way out of her difficulties and — with the support of the Cabinet — was embodied in the Bill she presented in November. It should be stressed at this point that all the Ministers were convinced that the onus of proof had now been decisively shifted from the client to the Employment Exchange. Indeed the Home Affairs Committee asked the Attorney-General, Sir William Jowitt, to make quite certain that this was the case.[71] The officials of the Ministry of Labour reached the same conclusion, albeit with different feelings. Bowers, the Accountant-General, complained that the new clause was 'likely to have a bad effect on the less fortunate workers; it will act as a soporific, whereas even their best friends would say they need a stimulus . . .'[72] In consequence the Cabinet viewed the attacks made on the new clause from the Labour back benches with genuine surprise and dismay. After his efforts to ensure the fairness of the new clause Jowitt was furious, and gave vent to his feelings in a phrase which was later to prove highly embarrassing: 'Are we to legislate on the lines that these people should think that they need do nothing themselves, that they should wait at home, sit down, smoke their pipes and wait until an offer comes to them?'[73] The truth was that for a substantial number on both the Labour and Liberal benches the answer to that question was 'yes', and they remained firmly opposed to any obligation being placed on the claimant beyond the acceptance of suitable work when it was offered. Their experience in recent years had convinced them of the need to remove all discretion from the hands of the Exchange staffs and Courts of Referees, and all vagueness from the regulations. In Hayday's words:

> never again would they support any condition, no matter how simple and reassuring the words may have been . . . that would permit of the commencement of a further period of cross-examination which would be bound to develop as the not genuinely seeking work section had developed.[74]

Confronted by an unlikely alliance of the left, the Trades Union Group and many Liberals, the government capitulated. The offending clause was withdrawn and reintroduced along the lines of the 'Hayday formula'. The 'seeking work' test was finally withdrawn on 13 March 1930. It had been part of the administration of insurance in one form or another for nine years and had been responsible for the disallowance of nearly three million claims.

Although the 'seeking work' test was never to rise from what Beveridge called its 'dishonoured grave',[75] the administration of insurance remained the centre of intense controversy. The growth in the numbers drawing benefit after the repeal of the test, and particularly the spectacular increase in successful claims by married women, was seized upon by Margaret Bondfield as evidence of the need for fresh measures.[76] The Ministry of Labour began compiling examples of abuse in June 1930 and in November she presented the Cabinet with a 42 page memorandum listing the loopholes in the existing regulations.[77] As Skidelsky notes, the impact upon MacDonald was 'formidable', and in January 1931 he told a TUC delegation:

> There is a very large and growing section of my letters protesting against the way in which insurance is being used coming from our own people. I am glad to see it, the people who have been with us building up the Labour Movement and agitating for unemployment insurance, the stories they write to me of neighbours or fellow-workmen abusing this are very heartening indeed.[78]

The result was the Anomalies Act of July 1931 which empowered the Minister to draft regulations governing the treatment of claims by married women, seasonal and casual workers, and persons on short-time. Although the Bill was bitterly contested by the parliamentary group of the ILP,[79] only the clause relating to short-time workers aroused any wider opposition and this was emasculated in the Commons.[80] In fact, of 299,908 claims refused under the anomalies regulations by April 1933, 250,920 were by married women, and the success of the regulations in excluding this group was a major reason why the National Government made no attempt to reintroduce the 'seeking work' test in the early 1930s.[81]

There is little doubt, then, that the abolition of the 'seeking work' test did enable some married women and seasonal workers to draw benefit, even though they were not looking for work at the time of their claim.[82] This 'problem', however, was effectively dealt with by the anomalies regulations which specifically applied to those groups, and Beveridge was later to condemn the imposition of the test upon *all* claimants as having been totally unnecessary. Viewed as an administrative measure, the test was a sledgehammer used to crack a relatively small — and often exaggerated — nut. However, to regard it as simply an over-zealous reaction by the Ministry of Labour to the dangers of abuse is to wrench the best from its political context and ignore the motives which lay behind the 'tightening up' of insurance. Fears of unrest had forced governments to make major concessions in unemployment relief by the early 1920s; concessions, moreover, which could only be withdrawn by throwing hundreds of thousands upon the Poor Law and risking its total collapse. Hence the 'seeking work' test, a deliberate and often brutal use of strict administration to reduce both the cost of relief and the threat to the incentive to work which was assumed to have arisen from its expansion. This use of the test was, of course, only part of the general reaction which followed the abatement of the fears of disorder and the collapse of the General Strike.[83] This in itself, however, does not account for the apparent lack of resistance to the 'tightening up' campaign, and an attempt must now be made to explain why the labour movement was unable to prevent — or even to modify — the operation of the 'seeking work' test on such a scale in the late 1920s.

IV

A major reason for the success of the 'tightening up' campaign between 1925 and 1929 was the fact that the legislative foundations had already been laid by the Labour Government in 1924. Throughout these years, the Baldwin administration was employing regulations which had been approved by Labour Ministers, and administrative machinery which they had perpetuated, and even praised for its impartiality.[84] The significance of this should not be underestimated. The Labour Government could, for example, have dealt with the problem of married women by introducing a measure along the lines of the anomalies regulations. Had it done so, the original rationale of the 'seeking work' test would have been removed and their successors could not have reimposed the test without their motives becoming obvious and the nature of the test itself being widely understood. Thus, the policy of the Labour Cabinet which stemmed, as noted earlier, from a failure to recognise the importance of the 'seeking work' test was in turn to delay that recognition still further.

In fact, of course, the Labour leaders in Parliament did not put forward any alternative to the 'seeking work' test until the Morris Committee provided them with a compromise formula in 1929. The campaign against the test in Parliament was conducted almost entirely by backbenchers, and the absence of front-bench support — together with the lack of interest in the issue in the House of Commons generally — meant that their protest could safely be ignored. Occasionally an individual case was reconsidered and minor changes in procedure were made from time to time, but that was all.

Outside Parliament, the anger generated by the means test diverted attention from the 'seeking work' condition before 1928. Both the NUWM and the TUC regarded the former as the more important issue, and this is not altogether surprising since the arbitrary operation of the means test was obvious to all, while many of the unemployed themselves regarded those disallowed as not seeking work with suspicion. The stories of scrounging and abuse which constantly appeared in the press were read by claimants — and contributors — as much as by anyone else, and, as a Labour back-bencher claimed in 1931, they resented 'more bitterly even than our political opponents any wrangling on the dole'.[85] The stigma of personal failing which became attached to those who failed the 'seeking work' test isolated them from the rest of the unemployed and inhibited protest. To persuade a man who had had to tramp round the district in order to retain his benefit that he should now jeopardise his position by joining in agitation on behalf of those who had failed the test was not an easy task. That task, moreover, would have been almost impossible if the majority of the unemployed had remained stoically optimistic of securing work in the near future, and that — as Hannington recalled — was often the case.[86]

The workpeople's representatives on the Local Employment Committees could do little to moderate the operation of either the means test or the 'seeking work' condition, and their position was accurately described by Arthur Hayday at the 1925 Trades Union Congress:

It is very well to say that you have a share in the administration. Your share is to do as the regulation bids you do, and the time is coming when you will have to consider seriously whether it is worthwhile befooling yourselves and running the risk of hostile criticism on the part of the men who cannot get extended benefit.[87]

In 1925 Hayday was primarily concerned with the means test, and the few Committees who did rebel — and were replaced by permanent officials — did so in protest against this rather than the 'seeking work' condition.[88] In fact, the only challenge to the operation of the 'seeking work' test in England came from the Boards of Guardians in areas where the 'pauper vote' had been carefully nursed to secure the election of members committed to the payment of generous relief.[89] Several Boards, chiefly in East London and the North-east, paid full outdoor relief to anyone refused insurance benefit as not seeking work, despite the Ministry of Health's insistence that those disallowed as malingerers should be offered the workhouse.[90] This practice, however, was confined to a small minority of Boards, and Glasgow remained the centre of opposition to the test.

The prompt recognition of the 'seeking work' test by the Clydeside MPs and the Parish Councils appears to have been due to the test's severe impact in Glasgow in the early 1920s. In Govan, for example, over 24 per cent of claims were being disallowed by October 1923, nearly all on 'seeking work' grounds. The position was similar in Bridgeton, Parkhead and South Side; indeed, the proportion of claims refused in Glasgow as a whole was consistently double the national average throughout the decade.[91] It was equally important, perhaps, that the test affected the skilled worker particularly badly in Glasgow, especially the engineers with whom Maclean and Buchanan had close contacts.[92] It seems likely that these circumstances sensitised the Clydeside MPs to the issue before anyone else.

The failure of the labour movement to prevent the use of the 'seeking work' test against the unemployed was thus rooted in a failure to recognise its importance until after the political conditions which made protest effective had passed. In the early 1920s, the movement as a whole defined its objective as the removal of the existing scheme of contributory insurance and the establishment of a system of maintenance. Its preoccupation was consequently with the level of benefits and the length of time for which they could be drawn. Apart from the means test, the conditions attached to benefits and the machinery for their administration seemed less important. During the decade the various sections of the movement came, at different times and by different routes, to realise the purposes for which those conditions and that machinery could be employed. The distraction of the means test, the divisive effects of the 'seeking work' condition itself, the distrust of the Clydesiders at Westminster, and the reluctance of the Labour Party to challenge the 'scrounger myth', all delayed that realisation until hundreds of thousands had been deprived of benefit.

Notes

1. W. Kendall, *The Revolutionary Movement in Britain 1900-21* (1969), p. 187.
2. W.S. Adams, 'Lloyd George and the Labour Movement', *Past and Present*, 3 (1953), p. 62.
3. K.O. Morgan, 'Lloyd George's Premiership: A Study in Prime Ministerial Government', *Historical Journal*, 13 (1970), p. 145; J. Saville, 'The Welfare State: An Historical Approach', *New Reasoner*, 1, 3 (1957), p. 12. For a contrasting interpretation, R.Blake, *The Unknown Prime Minister: The Life and Times of Bonar Law* (1955), p. 411 *et. seq.* Bonar Law thought the fears of his colleagues 'mere alarmism', an opinion shared by his biographer.
4. B.B. Gilbert, *British Social Policy 1914-1939* (1970), p. viii.
5. *Royal Commission on Unemployment Insurance. Minutes of Evidence* (1932), pp. 381-3.
6. B.B. Gilbert (1970), op. cit., p. 32.
7. Quoted in P.B. Johnson, *Land Fit for Heroes* (1968), p. 345.
8. P.R.O., CAB 27: 114. Cabinet Unemployment Committee 6 October 1921. Unpublished material in the Public Record Office appears by permission of the Controller of the Stationery Office.
9. *Daily Herald*, 2 December 1920. The earlier march is reported in the issue of 19 October 1920.
10. For an account: W. Hannington, *Unemployed Struggles 1919-1936* (1936), pp. 28-78.
11. For the origins of this organisation: B.B. Gilbert (1970), op. cit., p. 17.
12. P.R.O., CAB 24: 127 C.P. 3295.
13. P.R.O., CAB 24: 128 C.P. 3317.
14. Lloyd George Papers F 29/4/70. He later wrote to the Cabinet urging them to take prompt action to relieve the unemployed, 'the great majority of whom His Majesty understands honestly want to work'. P.R.O. CAB 24: 128 C.P. 3329,22 September 1921.
15. P.R.O., CAB 24: 127 C.P. 3285 6 September 1921.
16. For example, Lloyd George Papers F. 196/7/7 and F 223/2/-.
17. *Parl. Debates*, 5th ser., 26, 502. Originally the ratio was one to five.
18. P.R.O., CAB 24: 119 C.P. 2562 (Appendix 2).
19. An exception was Winston Churchill, who declared that it was 'rotting the youth of the country and rupturing the mainspring of its energies', and would be stopped by 'any Government that dares to do its duty'. Letter to Sir Arthur Steel-Maitland (19 September 1925), Baldwin Papers, Vol. 7, F 378-380.
20. E.W. Bakke, *Insurance or Dole?* (1935), p. 95.
21. *Royal Commission on Unemployment Insurance Interim Report*, Cmd 3872 (1931), Appendix 1. Since the twenties experienced a constantly falling price level, the rise in real value far exceeded the nominal increase.
22. Quoted in B.B. Gilbert, *The Evolution of National Insurance in Great Britain* (1966), p. 272.
23. The major source for both the means test and the 'seeking work' test discussed below are the circulars issued by Ministers to the Committees. The most important are the U.1 series, copies of which may be found in the House of Commons Library. In July 1923 they were codified and amended in LEC 82/2, and this in turn was later published by the Labour Government as *Unemployment Insurance: Directions to Local Employment Committees regarding Grant of Uncovenanted Benefit*, Cmd. 2104 (1924).
24. This, of course, did not appear in any of the circulars. See 'Unemployment Insurance Bill: Notes for Consideration', n.d., PIN 3, No. 12, P.R.O.

25. *Parl. Debates*, 5th ser., 192, 2336/7.

26. Speech by Arthur Hayday, 19 March 1923; *Parl. Debates*, 5th ser., 161, 2216.

27. These statistics, and those relating to the 'seeking work' test presented below, are based upon the writer's own calculations. The data has been drawn from the *Ministry of Labour Gazette*, the *Annual Reports* of the Ministry, Parliamentary Questions and memoranda in the Public Record Office.

28. This failure had several causes: the lack of technical knowledge on the part of the staff, the greater ease with which employers could recruit at their factory gates, and the hostile attitude of the newspapers anxious to preserve their 'situations vacant' columns.

29. Cmd. 2104, op. cit., p. 13. By 1924 less emphasis was being placed on documentary evidence than in the earlier circulars (referred to in note 23).

30. Circular U.1A. 505c (House of Commons Library). The distance which should be covered in the search for work was left to the discretion of the Committee, though single persons were usually expected to be prepared to move to another district.

31. E. Briggs and A. Deacon, 'The Creation of the Unemployment Assistance Board', *Policy and Politics*, 2, 1 (1973), pp. 43-62. Less than 1 per cent of the Committees' recommendations were rejected by the Minister.

32. *Parl. Debates*, 5th ser., 181, 1064.

33. These two conditions were designed to provide a criteria for the assessment of the claimant's attitude towards work, and are referred to below as the 'seeking work conditions'. Under the Act *covenanted* benefit became known as *standard* benefit, *uncovenanted* as *extended*.

34. *Parl. Debates*, 5th ser., 173, 2151.

35. P.R.O., CAB 24: 173 C.P. 234 (25).

36. The proportion for men was 14.9 per cent, for women 34.3 per cent. Part of the increase was due to the reintroduction of the means test.

37. 'Extended Benefit: Disallowances by some L.E.C.s', PIN 7 No. 79, P.R.O. For Stepney and Walworth Road respectively: *Parl. Debates*, 5th ser., 216, 1735 and 893.

38. The Controllers were 'to pass the hint in confidence to their Insurance Sections and Examining Officers'. These instructions were issued in November 1927 by T.W. Phillips, Deputy Secretary in the Ministry. *Deputation from Northern Poor Law Conference: Action on Points Raised*, n.d., PIN 7 No. 79, P.R.O.

39. *Report of the Unemployment Insurance Committee* (Blanesburgh) (1927). The nature of this compromise is examined briefly below.

40. The Insurance Officer and, in certain circumstances, the claimant, had a right of further appeal to the Umpire, a full-time post appointed by the Crown. The decisions of the Umpire formed a case-law binding on the Courts of Referees and Insurance Officers.

41. Total disallowances in 1927 were 891,843, including 182,465 under the means test. In the first year of the new Act the total fell to 615,378 of which 267,489 were for not seeking work and 136,284 for not having been employed for a 'reasonable' period in the previous two years. The amalgamation of *standard* and *extended* benefit meant that the overall disallowance rate fell considerably since relatively few claims to the former were refused.

42. Decision 1404/26 of the Umpire. This was reproduced in full as Appendix 3 of the Blanesburgh Report, op. cit.

43. In the south-east, for example, it proved 'more fruitful to call, ostensibly in error, at a neighbour's house'. U.1. 20909/35 (untitled), in PIN 7 No. 160, P.R.O. See also *Parl. Debates*, 5th ser., 223, 1024.

44. *Committee on Procedure and Evidence for the Determination of Claims for*

Unemployment Benefit (Morris), *Minutes of Evidence* (1929), p. 103.

45. See, for example, 'Deputation of Birmingham Unemployed', 17 August 1922, Lloyd George Papers F. 223/1/-. *The Administration of Unemployment Insurance* (1923), a joint report by the TUC and Labour Party, was highly critical of the means test but made no mention of the 'seeking work' test. A resolution criticising the test was submitted to the 1923 Conference by Middlesbrough Labour Party.

46. *Parl. Debates*, 5th ser., 138, 1199.

47. It was not investigated, for example, by the Labour Research Department. The proportion of claims which were disallowed in 1921 was just over 6 per cent, though this figure rose to 15 per cent after the introduction of the means test.

48. P.R.O., CAB 27: 135 U.1.2; *Parl. Debates*, 5th ser., 143, 460.

49. *Parl. Debates*, 5th ser., 143,459 and 2013.

50. F. Morley, *Unemployment Relief in Great Britain* (1924), p. 102.

51. TUC, *Annual Report* (1924), p. 109.

52. Labour Party, *Annual Conference Report* (1924), pp. 156-9. The *Daily Herald* greeted the proposals with the headline 'Cabinet keeps its promise to worker' (10 March 1924).

53. *Parl. Debates*, 5th ser., 173, 2127. For an example of the Clydesiders' earlier attacks on the test, *Parl. Debates*, 161, 170 (5 March 1923).

54. Although he was Shaw's chief critic in 1924, Maclean later quarrelled with the others and − distracted by a conflict with his Govan constituency − spoke little after 1925.

55. *Parl. Debates*, 5th ser., 211, 742.

56. *Unemployment Insurance Committee. Minutes of Evidence* (1927), p. 174.

57. For Bondfield's case see her autobiography: *A Life's Work* (1948), pp. 263-71. Ironically the employers on the Committee were also heavily attacked within their own organisation. See: National Confederation of Employers' Organisations: Circular Files N.C. 1989. The Files of the Confederation are located in the Library of the Confederation of British Industries, 21 Tothill Street, London S.W.1.

58. TUC, *Annual Report* (1927), pp. 283-8: Labour Party, *Annual Conference Report* (1927), pp. 35-6; *Daily Herald*, 29 April 1927.

59. For example, *New Leader*, 18 and 25 February 1927. None of the resolutions submitted to the 1927 Labour Conference attacking the Blanesburgh Report mentioned the 'seeking work' test as the reason for their opposition.

60. Hannington (1936), op. cit., pp. 172, 174, 180-200. Possible reasons for this mistake are discussed below.

61. House of Commons Standing Committee D., *Official Report*, 16 July 1925, 570.

62. The possibility of libel actions arose from the detailed accusations made by Buchanan concerning both the attitudes and behaviour of individual officials in the Glasgow Exchanges, and the bias shown by the 'pettifogging lawyers' who chaired the Courts of Referees in the area. A typescript of his original evidence is contained in P.R.O., LAB 2 BOX 1347 E.D. 29473/22.

63. Dowse, for example, notes that MacDonald had come to regard the ILP as 'impossibilist' and 'would not have bothered to understand anything it argued'. R.E. Dowse, *Left in the Centre* (1966), p. 134.

64. P.R.O., CAB 24/206 C.P. 253. See also: CAB 26: 396 Cabinet Committee on Unemployment Insurance Bill, 17 September 1929.

65. They 'agreed' its necessity, for example, at the second meeting of the all-party Advisory Committee on Unemployment Insurance on 8 September 1930. P.R.O., CAB 27: 429.

66. He first made the suggestion at the meeting on 8 September 1930 referred to in the previous note, and again in a memorandum on 23 September 1930, P.R.O. CAB 27: 429 A.C.U.1. 11. The Conservative and Liberal representatives opposed the Royal Commission unless drastic steps were taken to reduce the numbers on benefit in the interim. Thus MacDonald's denial to the TUC delegation in January that its appointment had been agreed in September was true, although the Commission was clearly more than a delaying measure for at least a minority of the Cabinet. See: R. Skidelsky, *Politicians and the Slump* (1967), pp. 262-4. P.R.O. CAB 24: 215 C.P. 318 (30); CAB 24: 216 C.P. 354 (30).

67. Between 9 September 1929 and 12 March 1930, 180,254 cases were referred to the Boards, of which 103,397 or 57.4 per cent were allowed benefit. The proportion of total claims which were disallowed fell from 7 per cent to an average of 4.6 per cent whilst the Boards were in operation. Their establishment was fiercely opposed by the senior officials of the Ministry. See: P.R.O., LAB 2 BOX 1584 1/F 3925.

68. Labour Party, *Annual Conference Report* (1929), pp. 171-6, 187-90.

69. *Report of Committee on Procedure and Evidence for the Determination of Claims for Unemployment Insurance Benefit* (1929), Cmd. 3415. A Minority Report by Arthur Hayday and Mrs Adams restated the case for the 'Hayday formula', whilst John Gregorson representing the employers pointed out — correctly — that it was beyond the Committee's terms of reference to propose a new clause.

70. Ibid., pp. 16-23.

71. P.R.O., CAB 23: 62 Cabinet 22 October 1929, 40 (29); CAB 26: 12 Home Affairs Committee 7 November 1929, H.A.C. 11 (29).

72. Letter to T.W. Phillips (25 November 1929) contained in Bill Papers, Vol. 2, PIN 3, No. 27, P.R.O. As a further precaution, Jowitt amended the clause so as to require the Exchange to show that the claimant would have had a 'reasonable' chance of securing the work had he sought it.

73. *Parl. Debates*, 5th ser., 232, 2688.

74. *Parl. Debates*, 5th ser., 232, 2605.

75. W.H. Beveridge, *Unemployment: A Problem of Industry*, Rev. ed. (1931), p. 280n.

76. Under the Act *extended* benefit was renamed *transitional* benefit and its cost was transferred from the Insurance Fund to the Exchequer. In the first three months the total numbers on transitional benefit doubled and those of married women increased sixfold; 38 per cent of the latter were normally employed in the cotton industry.

77. P.R.O., CAB 24: 216 C.P. 381(30). The evidence of abuse submitted by the Exchanges is collected in 'Bad Insurance Risks', LAB 2 1597 F 3243/31. The chief offenders were married women who, whatever their domestic circumstances, were now able to remain in benefit until the Exchange could find a job to offer them. Similarly, seasonal workers were alleged to be drawing benefit throughout their 'off season' even if they were not seeking work in that period.

78. 'Deputation to the P.M. from the General Council of the TUC regarding Unemployment Insurance', T 172 1769 P.R.O.; R. Skidelsky, op.cit., p. 238.

79. The 'revolt' was led by Buchanan, Maxton and Campbell-Steven, *Parl. Debates*, 5th ser., 255, 481-740. For the formation and role of the Parliamentary group, R.E. Dowse, op. cit., pp. 160-1, 171.

80. Again the opposition of the trade union MPs was crucial. *Parl. Debates*, 5th ser., 255, 605 and 1308.

81. *Report on the Operation of the Anomalies Regulations* (1933), Cmd. 4346,

pp. 2-10. No short-time workers lost their benefit under the regulations.

82. A similar, if less publicised, problem is posed by professional people who have retired early on generous occupational pensions and yet are able to sign the register and draw benefit. *Report of the National Insurance Advisory Committee on the Question of the Conditions for Unemployment Benefit and Contribution Credits for Occupational Pensioners* (1968), Cmnd. 3545.

83. Another element was the campaign to curb the dissident Boards of Guardians through the inspectorate and the district auditors; S. and B. Webb, *English Poor Law History*, Part 2, Vol. 2 (1963), pp. 912-25.

84. See, for example, TUC, *Annual Report* (1924), p. 110.

85. Speech by Mills, *Parl. Debates*, 5th ser., 255, 739. The same attitude is common amongst present-day recipients of social security benefits. For an example, V. Bottomley, *Families with Low Income in London* (1972), p. 8.

86. Hannington (1936), op. cit., p. 322. It is also likely that the 'seeking work' test was applied more severely to the unskilled worker than the more organised and better-represented skilled man.

87. TUC, *Annual Report* (1925), p. 404. In 1926 an attempt was made to formulate a common policy for the Labour representatives on the LECs, but with little result. TUC, *Annual Report* (1926), p. 130.

88. For an example, *Parl. Debates*, 5th ser., 188, 1403.

89. For this, A. Deacon and E. Briggs, 'Local Democracy and Central Policy: The Issue of Pauper Votes in the 1920s', *Policy and Politics* 2, 4 (1974), pp. 347-64. It must be remembered that Poplarism itself was roundly condemned by the Labour leadership. G.W. Jones, 'Herbert Morrison and Poplarism', *Public Law* (Spring 1973), pp. 11-31.

90. Poplar was the most prominent of these authorities, but others were equally forthright. Sculcoates, for example, told the Ministry in 1929 that it considered the test to be 'no better than an excuse to discontinue benefit'. *Summary of Replies to Questionnaire in respect of certain Unions regarding the relation of Out-door Relief to Unemployment Insurance Benefit*, PIN 7, No. 102, P.R.O.

91. The figures for 1923 are given by *Parl. Debates*, 5th ser., 170, 851. For later figures, ibid., 210, 173; 226,223.

92. I am greatly indebted to Mr Ian Levitt of Edinburgh University for information on the situation in Glasgow at this time. His research indicates that the shipbuilding employers and the Scottish Office were both convinced that the war had left a surplus of skilled labour on the Clyde and saw the 'seeking work' test as an opportunity to persuade those workers to move south.

2 THE TUC SPECIAL INDUSTRIAL COMMITTEE: JANUARY — APRIL 1926

John Lovell

The General Council which the TUC established in 1921 to replace the Parliamentary Committee was, as Bullock has said, 'rather to be looked upon as a representative body' than as an effective executive committee.[1] With 32 members it was too large to function as an executive, and from the beginning delegated much of its work to subcommittees, meeting only at monthly intervals to receive the latters' reports. In this situation, some of the Council's subcommittees came to exercise a very considerable influence, although in the 1920s the committee system was still extremely flexible and no single committee came to constitute a permanent inner cabinet for the Council as a whole.[2]

The most important task of the Council in its earliest years was to develop its powers to intervene in major industrial disputes — powers both to mediate and if necessary to co-ordinate defensive action in support of an affiliated union. Following the engineering lock-out of 1922, the Council delegated the job of formulating policy in this area to a subcommittee known first as the Joint Defence Committee and later as the Committee for the Co-ordination of Trade Union Effort.[3] This body remained in existence for several years and promoted a whole series of policies aimed at increasing TUC influence over the industrial activities of affiliated unions. In July 1925 it was investigating various general problems connected with sympathetic strike action — in particular the variety of agreements or contracts into which unions had entered with employers.[4] When the crisis developed in the mining industry, however, the General Council set up a new committee to deal with it, and the Co-ordination of Union Effort Committee passed into oblivion.[5]

The Special Industrial Committee (SIC) — the body formed to deal with the coal crisis — was established on 10 July 1925. It had nine members — Swales (Chairman of the General Council), Citrine (Assistant Secretary), Bromley, Hayday, Hicks, Marchbank, Poulton, Tillett and Walkden.[6] This Committee was to play a critical part in the events leading up to the 1926 General Strike. It has, however, never been properly assessed by historians. This is surprising, because the records of the Committee tell us much about the attitudes and relative influence of leading figures on the trade union side. It is the intention of this essay to make full use of these records for the first time. The Committee met seven times during the 1925 crisis, and pursued a policy of working for a peaceful settlement while at the same time preparing contingency plans to deal with a breakdown in negotiations. In the event, of course, the crisis was resolved by the government at the eleventh hour. The subsidy which the government offered to the coal industry was of a temporary nature − due to last only until May 1926. Its purpose was, ostensibly, to preserve the *status quo* until a Royal Commission had had time to investigate the problems of the industry. The General Council thus kept its Special Industrial Committee in being, and instructed it to 'apply itself to the task of devising ways and means of consolidating the resistance of the trade union movement should the attack be renewed'. After the 1925 Scarborough Congress there was a small but vital alteration in the Committee's membership. Pugh and Thomas replaced Poulton and Marchbank. As the new General Council Chairman, Pugh also replaced Swales as chairman of the Committee. In the months that followed the General Council left matters entirely in the hands of its Committee. Between the Scarborough Congress in the autumn of 1925 and 27 April 1926 the full Council did not discuss the mining situation once; it simply received the reports of the Committee during the course of its regular monthly meetings.

The Committee's task as defined by the Council after the 1925 crisis was, as we have seen, to devise ways and means of organising support for the miners, on the assumption that a serious crisis would arise when the subsidy expired. In fact, it paid scant attention to this problem. When, in December 1925, the Council referred to it the Scarborough Congress motion calling for increased General Council powers to coordinate industrial action, the Committee decided to take no action in the matter.[7] A similarly negative attitude was shown by the Committee in its dealings with the Co-operative Union. The latter was anxious to discuss the situation that would arise in the event of a stoppage. Many local co-operative societies had still not recovered from the miners' unions, money that had been advanced during the 1921 dispute, and the Co-operative Union therefore proposed a scheme whereby the whole trade union movement would offer a guarantee against further losses. The suggestion was turned down by the Committee, and although it was invited to produce alternative suggestions of its own, it declined to do so.[8] Despite promptings from Citrine, at no stage did the Committee give serious consideration to the problem of organising support for the miners, and in the end it was left to another subcommittee − the Ways and Means Committee hurriedly established by the General Council on 27 April 1926 — to improvise plans for strike action.[9]

If the SIC failed to prepare for a possible stoppage, it failed equally to provide the General Council with a policy of its own regarding the future of the coal industry — a policy which could form the basis of a settlement. When the Council met on 27 April, with only three days to go before the mining lock-out was to commence, it had nothing before it. As Bevin wrote later:

> The General Council found . . . that the only steps that had been taken were of a mediatory character. No definite proposals on the part of the Council itself had been formed and put down.[10]

Proposals relating to the reorganisation of the coal industry *were* subsequently drawn up, and were presented to the Conference of Union Executives on 29 April, but at this late hour the exercise had little meaning.[11]

The inactivity of the SIC during the period between July 1925 and May 1926 is quite remarkable, and, of course, stands in marked contrast to the preparations made on the government side. Fortunately, verbatim reports were made of the discussion at all the meetings of the Committee up until that of 27 April. It ought, therefore, to be possible to reach an understanding as to why the SIC behaved in the way it did.

The first point of interest to emerge from the reports concerns the role played by Citrine — the Acting Secretary of the TUC following the death of Bramley in October 1925. It was Citrine who initiated serious discussion of the mining situation. During the course of a routine discussion, on 19 January 1926, he suggested that a special meeting should be held 'to consider fundamental policy'.[12] This special meeting of the SIC took place on 29 January, and the Committee had before it a memorandum, prepared by Citrine, which set out a number of issues that had to be faced. The memorandum is well known.[13] It made the point that whatever recommendations the Royal Commission came up with regarding the reorganisation of the coal industry, a problem would still exist in the short run, because the reforms could not be implemented immediately. Much therefore depended upon whether the government would agree to continue the subsidy during the period of reorganisation. The SIC had not yet decided what its policy was regarding the subsidy, and Citrine saw this as its first task. Apart from this, the memorandum proposed a series of steps to be taken by the Committee. It should make preparations for a major stoppage, assume complete control of policy — this might entail having representatives of the Miners' Federation and the Labour Party on the Committee, and finally mount a large-scale publicity campaign to educate public opinion concerning the attitude of the labour movement.

Citrine's call to action was not favourably received. The only decision taken by the meeting on 29 January was to invite the Executive of the Miners' Federation to a further meeting — the proposal to co-opt miners' representatives on to the Committee was rejected. Thomas played the leading role in the discussion, and his attitude contrasted sharply with that of Citrine. In his view, the coal industry was first and foremost the affair of the Miners' Federation. He asked:

> Had they reached a stage when an industrial dispute affecting the largest union in the country was now handed over to someone else? If the SIC was dealing with the railway situation, he would decide it was time he cleared out.[14]

The example of the railways — Thomas's own industry — formed a constant theme:

> The mining situation was almost identical with that on the railways seven years ago. 158 companies were merged into four and we protected our men's interests by applying our minds to the problem of our people — that is the Miners' job.

Thomas was bitterly critical of the leadership of the Miners' Federation, and he suggested that the main task of the Committee was to get the miners to rely upon their own efforts. Bromley — the other railwayman on the SIC — strongly supported Thomas: 'The miners must not rely on the SIC. It might be their duty to say to the miners, "You have got to pull your weight in endeavouring to stave off the trouble." '[15]

In this atmosphere the issues raised by Citrine's memorandum were largely ignored. From the start Thomas poured cold water on the idea that the SIC should prepare contingency plans for sympathetic action in support of the miners. 'If they [the Committee] thought they could create the situation of last July', he said, 'they were living in a fool's paradise. These things could only be done once — that was mass psychology.' He suggested that talk of co-ordinated action amounted only to 'lip service', which was 'not much good to the miners, but could create a situation which would ruin the miners' case or deceive them'.

The meeting between the SIC and the Executive of the Miners' Federation was fixed for 12 February, and a copy of Citrine's memorandum was sent to the Miners' Federation on 3 February.[16] When the two groups met, Herbert Smith, the miners' President, began by saying that his Executive had not yet had time to consider the memorandum. Smith in fact was in no hurry, and he said so. The miners' programme — no wage cut, no increased hours, and maintenance of the national agreement — was the same as in the previous year. He was quite happy to await the report of the Royal Commission, and then 'see what might come from the other side'. He did not suggest to the Committee that there would be anything further coming from his side, and when he agreed to set up a subcommittee of his Executive to consult with the SIC, it was simply with a view 'to comparing notes from time to time'.[17]

Citrine was distinctly unhappy with this situation. Instead of waiting for the Royal Commission to report, he thought that the movement should be trying to influence it *before* it reported. The matter of the continuance of the subsidy he regarded as crucial. He argued that the SIC and the miners ought first to reach a definite decision that they were in favour of continued financial assistance, and then — in the time that remained before the Commission reported — mount an intensive publicity campaign advocating this policy. Thomas disagreed: 'The present was a time for careful tactics, not for launching out. Wait for the report.' In the end it was decided to adjourn the discussion for a week, presumably to allow the miners to give full consideration to the memorandum.

On 19 February the SIC and the miners' subcommittee resumed their discussion. Citrine's memorandum was considered again, but with little enthusiasm. Pugh thought it might be provocative to talk too much about the continuance of the subsidy. Hayday felt that the matter of the subsidy would have to be looked into in more detail, and that it was in any case 'premature to discuss the matter without knowing the lines of the Commission's report'. Even Smith was half-hearted in his support, and suggested that it was 'a little bit dangerous to decide on any definite policy'. Citrine made one final effort:

> Whatever the Commission said, there would have to be assistance during the interim period. Was it better to create public opinion on that or leave it until the Commission had reported? They would have to urge publicly that the Government could not dodge its responsibility — should they delay doing this? If they delayed, they could not influence the Commission's findings. He was convinced that a

Commission of human beings was susceptible to public opinion. They were postponing all the time without seeing where they were going while the other side was making adequate preparations for war, while talking of peace.[18]

It was to no avail. The meeting did agree to set up a subcommittee to handle publicity, but in the absence of policy there was nothing to publicise. Nothing more was heard of Citrine's memorandum on the Committee, and it was never even seen by the full General Council.[19]

After 19 February Citrine ceased to be a force on the SIC. He continued to attend meetings, of course, but played virtually no part in the proceedings. Indeed, between 19 February and 8 April his voice was hardly heard at all. Presumably he had been reluctantly forced to accept that his opinions as yet carried no weight. Still under forty years of age, and still only in the position of *Acting* Secretary of the TUC, he was the most junior member of the SIC. Even without this handicap he would have been at a disadvantage, for the views of a TUC official carried less weight than those of a general secretary of an individual union. Thus, when Citrine suggested that the SIC should be present at the meetings between the miners and the coal-owners, Thomas retorted:

That might be all right for Mr. Citrine who represents the General Council, but it was too dangerous for anyone else on the Committee who were responsible to their organisations.[20]

Despite all these difficulties, however, he might still have exerted an influence on the SIC had Bevin been a member of that body, for the two men thought alike, and they were to prove a most powerful combination in the years ahead. But Bevin only became a member of the General Council in 1925, and was not included in the membership of its SIC. The coal crisis came too soon for the two ablest British union leaders of the period to be able to play a decisive role. Had it been otherwise, the outcome would surely have been different.

It will be evident from the account of the Committee's activities so far given that its dominant member was Thomas. Thomas was a new factor in the situation, for he had not been on the SIC during the 1925 crisis, and it soon became clear enough that he did not favour further TUC involvement in the coal industry's problems. Ironically, however, the very date which marked the end of Citrine's activity on the SIC marked also Thomas's temporary loss of control over events. Thomas was absent from the meeting on 19 February, and that meeting took one critical decision. It was not prepared to anticipate the Royal Commission's report in the manner suggested by Citrine, but it was apparently prepared to anticipate it in a way desired by the miners. The latter had come to the meeting with one clear objective — to obtain from the SIC a definite statement in support of their three-point programme. Since the miners had the advantage over the rest of those present, in at least knowing what they wanted, they got their way. The SIC issued a press statement reaffirming its support for the miners' programme. The Miners' Federation thus obtained a TUC commitment to its three points, *in advance* of the Commission's report. That the SIC should have done this, and yet at the same time have rejected Citrine's memorandum, is a measure of its lack of direction. If Thomas had been present it is unlikely that the statement would have been issued, for he at least was capable of appreciating that the memorandum and the statement logically went hand in hand — and he would have argued strongly against both.

When the SIC met the miners again, on 26 February, Thomas tried hard to put the clock back. The publicity subcommittee had prepared a draft circular to be sent out to affiliated unions and this followed the statement in declaring TUC support for the miners' programme. Thomas argued against it, but Cook, the miners' Secretary, pointed out that it only repeated what had already been issued to the press. Thomas persisted, and Cook lost his temper — 'they ought to show a little guts in meeting the situation.' The railwaymen's leader was not deterred, however, and stuck to his objection:

> The Report wasn't yet out. They didn't want a statement that would compel them to climb down, he wasn't saying they would have to do any climbing down but it was better not to have to.

The implication of this last remark was not lost on the miners, and there ensued a full-scale row between Cook and Thomas.[21] In the end, however, the SIC agreed to phrase the circular in the same terms as the press statement, and Thomas had to accept defeat. Given the Committee's decision the previous week the defeat was perhaps inevitable, but it was a significant moment none the less. The TUC had now placed on record, both before the public at large and its own affiliated membership, its continued support for the miners' three points.[22] Its ability to revise its policy in the light of the Royal Commission's recommendations was thus impaired. The miners had won a major tactical victory.

The next meeting of the SIC took place on 11 March, and the full

Executive of the Miners' Federation attended. The Report had appeared the previous day, so that it was, presumably, no longer 'premature' to consider policy. The position adopted by the miners was simplicity itself. The Report recommended a reduction of wages, and this they would not accept. As to its other proposals, these were reasonable enough, but it was for the government and owners to initiate action on them — both Cook and Smith stressed this last point. It is clear, however, that the thing that interested the miners most was the attitude of the SIC. The Commission's recommendation regarding wages put the TUC's declaration of support to a severe test. Anxious to do nothing that would cause offence, the miners emphasised their willingness to consult with the SIC. They said that they wished to discuss with the Committee the nature of the lead that they should give to their districts.

Thomas was not to be drawn. He began by praising the miners for meeting the Committee so soon after the Report's publication. But he went on:

> The S.I.C. must recognise right away that they were amateurs. The support they could give to the miners was not on the technical side or on how they could do their business. Its ramifications must be and remain the miners' business and no-one else's.

He suggested that the miners should meet the SIC immediately they had formulated their policy; it was 'not for the S.I.C. to determine that policy'. Smith, of course, realised that Thomas was gently trying to disentangle the TUC from its commitment. He replied:

> There were some questions that were miners' questions, but they were joint partners there and they wanted to stand together and make them joint questions. They would not declare any policy as Miners as a set policy, until they had consulted the S.I.C.[23]

It was Bromley who raised on behalf of the SIC the delicate question of the Report's recommendation on wages. He referred to there being good things in the Report for the future — Thomas had called it a 'wonderful document with tremendous advantages' — and then commented:

> But the interim, according to the Report, should be bridged not by a subsidy, but by wage reductions. In that case he would like to say

to the Government — let us see your legislation which will give us a
secure future if we are to submit to something to our detriment.

The implication, of course, was that the miners might consider accepting
the Report as a whole, including the reductions. Cook was quick to
denounce Bromley's suggestion, calling it 'very previous', but Smith and
Richards (a member of the Miners' Executive) made no objection. The
latter's comment is of some interest:

> Bromley had rightly visualised their eventual position if the Cabinet
> accepted the entire Report. Then they would be in a serious situa-
> tion. But for the present, they should say the responsibility was the
> Government's.[24]

The meeting ended with no firm conclusion having been reached.
Thomas and Bromley concocted an innocuous press statement, which
was agreed, and Pugh suggested that 'they could do nothing but await
events'. Events had in fact turned out so far exactly as Citrine had fore-
seen. The interim period, for which it now appeared there was to be no
subsidy, provided the fundamental obstacle to a settlement on the basis
of the miners' three points.

The most important event to be waited upon was a statement of the
government's attitude towards the Report. This came on 24 March, at
a meeting between the Prime Minister and the two sides of the industry.
Baldwin stated that the government would be prepared to give effect to
the Report's recommendations, provided that the owners and miners
accepted them. By throwing the responsibility on to the owners and
miners the government, of course, greatly reduced the chances of a
peaceful settlement. The 'serious situation' envisaged by Richards, in
which unreserved government backing for the Report would make it
difficult for the miners to avoid a compromise on wages, was no longer
a possibility. The SIC met on 25 March to hear the Miners' Federation
officials report on the meeting with Baldwin. Tillett was one who recognised the gravity of the situation. He suggested that the 'S.I.C. should
inform the movement of the seriousness of the position'. He also
suggested that it was time the Committee considered what 'bargaining
authority' the miners were to have from the movement. Thomas, however, immediately challenged these suggestions: 'Bluff wasn't going to
carry them anywhere: just as in the Triple Alliance, they could only do
it once.'[25] He got his way, and no action was taken.

On 6 April the owners issued a detailed statement of their attitude concerning the Royal Commission's recommendations. They expressed a qualified adherence in principle to most of the measures proposed, but remained convinced that an extension of working hours was imperative. As to wages, they said that they were prepared to enter immediately upon negotiations for a national wages agreement, but on the basis that minimum percentages should be settled in the districts and then submitted to a national conference for approval. The national minimum percentage was to go. After statements by the government and owners, the ball was now definitely in the trade union court.

The SIC met the miners' subcommittee again on 8 April, but before the miners arrived the Committee met by itself in order to decide what line to adopt. It had run out of events to wait upon. The Report was out, the government had made a statement, the owners had made a statement, there was nothing else left. At the previous meeting on 25 March Pugh, as chairman, had expressed the view that 'it was no good talking about policy at this stage'. Now, however, he was prepared to give the Committee a clear lead for the first time. Even so, it is evident that his hand had to some extent been forced by the speeches that Cook had been making — to the effect that the transport and railway workers were ready to come out in support of the miners. Pugh told the Committee: 'Cook in his speeches was assuming that they were in the position of last July. That was not the case. They now had a document 70% in the miners' case.'[26] Pugh had made up his mind that the Report had changed everything, and that the miners would have to negotiate on the basis of it.[27]

> It was a profound mistake to think that the whole trade union movement could be brought out to support a subsidy. Today they had to speak frankly [to the miners] as to their policy.

Thomas was delighted, and announced that he was 'pleased that Pugh had faced up to the situation'. He went on to say that he thought a strike was virtually out of the question, and that the job of the SIC was 'to intervene with the Government to bring both sides to a margin of difference, which none of them knew now'. The alternative to a negotiated settlement he characterised in lurid terms — 'a week of bloodshed' and 'a whirlpool into which he was being dragged . . . which was certain to drown him'.[28]

It was left to Citrine, who had hardly spoken a word since 19 February, to point out the extent to which the views of Pugh and Thomas diverged from the declared position of the TUC. When Pugh emphasised

again that a stoppage could not be called to force a subsidy, Citrine
commented:

> If that was the opinion of the S.I.C., the miners ought to be told as
> they genuinely imagined they were going to get the same kind of
> support as last July.

When the miners joined the Committee, Pugh made a statement to
them, repeating the points he had made to the Committee. During the
course of this statement he implied that TUC backing for the Miners'
Federation would become necessary only 'if an attempt was made to
enforce upon the industry the conditions which the owners had suggested to the Coal Commission'.[29] In reply, Smith said the miners were
favourably disposed towards most of the proposals put forward in the
Report, but that they remained adamant concerning their 'three essential points', and he asked 'the General Council to stand by the miners
and protect them on those points'. To Thomas and Pugh this response
was totally unacceptable. Pugh remarked: 'The attitude of the Miners'
Federation was that there was to be no negotiations on those three
main questions raised. Those matters were a subject of negotiation.'
The tactic of pressing the miners to negotiate on their main points,
however, now encountered a serious obstacle. Smith pointed out that
the miners could not open negotiations on wages without sacrificing
the principle of national agreements, because the owners had made it
clear to them that the miners would have to apply to the districts in
order to fix minimum percentages. Thus, in so far as they were prepared to discuss wage reductions at all, they could not do so without
accepting district agreements in advance. The SIC could find no way
around this block. In the end the miners withdrew in order to allow the
Committee to consider their request for support on the three points.
The Miners' Conference was meeting on the following day, and they
wanted to be able to make a positive statement regarding the TUC's
position.[30]

With the miners gone, the Committee did not take very long to make
up its mind on the question of a declaration of support. In Pugh's view,
such a declaration would prejudice negotiations. Thomas and Hicks
agreed. Only Swales, the left-winger who had been chairman of the
Committee the previous summer, was in favour. Swales had been absent
from a number of the earlier SIC meetings, but he now spoke out in
support of the miners. He thought a declaration would strengthen their
hand in negotiations, and saw no reason for departing from the policy

of the previous year. His was a lone voice, however, and the Committee decided not to endorse the three points. Instead, a letter was dispatched to the Miners' Federation expressing the view 'that matters have not yet reached a stage where any final declaration of the General Council's policy can be made'.[31] In Pugh's mind, the owners' refusal to embark upon national negotiations constituted the crucial problem. If this could be overcome, progress might be possible. This view was based on a misunderstanding of the miners' position, as Pugh painfully discovered in the days ahead.

The SIC met the miners again on 14 April, and Smith gave a report on the meeting that had taken place between miners and owners on the previous day. The meeting had ended in deadlock, and the owners were now approaching the miners' district organisations with a view to negotiating wage reductions. Furthermore, they were taking steps to end existing contracts on 30 April. The situation was extremely grave, and Smith renewed the request that the TUC should reaffirm its support for the miners' programme. Pugh's response was to try to get back to the Report, and to what he saw as the main obstacle to its implementation — the owners' attitude to national agreements. Thomas supported Pugh. He said that the Committee was unable to make the sort of declaration that the miners wanted. Instead, he suggested that the SIC should approach the government with a view to bringing pressure to bear on the owners. Confronted by what he regarded as evasions, Smith became exasperated. He said he did not know whether Thomas was misunderstanding him wilfully. Was he to understand 'that the declaration made on February 26th was dead and forgotten?' All he was asking was that they should reaffirm that decision. 'When they had reaffirmed that decision, any practical help they could give would be welcomed.' The atmosphere had now become extremely strained, and Hicks tried to calm things down by vague reassurances to the miners. No more than Pugh and Thomas, however, was he prepared to give a definite commitment. Pugh explained that while the SIC was not going back on earlier statements, it believed that

> the time had not arrived yet when it was a case of giving effect to declarations ... The Committee did not accept the owners' attitude as final, or the right attitude. He thought they ought to bring the whole thing back to central discussion.[32]

Pugh, however, was unaware of the significance of 'central discussions' for the Miners' Federation. He quoted extracts from the Report which emphasised the supremacy of the national negotiating machinery, but appeared to regard that machinery as an end in itself, whereas its value for the miners was that it maintained the uniform national minimum percentage on base rates. When Cook tried to point this out, Pugh thought he was simply confusing the issue — 'they were dealing with the question of national agreements, and Mr. Cook was dealing with the factor of wages.' It was left to Straker (a member of the Miners' Executive) to clarify the position. He explained:

> They had to consider as a matter of principle whether they had to agree, either by national machinery or any other, to varying district minima, or whether, national machinery or otherwise, they had to refuse to agree to such minima and stand for one uniform national minimum percentage on pre-war wages. They wanted to know whether the TUC would support them in maintaining the principle that there should be no variation in the minimum applying to every district. If they said they had to go into it, then that implied that the Committee believed that under certain circumstances they might agree to a difference in the minimum. The miners stand against that on principle as a Federation.

His eyes finally opened, Pugh remarked that if 'that was the essential point, they had better discuss it'.[33]

In the event, however, Straker's lucid exposition of the miners' position made no difference to the Committee's policy. Thomas and Pugh were resolved not to give the miners a firm declaration of support. They were also convinced that the best course of action was to intervene with the Prime Minister, with a view to persuading him to bring pressure to bear on the owners to resume national discussions. Baldwin was interviewed by the SIC that evening (14 April).[34] He agreed to see both the Miners' Federation and the Mining Association and to use his influence to secure a resumption of negotiations.

A week later negotiations had still not been resumed, and so, the Miners' Federation having nothing to report, the SIC met alone. The absence of the miners afforded an opportunity for uninhibited discussion. Pugh suggested to the Committee that it was not going to be possible to sustain the existing wage level in the industry:

> He could not see the Miners getting out of the difficulty on the principle of 'not a penny off wages'. Even when they got to the smallest point [of difference] possible it still meant some adjustment

in wages.[35]

As to the remaining items in the miners' programme – national agreements and hours – he thought these *could* be upheld. Pugh's view of
national agreements, however, still took no account of the uniform
minimum percentage. Tillett and Swales were distinctly unhappy with
this line, and the latter pointed to the significance of the national minimum for the survival of the Miners' Federation: 'He could not see the
Miners agreeing to accept a reduction for one section of the men to ease
off the other. That was going to split the Union.'[36] But Pugh and
Thomas defended their viewpoint by pointing to the implications of the
miners' programme. If wages remained unchanged two possibilities existed: either the industry would have to face a much higher level of unemployment, or the government would have to renew the subsidy for an
indefinite period. When seen in the light of this choice the miners'
programme was, in their view, simply untenable.

The dominant group on the SIC thus regarded the miners' position
as untenable, but the problem remained as to how the TUC could be
released from its commitment to this position. No way out had yet
appeared, and the threatened mining lock-out was now little more than a
week away. Bromley was one who felt that the Committee was drifting
helplessly towards disaster:

> They could not move. Undoubtedly they had to come to something
> which he feared was not what the Miners want. He believed all of
> them would be willing to throw all their troops into the firing line if
> they felt there was a reasonable chance of winning after. The Miners
> would not release them. They were holding position . . . He thought
> it was a good thing the General Council was meeting.[37]

The last sentiment was undoubtedly echoed by certain Council members not on the SIC. Bevin, for example, felt so out of touch with
developments that on 21 April – the same day as the SIC meeting
described above – he contacted Cook to find out what was happening.[38]

As a result of Baldwin's leisurely promptings, the Mining Association
and Miners' Federation did get together on the morning of 22 April.
The meeting was not a success, for it transpired that the Prime Minister
had been able to achieve little in the direction of modifying the owners'
attitudes. They presented the Federation with a draft national agreement, but it did not provide for a continuance of the national minimum
percentage, and the miners refused to discuss it. When asked for infor-

mation concerning the minimum percentages to be offered in the districts, the owners agreed to provide the Federation with details. The miners reported on this situation to the SIC on the evening of 22 April, and they brought with them the details of the wages offered. It seems that they definitely felt they had reached the end of the road, and they were certainly in no mood to tolerate SIC evasions. Smith told the Committee that he thought the miners had been 'side-tracked', for the intervention of Baldwin had achieved nothing — the owners would not discuss wages except at district level. So far as the information regarding the district proposals was concerned, 'the reductions were too serious for the Miners to give any consideration to them.'[39]

The position was one of absolute deadlock, but Pugh was desperate to salvage something. If, he suggested, they left aside for a moment the details of the district wage cuts, was it not the case that negotiations had broken down because the owners were not prepared to consider a national settlement? But Smith would not be drawn away from the wage issue. He said he wanted to be quite fair to the Committee:

> They were now within a week of the termination of the contract. There was no room for a reduction. The Miners did not object to meet, but they could not stand for any reduction in wages.

Pugh pressed him on the question of the Federation's willingness to negotiate, on a national basis. Smith repeated that he would meet the other side, 'but he could not agree to a reduction in wages'. This was the most rigid line the miners had so far taken with the SIC. In order to deal with it, Thomas intervened with the unemployment argument. The existing rate of wages, without a subsidy, would put thousands out of work. How did the miners react to that? Smith met the challenge without flinching:

> If the Miners retained their position for no reduction of wages, they were going to put upwards of 200,000 men out of work. They realised all that . . . It was a big proposition, but as they told the Owners, they had to face it. They were determined that if the country wanted coal, it had to give the men who got it a respectable living.

There was no way round the miners' position, and Smith emphasised this further by remarking that he did not want to be told afterwards that it was understood that the miners would be prepared to compromise on wages. 'They had nothing to compromise', he said.[40]

Smith's statement produced its effect. Thomas and Pugh now agreed that the owners' terms were impossible. They suggested that the only course open was to get the government to intervene once more. Cook demurred at this, suggesting that the first course of action ought to be to inform the movement concerning the owners' terms since 'it seemed that they were not far from the time when they would be forced into a conflict.' But Smith, sensing that the critical moment had passed, was prepared to be more conciliatory: 'The Miners had no objection to their friends the S.I.C. seeing the Government, but they expected them to let the world know tomorrow or that night where they stood.' The SIC then went to see Baldwin, and returned later in the evening with the news that he was prepared to convene a meeting of the two sides of the industry on the following morning. It was apparent, however, that the SIC and the miners had widely differing expectations concerning the outcome of this meeting. The Committee saw it as inaugurating a serious process of negotiation, but for the miners it was little more than a gesture. Smith's main concern in fact was to arrange the next meeting with the Committee: 'He wanted to suggest that it was high time they ought to begin to get to close quarters with the general movement.'[41]

In retrospect, it seems clear that the meeting between the SIC and the miners on 22 April marked a decisive step on the road to the General Strike. The Committee had at no stage since January really believed in the tenability of the miners' position, and up until 22 April a withdrawal of support was always a possibility, even if a remote one. At that meeting the miners had been pressed hard, but in the end it was they who carried the day. The SIC leaders had not, of course, changed their convictions, but they had conceded ground, and time would not permit them to recover it.

The time factor was borne in on the Committee when it assembled late on the following afternoon, to await the appearance of the miners with news of the negotiations.[42] The meeting considered the need to summon a Conference of Union Executives. Pugh seemed to think that it could be left to the General Council to take the decision, but Hicks and Bromley thought that the matter was too urgent to wait until 27 April. It was therefore agreed that the SIC should summon the Conference itself; it was called for Thursday 29 April — the day before the mining lock-out. The decision was the most important the Committee had yet taken. When the miners arrived, they reported that negotiations had broken down again. A fruitless discussion ensued, the verbatim report of which simply peters out — it is marked 'incomplete'. The SIC tried to be constructive. Pugh suggested that if it were possible to distinguish between that section of the industry which could retain present wages without a subsidy, and that section which could not, it might then be possible to persuade the government to provide some financial assistance for the latter. But Smith was unwilling to pursue the discussion:

> He repeated what he had pointed out last night, that it [no reductions] would mean from 150,000 to 200,000 men out of work . . . Whatever figures they had, they still came back to the fact that they would have to go down with a reduction in wages unless some people came out of the industry.[43]

He was prepared to leave it at that. The meeting adjourned with only the uncertain prospect of a renewed initiative by Baldwin standing between the SIC and the crisis it dreaded.

At this juncture Baldwin did in fact make a significant move. He invited Pugh down to Chequers on Sunday 25 April, and followed this up by meeting the SIC at noon on Monday.[44] It became clear that he wanted the Committee to exercise a moderating influence upon the miners, and to this end actually proposed that members of the SIC should be associated with the miners' negotiating team.[45] It was a strategy doomed to failure. The SIC had no influence with the miners, and in any case the meeting with Baldwin had aroused suspicions.[46] When the two groups renewed contact on the Monday evening the atmosphere was exceedingly strained, and the verbatim report again peters out, with the note 'unfinished' written upon it. In the discussion the same ground was gone over as had been gone over so many times before, and the only positive outcome was the miners' agreement that the SIC should be associated with them in negotiations.[47]

In the event the owners vetoed the proposal to involve the SIC directly, but the episode was revealing none the less.[48] The idea that the Committee should be represented in negotiations had been discussed by Citrine and his staff back in February, but he did not bring the suggestion before the Committee until 23 April.[49] Pugh and Thomas had then opposed it. The reason Pugh gave for his opposition is of some interest:

> The difficulty was that if they took part in the negotiations they would have to have a policy. At present the Committee had none. All they had done was to endeavour to get the thing back to discus-

sion. It was no good going into negotiations unless they knew what their policy was.[50]

Six months had elapsed since the 1925 Trades Union Congress, a week remained before the lock-out notices took effect, yet the SIC did not know what its policy was! Citrine's proposal was not therefore entertained by the Committee, but when, as we have seen, virtually the same proposal was made by Baldwin three days later, Thomas and Pugh accepted it. The problem as to policy remained, however, so Pugh proposed that a subcommittee should be set up, representing the SIC and the miners. The subcommittee's task was 'to examine the whole of the factors relating to the Commission's Report, and to get something constructive on paper'. Pugh put this scheme to the miners at the meeting on 26 April. Their reaction was one of incomprehension.[51]

The General Council met on 27 April, and the crisis moved into its final phase. This essay is not concerned with the rush of events in the last few days preceding the strike. Its concern has been with the months of inactivity which paved the way for the final episode. The reasons for this inactivity will, it is hoped, have been made apparent by the account of the Committee's proceedings given above. It is clear, for example, that the presence of Thomas on the Committee was a vital factor. He dominated the rest, and his influence was of an almost totally negative kind. He did not believe in co-ordinated union activity and did his utmost to prevent discussion of it. But he had little that was constructive to offer in its place. The influence of Thomas might have been counteracted by an effective chairman, but Pugh certainly did not fall into this category. Pugh delayed decisions for as long as he could, misunderstood basic issues involved in the dispute, and in the end simply reinforced Thomas's influence on the Committee. It was, frankly, a record of incompetence. Citrine was silenced at an early stage, Bromley supported Thomas, and the rest were of little account, although Swales did offer some opposition.

Thomas's influence has been described as negative, yet it had one positive aspect. Thomas believed in the fairness or neutrality of the government, and therefore rested his hopes for a peaceful settlement upon government intervention in the dispute. Pugh seems to have shared this view to some extent, as did certain other members of the Committee. The miners, however, did not believe in the government's impartiality. The lack of this common assumption does much to explain the mutual incomprehension and exasperation that characterised the relationship between the SIC and miners throughout the period covered by this essay. The divergence of viewpoint emerged explicitly on a number of occasions, but one in particular, in early April, is especially memorable. The episode in question deserves to be quoted in full, and will serve as a fitting conclusion:

> Mr. Cook said that in his opinion the Government would accept the owners' interpretation [of the Report]. The Government and the owners were one in this issue.
>
> Mr. Thomas asked what proof there was of that.
>
> Mr. Cook said that otherwise the Government would have agreed to carry out the Report and not have made it conditional on the agreement between the owners and miners.
>
> Mr. Thomas said there was no hope of a settlement if that was Mr. Cook's view.[52]

Notes

This essay is based mainly on unpublished material from the files of the Trades Union Congress.

1. Alan Bullock, *The Life and Times of Ernest Bevin*, I (1960), p. 288.
2. There is a valuable account of the development of the TUC's committee system in V.L. Allen, 'The Reorganisation of the T.U.C., 1918-27', *British Journal of Sociology*, XI (1960).
3. General Council Minutes, 1 March, 21 March, 4 April 1922. The Joint Defence Committee was composed of two representatives from each of the six Group Subcommittees of the General Council. In 1924 the Chairman of the General Council became Chairman of the Defence Committee, *ex officio*, Joint Defence Committee Minutes, 24 March 1924.
4. Joint Defence Committee Minutes, 16 July 1925. This was a general investigation and was not directly connected with events in the coal industry — discussion of the problem had begun in February 1925.
5. It is obviously not a coincidence that the Defence Committee ceased to function from the time of the appointment of the Special Industrial Committee. The task of co-ordinating action had passed from the former body to the latter.
6. Membership of the SIC was weighted towards the transport unions — the unions most likely to be involved in any sympathetic action. Equal representation of the Group Subcommittees was thus abandoned. These bodies had not developed as originally planned, and this no doubt was one reason why the Defence Committee was not retained.
7. Bullock, op. cit., p. 290. The various attempts that were made in the 1920s to increase the General Council's powers are discussed in John Lovell and B.C. Roberts, *A Short History of the T.U.C.* (1968).
8. Special Industrial Committee, Verbatim Reports of Meetings, 8 and 23 April 1926. Swales was the only member of the Committee who showed an interest in this question.
9. The Report of the Strike Organisation Committee, issued in May 1926, contains this comment: 'The Strike Organisation Committee desire to emphasise

that the organisation was of necessity improvised. The date upon which we were first asked as a Ways and Means Committee to consider the question in the event of a general dispute, was 27 April, and prior to that date, no consideration had been given to the possibility of such an eventuality.'

10. Bullock, op. cit., p. 299.
11. There was, however, an eleventh-hour attempt to get these proposals discussed in the House of Commons on the evening of 3 May. See Bullock, op. cit., pp. 314-15.
12. SIC, Verbatim Reports, 19 January 1926.
13. The memorandum is reprinted in full in Lord Citrine, *Men and Work* (1964), pp. 146-53.
14. SIC, Verbatim Reports, 29 January 1926.
15. Ibid.
16. Citrine's account given at the Special Conference of Executives, 20 January 1927. Report of Proceedings, p. 41.
17. SIC., Verbatim Reports, 12 February 1926.
18. SIC, Verbatim Reports, 19 February 1926.
19. Citrine's account at the Special Conference, 1927. Report of Proceedings, p. 41.
20. SIC, Verbatim Reports, 23 April 1926.
21. SIC, Verbatim Reports, 26 February 1926. For Cook's hostility to Thomas see also Citrine, *Men and Work*, p. 153.
22. For the text of the circular of 26 February see the Special Conference, 1927. Report of the General Council, p. 5.
23. SIC, Verbatim Reports, 11 March 1926.
24. Ibid. Richards' comment brings out well the contrasting attitudes of the miners and the SIC. For the former a 'serious' situation would be one in which they were obliged to compromise. A compromise, however, was just the thing the SIC hoped and worked for.
25. SIC, Verbatim Reports, 25 March 1926.
26. SIC, Verbatim Reports, 8 April 1926.
27. See Bullock, op. cit., p. 295.
28. SIC, Verbatim Reports, 8 April 1926. This was by no means the only occasion upon which Thomas indulged in lurid descriptions of impending disaster. See Citrine, op. cit., pp. 157-8.
29. SIC, Verbatim Reports, 8 April 1926.
30. Special Conference, 1927. Report of the General Council, pp. 5-6.
31. For the text of the letter see ibid., p. 6.
32. SIC, Verbatim Reports, 14 April 1926.
33. Ibid.
34. See Thomas Jones, *Whitehall Diary*, II (Oxford, 1969), pp. 13-14.
35. SIC, Verbatim Reports, 21 April 1926.
36. It was clear that under a system of district settlements miners in the export coalfields would fare very much worse than those in regions producing for the home market. Such a system was therefore felt to constitute a threat to the very existence of the Miners' Federation.
37. SIC, Verbatim Reports, 21 April 1926.
38. Bullock, op. cit., pp. 297-8.
39. SIC, Verbatim Reports, 22 April 1926.
40. Ibid.
41. Ibid.
42. Arthur Henderson attended this and subsequent meetings as an observer from the Parliamentary Labour Party.
43. SIC, Verbatim Reports, 23 April 1926.
44. The story of Pugh's visit to Chequers is told in Thomas Jones, op. cit., pp. 22-3.

45. Baldwin put his proposal in the following terms: 'What I want to put to you is whether you have any influence that can bring about real negotiations. I do not know if it would be of any help if you were to associate with the miners one or two of your own number who perhaps are more useful in negotiations.' Verbatim Reports of Interviews with the Prime Minister in connection with the Mining Crisis, 26 April 1926.

46. The miners had expected to meet Baldwin that day. Instead, they found out that he was meeting the SIC. Furthermore, Jones informed Cook during the afternoon that a future meeting between the miners and the Prime Minister would depend upon the outcome of the miners' discussions with the SIC. Jones presumably had in mind the Prime Minister's proposal regarding SIC representation at negotiations, a proposal which the Committee had agreed to put to the miners. None the less, the latter must have suspected that Baldwin had commissioned the SIC to put pressure on them to modify their position. SIC, Verbatim Reports, 26 April 1926.

47. SIC, Minutes, 26 April 1926.

48. News of the owners' veto was conveyed to the SIC by Baldwin. Verbatim Reports of Interviews with the Prime Minister, 27 April 1926.

49. The suggestion was actually made by Tracey, of the TUC Press Department, at a TUC and Labour Party staff meeting held on 18 February. Citrine was present and drew attention to the suggestion in his summary of the main conclusions arrived at by the meeting. Notes on Discussion on Strategy — Mining Crisis, 18 February 1926.

50. SIC, Verbatim Reports, 23 April 1926.

51. SIC, Verbatim Reports, 26 April 1926.

52. SIC, Verbatim Reports, 8 April 1926 .

3 THE STRIKER STRICKEN

G.D.H. Cole

Preface by Margaret Cole

The 'Operetta' which follows was written almost entirely by G.D.H.
Cole in a few days in late July 1926, for performance by some members
attending the summer school run by the Tutorial Classes Committee of
the University of London: he was Director of the school, and the
operetta was performed as a part of the entertainment on the Friday
evening before the school broke up. Entertainment of this kind was no
new thing. For a few years, mainly under the influence of Guild Socialists and workers in the Labour Research Department who were also
engaged in adult working-class education, summer schools often ended
with an evening in which a few of the members of the school performed
for the benefit of the rest.

It began in the year 1921, when the Fabian Society offered a week
of the Fabian Summer School to the Guild Socialists to organise as they
pleased; and the days of political discussion ended with a revue called
The Homeland of Mystery, based on the visit recently paid by George
Lansbury to revolutionary Russia, and produced in fine style, with
scenes painted by Lovat Fraser and Arthur Watts, costumes largely provided by Joseph Thorp, and a ballet composed by Rose Cohen, who
was a friend of Sylvia Pankhurst and a clerk in the Labour Research
Department, and danced to music from *Prince Igor*. Other, slightly less
impressive, efforts followed in later years; but the unprecedented situation made *The Striker Stricken* into a much more enduring piece of
work.

All the revues etc. naturally had a political content; and a left-wing
bias, with considerable sympathy for the USSR — which does not mean
that they were completely uncritical. *The Homeland of Mystery*, for
example, included a song sung to a tune from *Patience*, of which one
verse ended:

> And everyone will say,
> As you walk your bombstrewn way,
> When the Proletariat dictates, and the Proletariat's ME,
> Why, what a very comfortable kind of State that kind of State will be!

and another which went to the tune of *Under the Deodar*, began:

> Under the Commissar,
> But under very far —
> Intelligent — intelligent — intelligentsia — We are!

both of which might seem to anticipate much later criticism of the
Soviet system. On the other hand, I remember William Paul, the best
voice in the Communist Party, lambasting Bottomley of *John Bull*; and
Mrs Veitch, wife of Colin Veitch the footballer, imitating Marie Lloyd
in a song which ended:

> I'm one of the ruins that Horrabin knocked about a bit.

The whole atmosphere in these and other revues was one of friendly
knock-about; and as the songs were almost invariably set to well-known
tunes, some traditional, some from Gilbert and Sullivan operas and
Hymns Ancient and Modern, and some to current popular hits, amateur
pianists could easily help to train the choruses, and the whole audience
could 'participate' (though that ambiguous term had not yet been
invented) without any strain; it was a lively and a happy exercise.

In July 1926, however, the case was different. It was not very long
since the calling off of the General Strike; the miners were still locked
out, and the general mood of those attending the London summer
school, tutors and students alike, was one of strong political indignation. The Director of the school immediately started to compose his
angry operetta; and in this case the composition was not, as in earlier
entertainments, a co-operative effort, but 'all his own work' — owing
to the sudden death of my father I was unable to be present when the
school opened, and in the end contributed only a little of the dialogue.
In performance it was a great success, and was immediately seized upon
by other organisations. It could not be printed, first because it was
clearly libellous in parts, and secondly because it transgressed the
Emergency Powers Act, which was then still in force, and the author
(and possibly some of the performers) would have been liable to heavy
penalties — including transportation beyond the seas! But it toured the
Durham coalfield during the late summer, and was subsequently performed at various Labour and educational gatherings, the latest so far
as my knowledge goes being at Ruskin College in early 1959, a little while
after its author's death.

It may be regarded therefore, as 'first-hand' evidence, in that it presents, and presents accurately, the views and beliefs of the bulk of the labour movement at the time when it was written. More facts have, of course, come to light since then, with the publication of various diaries and Cabinet papers. The bulk of these, however, refer to the pre-strike preparations of the government and their supporters, with which the operetta is not concerned. I would, however, wish to put on record that the text, including some of the songs, is certainly unfair to Walter Citrine. Citrine was then only Acting General Secretary of the TUC; Fred Bramley, secretary after C.W. Bowerman, had only died in the previous October and Citrine had yet to be confirmed in his place; so nobody knew very much about him, and it was assumed that he was as ill-prepared and apprehensive as other union leaders. It was not until the publication, after many years, of his own reminiscences that we were able to see how hard he had in fact tried to induce his colleagues to be a little more realistic. So I hope that Lord Citrine will now accept a very belated apology for what I know is a misleading presentation of him. I had had a thought of altering the name, but it is wrong to tamper with historical documents.

In view of all that has been published about the General Strike in its jubilee year, in books and other media, I do not think it necessary to add another narrative piece here. I should only like to emphasise what some of the 'reconstructions' have omitted, its relation to the general economic situation and to Labour strategy in general. In 1948 I wrote:

It was the last blow of insurrectionism, of 'direct industrial action', belief in which had been for so long part of the cardinal faith of the Left. Ever since, in 1920, the threat of direct action had stopped the Polish war, the Left had not ceased to believe that *the industrial movement*, if really determined and united, could make its will prevail; and further that someday the opportunity would come, and the shame of Black Friday (when the unions, except the miners, were neither united nor determined) be avenged; and this belief was only strengthened in 1924-5 after MacDonald's first government had come to its inglorious end, while at the same time the period of post-war wage-cuts seemed to be over and many groups of workers were making tentative forward moves. When the strike failed, in spite of the most impressive exhibition of working-class solidarity seen since the days of Chartism, and when, after much post-mortem discussion, it gradually became clear that it could not possibly have succeeded, the long dreams of Syndicalists, Direct-Actionists, and the rest of them withered and died.

I could only add to this that the climb-down of the government in July

1925 and the nine months subsidy to the coal industry was wrongly
interpreted by the workers as a victory, not a pause for making more
effective anti-strike preparation.

N.B. The *Prologue* printed here is not the original Prologue, the text of
which has not survived. New Prologues were written for each performance: on internal evidence, this one was written for a University Labour
Club.

THE STRIKER STRICKEN:

or

THE THIRTY SLEEPERS OF ECCLESTON SQUARE

being

THE OPERATIVES' OPERA

IN THREE 'OPS

Come, and 'op it as you go.
Milton.

Prologue

ACT I

High Life — Downing Street

ACT II

Middle-Class Life — Eccleston Square

ACT III

Low Life — Heaven

Prologue

Immortal Bacon wrote 'The play's the thing,
Wherein I'll catch the conscience of the king.'
These latter days, our king is Henry Dubb,
Here personated by the Labour Club.
And 'tis your consciences this play's to snatch,
Brands from the burning; if you here may catch
Out of this Nine Day's Tangle what of moral
May make you wiser by the next big quarrel.
Indeed, this play we shortly mean to act
Is less than half a play, and more a tract.
Figure some spirit, free from mortal cares,
Who stands above the world, and our affairs
Surveys impartially. Whom did he praise,
Whom censure for the doings of those days?
Did he not rather shake his sides to see
All men the sport of some mad destiny
Unknown, and far beyond our mastery?

So has our author ventured to put on
The guise of immortality, and don
That spirit's mantle, making food for fun
Not this or that, but all and everyone.

This play's to show you how the strike began
And how it ended — hopes and fears that ran
Their course and died — some censure, some laudation.
Some sense, some satire, some exaggeration
Went to its making. Much of it is plain
Matter of fact, with here and there a grain
Of plausible invention. Not all true,
I grant, but true enough for the end in view,
Which is to serve the truth in things that matter.
One can't be just, and write effective satire.

Well, here's the play. The actors' sole inducement
To act it is their own, not your amusement.

But, if you like it, that will please us all;
And, if you hate it, that's your funeral.

Scene I. The Class Struggle

The scene is divided into two sections. In the left section, a Labour
College Class is in progress, in the right section a W.E.A. class.[1] A Tutor
is standing immediately in front of the partition, and is taking both
classes at once, but in quite different ways.

The Labour College students look very proletarian, the W.E.A. students highly respectable.

The Tutor gesticulates silently to each group by turns. To the
Labour College Class he makes the violent gestures of the propagandist;
to the W.E.A. his gestures are suggestive rather of mesmeric passes.
Under both influences, the two Classes go gradually to sleep and begin
to snore.

Tutor: Wake up, wake up. The play's beginning. You've got to sing
          your choruses now. Come on, I'll give you the note. (goes to
          the Piano)

The Labour College students sing:
          ('Tarpaulin Jacket')

          There is only one side to all questions,
          There is only one way that we know, we know.
          For our tutor has frequently told us
          The bloody old bosses must go.

The W.E.A. students reply:

          Our minds are much deeper and broader,
          We know that the class war won't wash, won't wash.
          For we've learned to revere law and order,
          And our tutor says Marx is all bosh.

Both sing together:

          But we're both of us quite of opinion
          We need far more educating, — cating;
          For whatever one learns when one's learning,
          It's evident learning's the thing.

From each Class a student rises and comes to the front.

('When I, good friends, was called to the Bar', from *Trial By Jury*)

Pleb (sings):

> When I joined this Labour College Class,
> And I couldn't have joined a worse one,
> I was, as many young workers are,
> An unclass-conscious person.
>
> I was top of the class at school — nuff said —
> I worked for the boss like a booby.
> And now I'm a Red and I'm thoroughly fed,
> And I work for the good time *to be*.

Pleb Chorus:

> But now he's a Red and he's thoroughly fed,
> And he works for the good time *to be*.

W.E.A.er (sings):

> When I signed the pledge for a three years course
> I'd a chap named Ross[2] for tutor.
> He taught me Keynes instead of Marx,
> And I wish he'd been astuter.
> For now my mind's in the deuce of a mess
> And I don't know what I'm thinking,
> And my joie-de-vivre grows less and less
> And I've taken of late to drinking.

W.E.A. Chorus:

> His joie-de-vivre grows less and less
> And he's taken of late to drinking.

Pleb (sings):

> You see what comes of a Class that's un-
> der the Board of Education.
> It makes your mind come all undone
> And it spells for the boss salvation.

W.E.A. er (sings):

> Oh shut your mouth, I've the devil's own drouth,
> And away to the pub I'm wending.
> Come away, old chap, to the nearest tap,
> For, thank God! the class time's ending.

Chorus of All Together:

> Yes, away to the pub or the workmen's club,
> For, thank God! the class time's ending.

ACT I   High Life — Downing Street

The scene takes place outside the doors of Numbers 10 and 11 Downing Street. A crowd of sightseers, held in check by large policemen, is to be imagined in the distance. As the curtain rises, the growls of the crowd and shouts of 'Move on, please!' and so on, are heard off.

Enter from opposite sides A.J. Cook and Herbert Smith.[3] They bear some resemblance to Tweedledum and Tweedledee.

Cook: That you, Herbert?
Smith: Aye, lad.
Cook: We must stand firm.
Smith: Aye, lad.
Cook: Shall I state the miners' case to the Prime Minister?
Smith: Aye, lad.
Cook: Then what I'll say is this:

Song
('It was many years ago')

Not a penny off the pay,
Not a second on the day,
So the Conference instructed, and we mean to stick to that;
And we won't go down the shaft
Till the honour of our craft
Has been satisfied by everybody saying aye to that.

They'll all have to say aye to that, won't they?

Smith: Aye, lad. And then I'll tell him this:

Song

('Don't go down in the mine, Dad')

We won't go down the mine, Stan,
For you and your coal-owning crew.
Put that in your pipe, lad, and smoke it, my boy,
You can take it from me that it's true.
I've summat to tell 'ee from me and my mates,
And as sure as the sun do shine,

66

We're swearing by Heaven until we get seven
No miner will go down the mine.

Cook: Bravo!

At this point a great noise is heard off, of mingled cheers and
booings. Enter, theatrically, the Rt. Hon. J.H. Thomas, followed by the
Rank and File, who slouches in whistling and lies down on the floor in
front of the stage.

Chorus (off)

('The Lord High Executioner', from *Patience*)

Behold the Lord High Constitutionist,
The leader of the railwaymen in unity,
The scourge of every revolutionist,
Who always flouts his members with impunity.
Defer, defer, to the Lord High Constitutionist,
Defer, defer, to the Lord High Constitutionist,
To the Lord High Constitutionist!

Thomas: That's me! (To Cook and Smith) What's that I heard you
          saying?
Cook & Not a penny off the pay,
Smith: Not a second on the day!
Rank &
File: 'Ear, 'ear!
Thomas (To Rank and File):
          Go away, my man. You're not wanted 'ere. These are matters
          to 'igh for you. (Rank and File only whistles)
Cook: Not a penny off. . .
Rank &
File: 'Ear, 'ear!
Thomas: Reely, you mustn't say that. It's not playing the game. If you
          won't give up your wages, 'ow can the Trade Union Movement
          rise in its might to defend them?
Smith: Not a penny. . .
Thomas (slightly rattled):
          I've heard that before. Come now, be sensible. When I reduce
          my railwaymen's wages, no one grumbles. Can't you take a

more statesmanlike view?

Cook: Not a penny. . .

Thomas: Speaking with a full sense of my responsibility, I say that in
              my 'umble opin . . .

Rank &
File: Cut it out, Jimmie.

Thomas: . . .ion this attitude makes my position impossible.

Cook: Not a penny. . .

Thomas: Now do 'ear reason. You say not a penny. Why not a 'apenny?

Cook: Not a bloody franc[4] so there.

Thomas: But you must consider my position. I promised Lady Astor. . .
              Really, I ask you . . .

Song

('Three Cheers for the Red, White and Blue')

In the name of the great T.U.C.
I entreat you, dear friends, to agree;
If you won't let the owners cut your wages,
Why the 'ell won't you let the T.U.C.?

You must work for the community
Without counting the hours or the fee,
If you won't work long hours for lower wages,
Where the 'ell will the Hempi-er be?

Enter in haste Lady Astor.[5] Without noticing Cook and Smith, she
goes straight up to Thomas.

Lady Astor: I say, Jimmie?

Thomas: Yes, Nancy?

Lady Astor: Is it O.K.?

Thomas (aside):
              'Ush, don't speak so loud. They're 'ere. No, they won't
              see reason, yet.

Lady Astor: Well, shall I try? Tact is my middle name.

Thomas: No, I think you'd better not, If I can't deal with them,
              nobody can. I tremble for the Country's future.

Song

('Prythee, pretty maiden', from *Patience*)

Lady Astor: Prythee, Jimmie Thomas, prythee tell me true
                (Hey, but I'm Nancy, don't I take your fancy?)
                Can't you stop these miners making a to-do?
                Tell your fancy Nancy, O.
                O my Labour Viking,
                Can't you stop them striking?
                Teach them sycophancy, O.

Thomas: Nancy, dear, my 'eart is full of misery,
                (Hey, but I feel a very dismal Jimmie)
                For Cook and Co. are Communists, and pay no heed to
                    me;
                They've no use for Jimmie, O.
                Much against my liking
                They're intent on striking,
                All around Reds hem me, O.

Lady Astor: Then, my darling Jimmie, I must do and dare,
                (Hey, but I'm Nancy, I shall take their fancy)
                Ask them in to dinner at St. James's Square,
                All with fancy Nancy, O.
                Bring me half a dozen
                Leaders in to cozen
                With my necromancy, O.

Thomas: Try it on, dear Nancy, try it on to-night,
                (Hey, but I'm 'opeful, I'm your 'opeful Jimmie)
                But Herbert Smith's a nut to crack, so crack with all your
                    might,
                Oh, save your Jimmie, O.
                Have a pretty parley,
                Nobble Cook and[6] Varley,
                All for love of Jimmie, O.

                Let me introduce you. Mr. Cook . . . Lady Astor.
                Lady Astor . . . Mr. Smith.

Lady Astor: Well now, Mr. Cook, this surely is interesting. I've been
                just longing to meet you ever since I left New York. About

the poor miners, you know; I'm so interested in miners.
Now, I tell you, you simply must come round and have a
little talk with Waldorf. He'll be tickled to death to see
you.

Cook & Smith (As before):

Not a penny off the pay,
Not a second on the day.
No, we thank you very kindly, but we will not come to
    dine.
Though the Carpenter you be,
And the walrus J.H.T.,
You're mistaken, we're not oysters. We respectfully
    decline.

Lady Astor: Young men, you surely have spat an earful. You boys
make me tired. I shall go and join the O.M.S.[7] (Flounces
off)

Thomas: There! A matchless opportunity absolutely thrown away!
One would suppose you *wanted* a strike.

Cook: Now, Jimmie, no more of your games. I'll let you know
how I feel about it.

Song

('I am a Pirate King', from *Pirates of Penzance*)

I am the miners' king,
And this is the song I sing.
You've got to strike, a thing you don't like, at
    the call of the miners' king.
For I am the miners' king,
And a General Strike's the thing,
And there isn't a doubt that they'll all come out
    at the call of the miners' king.

Thomas: An 'umbler man by far
Is J.H. of the N.U.R.,
But I know what's what and you're talking rot
    and you dunno where you are.

> For I am the Railway Czar,
> And a General Strike I bar,
> And though it seems odd, I'm a little tin god
>   to the boys of the N.U.R.

Loud huzzas are heard off. Enter George V and the Prince of Wales.
Mr. Thomas prostrates himself.

Cook: I am the miners' king. . .
Thomas: 'Ush! 'ush! 'Ats off in the presence of Royalty! Your
             Majesty, I am honoured. Your Royal 'Ighness, I am
             deeply gratified. I hope you have come to give us the
             benefit of your advice in this distressing situation.
Cook: I am the miners' king . . .
Thomas.   Shut up, you fool!
George (Clearing his throat):
             Chrmmm!
P. of W. (in a squeaky voice):
             Go on, father!
George (sings):

> I am a *minus* king,
> I'm minus everything,
> If it weren't for the Press, you never would guess
>   I was even a *minus* king.
> But I *am* a minus king,
> And I claim the right to sing,
> If you hear me out I'll tell you about the woes of a
>   minus king.
>
> I'm minus everything,
> I never can have my fling,
> I have to be good as an idol of wood, while my Ministers
>   pull the string.
> Poor Kaiser Bill was a king,
> And Nick, and the Chinese Ming,
> But I've nothing to say, so I'd better give way to
>   Mammon, the only king.

Thomas: I'm sure your Majesty has my 'umble veneration to the
             last.
George: Now, look here, Mr. Thomas, is this quite fair? You have

been presented at Court, and you have your court dress
on, and here I find you making a disturbance on poor
Mr. Baldwin's doorstep.

Thomas: Please, sir, it wasn't me. It was 'im. (Pointing to Cook)

George: Is this so, Mr. . . . I don't think I have the pleasure of
your acquaintance?

Cook: Not a penny off the pay,
Not a second on the day . . .

George: Now, I seem to have heard that before somewhere.

P. of W.: Wasn't it at the Empire, father?

George: Ah, yes, Mr. . . . hmm . . . we greatly enjoyed your turn.
Let me see, do you know my son, Prince Charming? I
should like you to hear him sing. He's been wanting some
advice from a professional. You see, I'm thinking of
sending him on the halls if all else fails. Sing something,
Charming. What about 'Roses in Picardy'?

P. of W. (falsetto):
Put me among the girls . . .

George: No, no, not that one. Sing the one about our family. It
always goes down with a middle-class audience.

P. of W.: Oh, very well.

Song

('Tit-Willow', from *The Mikado*)

In Buckingham Palace a Queen and a King
Live deeply revered by the nation;
And our middle-class monarchy makes us a thing
Deserving the world's admiration.
For while Mary is opening her daily bazaar,
And George's *bons mots* can be read in the *Star*,
No wonder the bourgeoisie shouts out Huzza!
Which implies a discreet approbation.

When I was a child, I remember mamma
Adjured me always to endeavour
To model myself on poor darling papa,
And cultivate virtue for ever.
Of course, she would say, your poor father's a fool,
My dear boy, and no more than a suitable tool
For helping the Baldwins and Churchills to rule,

So be good, and let others be clever.

I took ma's advice, and I'm well on the way
To make a most popular puppet;
Though Kaisers and Czars put their crowns up the spout
I bet you all mine's never up it.
But sometimes I weary of doing so well,
And I've one bitter grief that no comfort can quell —
I never shall meet poor grandfather in hell,
For to heaven I'm destined to hop it.

George: I am sure you will agree with me, Mr. Cook, he has a beautiful voice. And so popular with the ladies. But at present his mother won't hear of it.

Thomas: Your Majesty, this is Mr. Cook, the miners' leader, not a performer from the Holborn Empire.

George: Er. . . er. . . Oh, yes, of course. (Brightly) And do you really eat babies, Mr. Cook? They tell me you do.

Smith: No, lad, he eats kings and queens, and especially princes.

P. of W.: Oh, how frightfully funny you are, Mr. Smith! If there's a miners' strike, daddy, I shall send sixpence to the miners out of my pocket-money.[8] After all, the taxpayers have to pay it.

George: I don't know what your dear mother will say.

At this point there is a very loud noise off, accompanied by a blare of trumpets. Enter Mr. Stanley Baldwin, followed, in marching array, by Churchill, and other Ministers.

Baldwin: Your Majesty, this will never do — hobnobbing with notorious Bolsheviks on the steps of Downing Street. If you do this kind of thing, how can we play you as our last card against the miners? You must go away at once.

George: Come along, Charming,[9] or we shall be late for family prayers, and your mother hates that.

(Exit the House of Hanover)

Cook: Come away, Herbert, I don't like the look of them.

(Exeunt Cook and Smith)

Thomas: No! You must stop and talk to them!

(Exit in pursuit)

Rank & F.:   Yah, boo! (Exit in pursuit of Thomas)

Song

('Duke of Plaza Toro', from *The Gondoliers*)

Baldwin: In enterprise of class-war kind
              When Socialists need beating,
              Their leaders with my spells I bind,
              The rank and file with cheating.
              And when away their leaders run
              I term their action manly,
              The softly-soaping, ever-hoping, leader-doping hypocrite,
                  the British Premier Stanley.

              My pipe, my pig, my talking big
              About the paths of duty,
              Invest my Tory premiership
              With beams of moral beauty.
              And this is how from day to day
              I diddle them so cannily,
              The smug and sainted, dazzle-painted, never-tainted
                  moralist, the British Premier Stanley.
              For dishing Labour folk, aha,
              My pigs are all in poke, aha,
              The smug and sainted, dazzle-painted, never-tainted
                  moralist, the British Premier Stanley.

As the song dies away, Cook and Smith are heard singing off:

              Not a penny off the pay,
              Not a second on the day . . .

Baldwin (declaiming):

              Is that the song that made a perfect peace,
(aside)   (And stacked my coffers full of dividends?)
(aloud)   O friends, O friends, be friendly to your friends,
              Who, being friends, would, if you would be friendly,
              Befriend you into Paradise, and make
              This land of ours a garden, bringing forth
              Brave flowers of steel and iron, copper grass,
              Brass sunflowers in their splendour and the show
              Of cotton asters sown in woollen mould,

                          While all around the aromatic scent
                          Of boiling oil should mingle with the balm
                          Of smuts descending from the factory stacks,
                          Or coal-dust sparkling in the laden air.
(more   This vision of our England that might be
impressively) Haunts me; the passion of a life's devo-
                          tion to the welfare of my fellow men.
(slowly and   But how shall these things be, you ask me? Thus: —
with deep   Let but the lamb inside the lion lie down;
eloquence)   Let but the worker gratefully present
                          To him who hath his body safe, his soul;
                          Let Capital and Labour both agree
                          To act upon that principle which made
                          Our Empire (*cheers off*) what it is (or used to be),
                          That holy principle that when the boss
                          (To use a vulgarism) throws the dice,
                          Then it is heads he wins and tails you lose.
                          Do this, and of my garment kiss the hem.
(crescendo)   Do this, and I will build Jerusalem.

During Baldwin's speech, Jix and Winston[10] have shown growing im-
patience.

Jix: I suppose this sort of thing has to be done, but I do wish
                Stanley wasn't such a mutt.
Winston: My dear Jix, let him have his head, that's the stuff to give
                'em. Bless you, they like it. Meanwhile, how are the
                preparations for breaking the Strike going?
Jix: They haven't declared it yet. You know, I'm half afraid
                they're going to cry off.
Winston: Don't suggest such horrid possibilities. They can't back
                out now. Besides, we must have blood. Fee, fi, fo, fum, I
                smell the blood of an Englishman, eh, Jix?
Jix: Provided he is one of the lower classes, I am with you.
                The O.M.S. has taken to killing flies for want of some-
                thing to do.
Winston (yawning):
                I wish I could kill time. It seems centuries since Gallipoli.
Jix: No levity, I pray. This is no joking matter. The Reds are all
                around us. The very fabric of civilisation is crumbling.
                Murder, rapine, anarchy, even leaflets, are being dissemi-

nated. Every other woman you meet has a Moscow crop.
Whenever I raid a night-club nowadays, I find incriminating letters lying all over the place.

Winston: What, Red letters?[11]

Jix: Well, not exactly. But the position is serious. We must act, let me tell you.

Song

('Shenandoah')

Oh, Communists, I long to jail you;
Arise, you middle classes.
Oh, Communists, I mean to jail you;
I'll see you put away
In the Scrubs or Brixton.

For seven long years I mean to jail you;
Arise, you middle classes.
When you come out again I'll jail you;
There'll be no room for more
In the Scrubs or Brixton.

Winston: That's right, my boy, I like your spirit. What this country wants is a touch of Mussolini.

Song

('Humoresque', by Dvorak)

Joynson Hicks would like a teeny
Weeny touch of Mussolini
Just to teach the workers what is what.
England's messes and distresses
Must be cured by O.M.S's,
Give it to the workers hot.

Blackleg gaily, hustle daily
Agitators to Old Bailey;
Preferably shoot the blooming lot.
Middle classes, be not asses,
Rise *en masse* to down the masses;
Raise on high the Fasces.

Rank & F.(appearing suddenly from the wings):   ROT!

During this song, Cook and Smith have re-entered, and Baldwin has been conversing with them with apparent amiability.

Winston (seeing what Baldwin is doing):

> Stanley, we're here to tell you this thing must stop. We don't mind you singing psalms, but we won't have you talking to those fellows behind our backs. If they aren't engaged in a conspiracy against the community, they damned well ought to be, and we mean to smash 'em for it.

Baldwin (to Cook and Smith):

> As you know, I am a man of peace, but in view of what my colleague says, perhaps we had better postpone our little conversation. Very pleased to have met you all the same.

Cook &
Smith: Not a penny off the pay . . .

(Enter Thomas in great haste, carrying an olive branch)

Thomas: What's this I hear? From far and near the rumour flies
> around me
> That war's declared and Strike's prepared. My Baldwin,
> you astound me!
> It can't be right to let them fight on minor points like
> wages,
> Especially when you and I and Mond[12] and all the sages
> At heart agree that there must be — we will not say
> reductions —
> Say, readjustments based on trust, accepted without
> ructions.
> Oh say, oh say, oh tell me, pray, unfounded is the story,
> You cannot mean to fill our land with carnage red and
> gory?

Baldwin: As a man of good will I with sympathy thrill when I hear
> you, dear Jimmie, declaiming.

Jix: Quick, Winston, speak out, or he'll veer round about, and
> at peace in a minute be aiming.

Winston: Let us give him no choice, with no uncertain voice let us
> tell him the answer is NO.

Jix: Or the men of the Suburbs will kick up such hubbubs that

> Baldwin will certainly go.

Baldwin: If I mayn't speak of peace will you tell me, oh please,
                what it is that you want me to do?

Jix: You must fright 'em and smite 'em and so disunite 'em
                that they'll be completely napoo.

Baldwin (to Thomas):
                My colleagues feel strongly, and rightly or wrongly
                I feel I shall have to say 'Shoo!'

(Baldwin and his colleagues shoo Thomas off the stage. As soon as
he is gone a great noise of wailing is heard off, and two frenzied beings
leap upon the stage. These are Lords Beaverbrook and Rothermere,
bearing placards one saying 'Red Ruin', and the other 'Red Plot Unmasked'. They rush to the front of the stage.)

Rothermere: All, all my leaders gone at one fell swoop!
Baldwin: What's up?
Rothermere: Red revolutions up! Blood, Blood, Blood!
Beaverbrook: The workers are rising in their millions.
Rothermere: They have occupied the Strand.
Beaverbrook: They have mounted machine-guns on top of the Nelson
                Column.
Rothermere: Red agents are sacking the National Portrait Gallery.
Beaverbrook: The restaurants . . .
Rothermere: the theatres . . .
Beaverbrook: the banks . . .
Both
together: . . . are in their hands!
Rothermere: Ramsay MacDonald is leading them, waving his blood-red
                sword.
Beaverbrook: They are disembowelling the statues in Parliament Square.
Rothermere: The Thames is running with blood.
Baldwin: Stop! What has really happened?

(Dead silence for a moment)

Both: Natsopa[13] has suppressed the *Daily Mail*.
Jix (with a loud wail):

                Ah! Oooo — ooo — ooo! The middle classes will starve!
                What will they have for breakfast?

Winston: Never mind, Rothy, I'll bring out a paper of my own and

beat you at your own game. A hundred to one I can tell
more lies than you in nine days.

Jix: But seriously, this is our chance. In face of this, Baldwin,
you see we must break off all negotiations.

Baldwin (His head upon his breast):
Vicisti, Gadaraee.

Rothermere & Beaverbrook:
Huzza! We'll go and tell everybody about it.

(Exeunt, shouting 'Red Plot Unmasked! All negotiations at an end!'
etc. Music is heard, and then enter Thomas and Citrine, representing
the might of the T.U.C. They carry banners marked 'United we Stand,
Divided we Fall', and 'Defence, not Defiance'.)

Song

('The Church's one Foundation')

Thomas: The miners' one salvation
Citrine: Is in the T.U.C.
Thomas: By our collaboration
Citrine: The world shall be set free.
Thomas: We did not want to call a strike
Citrine: We are not Bolshevik.
Together: Our mere imposing presence
Is meant to do the trick.

Citrine: We bounce and blare and bluster,
Thomas: Exceeding big we talk;
Citrine: But we are all a-fluster,
Thomas: Our livers white as chalk.
Citrine: And so we come here marching
Thomas: With banners and with band,
Together: To ask Baldwin to lead us
Into the Promised Land.

Thomas: Right Honourable Sir, permit me to introduce you to a
deputation from the Trades Union Congress.

Rank & File (entering suddenly):
Shurrup, Jimmie!

Cook & Smith   (off):
Not a penny off the pay . . .

Rank & F.:   'Ear, 'Ear! (he is ejected)

Song

('Medieval Art', from *Patience*)

Thomas &   We want to find a formula to end this senseless fight;
Citrine: We feel a little commonsense will put the matter right.
              To take a stiff, unyielding view is far from our intent —
              Halfway we come to meet you.

Cook (appearing from the wings):
              Not a minute, not a cent!
Winston: You hear them, Stanley. When they speak you'd think no
                   harm was meant,
              But mark the sequel. Mark how Echo answers 'Not a cent'.
Jix: Tell him off, Stanley, or I resign.
Winston: Same here. Tell him off, or we both resign.
Baldwin: As Mr. Thomas knows, in goodwill I shall never fail;
              But further talk is useless. What about the *Daily Mail*.
Thomas: The *Daily Mail*?
Citrine: The *Daily Mail*?
Rank & F (from the wings):
              There ain't no *Dily Mile*.
Thomas: Why, what's the matter? Tell me not Lord Rothermere
                   doth ail?
Jix: Alack, the *Daily Mail* this night has gone and kicked the
                   pail.
Winston: The middle classes gasp for breath. They fade, they faint,
                   they fail.
              How can they wash their breakfasts down without the
              Daily Mail?
Baldwin: In circumstances such as these, all patriots confess
              The time for talking's over. To your standards, O.M.S!
Thomas: Yet hear me, hear me! We beseech thee, hear us NOW,
                   O Lord!
Baldwin: The time is past, the die is cast; I must not hear a word.
              The laws are silent, arms resound. On Winston I confer
              For the duration all the powers of High Commissioner.
              And for myself I hereby swear that I will never cease,
              While Winston wipes the workers out, to sing the songs of
                   peace.
              Bring me my harp of charity, my trombone of goodwill,
              I'll keep them quiet while of blood my Winston
              has his fill.

Thomas: Alas, alack, alas, alack. They've been and called our bluff.
              Strike, workers, strike, but gently. (Aside) Someone say
              we've had enough.

As the curtain falls, the workers off are heard singing:

Song

('The Volga Boatman')

Strike away, lads, strike away, lads,
   A long, strong strike all together;
Strike away, lads, strike away, lads,
   A long, strong strike all together;
Now at last the giant moves,
Now at last the giant moves,
Strike all together, strike all together,
   A long, strong strike all together.

ACT II Middle-Class Life — Eccleston Square

The scene is laid in Eccleston Square. At the back are the doors of Nos.
32 and 33. As the curtain rises, the stage is empty, and voices are heard.

Rank & File (off)   **Chorus**

> **Strike** away, lads, strike away, lads,
> A long, strong strike all together,
> Strike away, lads, strike away, lads,
> A long, strong strike all together,
> Now at last the giant moves,
> Now at last the giant moves,
> Strike all together,
> A long, strong strike all together.

Middle Classes: **Chorus**

> ('London's Burning', sung as four-part round)

> London's striking, London's striking,
> Bring blacklegs, bring blacklegs,
> Scab, scab, scab, scab,
> O for Mussolini.

Labour Leaders (entering):   **Chorus**

> ('Oh, dear, what can the matter be?')

Thomas: Oh dear, how did we manage it?
            Oh dear, how did we manage it?
            Oh dear, how did we manage it?
All: Blest if they haven't all struck!

Thomas: Oh dear, isn't it terrible?
            Oh dear, isn't it horrible?
            Oh dear, isn't it worriting?
All: Maybe they'll shoot us all down.

Citrine: Oh dear, how get 'em back again?
Thomas: Oh dear, how get 'em back again?
Citrine: Oh dear, how get 'em back again?
All: Deary me, blest if I know!   (Exeunt)

Rank & File   Chorus

('Great Tom is Cast')

> The die is cast,
> And not a man in all the city works,
> Till triumph's won.

The doors at the back of the stage open, revealing Ramsay MacDonald at the door of No. 33 and Ernest Bevin at the door of No. 32.

Song

('Modern Major-General', from *The Pirates of Penzance*)

Bevin: I am the very pattern of a boss for this imbroglio.
        In the coming Labour Government I'll take the Chief's portfolio,
        Don't talk to me of Ramsay Mac, or Lansbury, or Henderson,
        With my services available there are no other tenders on.
        I run the show, I larger grow, my boots are far too small for me.
        I stand no nonsense from the rest; no order is too tall for me.
        'Tis I decree no tram shall be or bus in all the city, boys,
        Away with Pugh and Thomas too; I am the Strike Committee, boys.
Voices off: Away with Pugh and Thomas too, for Ernie's the Committee, boys.

(Confused cheers and booing: then silence)

Song

('Au clair de la lune')

MacDonald: On this sad occasion
          I can only pray
        Peace may come ere morning,
          Strife may fly away.
        All this mad confusion

> Cannot but postdate
> Peaceful evolution
> To the Labour State.
>
> In the House of Commons
> Lies the better way,
> Never mind your hours,
> Never mind your pay.
> There all's done in order,
> Tape is pink, not red,
> Here I am not wanted,
> I shall go to bed.

Rank & File (appearing from the wings):
'Ear, 'ear!

MacDonald: Ah, my man, you will live to regret this day. I wash my hands of it. *This is a war I have not sought.* [14]

Rank & F.: Not 'arf, guv'nor. (Exit MacDonald. Rank & File makes a derisive gesture.)

Song

('Crossing the Bar')

Rank & F.: Sickle and Soviet Star,
> And one good strike for me,
> And may I have a hammer or crowbar
> On me when I'm M.P.
> The House of Commons is a rotten place
> Where rotten leaders are;
> I hope to bash that Winston in the face
> When I'm a Commissar.

Citrine: Hi, you! Come here. (Rank & File slouches up)
Now which of us is running this strike, you or me?

Rank & F.: Call it running, guv'nor? 'Tain't running, it's a bleeding crawl. 'Owever, I leaves yer to it. I'm a one for Party discipline, I am. But if I weren't, strike me pink if I wouldn't biff yer round the ear'ole. Garn! Call this a General Strike? Know what I calls it? I calls it a blooming Church Parade. Fakers, the 'ole bleeding lot of yer! So long, guv'nor. (Exit)

Citrine: Ingratitude, thy name is workman . . . Now to business.

Boy! (enter a T.U.C. despatch rider)
Take this note to the Prime Minister at once. It's a peace
offer.

Rider: It's only half an hour since I took the last one, and the
letter-box at Downing Street is full.

Citrine: Never mind, take it. Quick!

Enter Thomas with a large envelope.

Thomas: Stop, boy! I want you to take this letter to the Prime
Minister at once. It's a peace offer.

Rider: Am I to wait for an answer? There's six of our messen-
gers waiting on Baldwin's doorstep already.

Thomas: Yes, wait. Be off with you. (Exit boy) How long do you
think we can hold out? I suppose they're drifting back?

Citrine: Well, there's no exact news. In fact, all our messages from
the country say they aren't. But of course they must be.

Thomas: The pressure of public opinion is dreadful. Did you hear
the B.B.C. last night?

Citrine: And this morning the *British Gazette* accuses the General
Council of being Bolshevik.

Thomas: And now the Russians want to help us win the Strike.

Rank & File (putting his head round the corner):
Ooo-er!

Thomas: It's frightful. Think what would happen if we won. The
Constitution might be overthrown.

Citrine: But we're not attacking the Constitution. This is a Purely
Industrial Struggle.

Thomas: But the *Times* — have you seen the *Times*? It's positively
rude to me this morning.

Citrine: It can't last long. We must put our trust in the men of
goodwill.

The strains of 'Onward, Christian Soldiers' are heard off. Enter the
Archbishop of Canterbury[15] with attendant clerics in procession.

Song

('Onward, Christian Soldiers')

Archbishop: Onward, Christian peace-makers,
Stop the floods of gore,

> In the name of Garvin[16]
>> Strikes shall be no more.
>
> We are not united,
>> Many Churches we,
>
> But we all upon one point
>> Are able to agree.

Chorus: Onward, Christian peace-makers,
              Stop the floods of gore,
              In the name of God and Garvin
              Strikes shall be no more.

Archbishop: I want to see Mr. Cook.
Citrine: I am sorry, your Grace, I am afraid he is not here.
Archbishop: Where is he?
Citrine: I don't quite know. You see — well —we're . . . not
            exactly — I mean the matter is now entirely in the hands
            of the General Council. Of course any reasonable offer
            will be accepted. (Adopting the pose of an auctioneer)
            Well, gentlemen, what offers? I am instructed to dispose
            of this General Strike — this perfectly good General
            Strike — at a considerable sacrifice.
Rank & File (appearing again):
            'Oo's sacrifice? Not yours, old cock.
Citrine: As I was about to say . . .
Cook & Smith (marching on):
            Not a penny off the pay,
            Not a second on the day,
            Though both laity and clergy intercede for compromise;
            To our slogan we shall stick
            And you'll drop a mighty brick
            If you go about hobnobbing with these obsolescent guys.
Citrine: Damn!
Archbishop: Ahem! I beg your pardon . . . Ah, here is Mr. Cook. These
            gentlemen were just saying that they were ready for the
            miners to make great sacrifices. Most gratifying — most
            Christian. Ah, dearly beloved brethren, the Scripture
            moveth us . . .
Cook: Cut that all out. Not a penny . . .
Archbishop: Dear me, this is most distressing. Pardon me, but which of

	you *is* empowered to settle this strike?
Citrine:	We are.
Cook &	
Smith:	No, we are, and we won't.
Citrine:	I tell you I am.
Cook:	You're another.

Rank & File (appearing):
          Yah, faker!

In the course of these pleasantries, the Archbishop and clerics, holding up their hands in horror, steal off the stage on tiptoe. Scarcely have they gone when fresh music is heard off. Cook and Citrine, who have almost come to blows, cease their pantomime as there enters the entire Liberal Party (three decrepit individuals).

Song

('From Greenland's Icy Mountains')

Liberals: We are the Liberal Party,
                The chosen people we,
            The country is behind us,
                It backs our policy.
            At least we feel quite certain,
                Our rule it would prefer,
            If we knew what we wanted,
                Or who our leaders were.

            We are the Liberal Party,
                We are but two or three,
            But some of us are Asquithites,
                While some prefer L.G.
            And some of us are Tories,
                And Kenworthy's[17] a Red,
            And there is always Pringle,[18]
                But most of us are dead.

            We are the Liberal Party,
                That's me, and me, and me,
            We get no votes, we lose our seats,
                What bloody use are we?
            We put up Sir John Simon,
                To curse the T.U.C.,

And the Earl of Oxford bars the Strike,
But we're not sure of L.G.
We *were* the Liberal Party . . .

Everybody: Oh, for God's sake, stop!
Citrine: What have you come here for?
Liberals: We don't know. (They slowly turn and exeunt)
Citrine: Then you'd better go back.

Music off. Enter Sir Herbert Samuel and Sir William Beveridge.

Samuel (recitative):

A word, allow me, kind ladies and gentlemen.
I have a word to say about this impasse.
Do not forget there was a Coal Commission,
Composed of men well tried in great affairs,
And all of proved devotion to the State,
Who put their mighty wits to solve the problem.
We with wide minds surveyed the whole affair,
And then reported.
And all would now be well had but the parties
Accepted our report.
I was the Chairman,
And now I'll go one better than before.
First, I will call on my colleague, the Director of the
London School of Economics, to introduce the question.

Song

('The Heavy Dragoon', from *Patience*)

Beveridge: If you're wanting a cure for this creeping paralysis
Known to the Press as the General Strike,
You must subject the problem to closest analysis,
Though 'tis a method you greatly dislike.
First, the coalowners must never be rude again,
Calling you Bolshies and saying you shirk;
Then in return you must give them a cruder gain,
Let them cut wages and go back to work.
Kiss and be friendly, boys, stop all this bickering;
Call off the Strike ere the zeal for it's flickering;
Put away anger, no more of this snickering;
Celebrate peace with a mutual liquoring.

Cook, Smith and Richardson, Varley and Co.,
Peace when I offer you do not say no.
Say yes, yes, yes,
Please to be rational, not international;
Banish with scorn all appeals that are passional;
Take lower wages and don't commit tort,
And seek to be saved through the Samuel Report.

Cook & Smith (appearing from the wings)

Not a penny off the pay,
Not a second on the day,
No more Sankey hanky-panky now the Unions all
    combine,
For the bosses' day is past,
It's the workers' turn at last,
So be off with you to blazes; for we won't go down the
    mine.

Citrine (to Samuel)

You see, they won't. We don't know what to do.

Samuel: This is terrible. Let me think. (He thinks.) Hush! I have it.

Song

('Tit-Willow', from *The Mikado*)

(To audience)

Right here in my pocket I've just what they want;
    In a minute I mean it to hand 'em.
It's short and it's sweet and it's perfectly neat;
    It's precisely the bait that will land 'em.
I showed it to Baldwin and he said with joy,
'If they swallow that, then why worry, my boy?
Don't commit me, of course, but 'twill do to decoy.'
    Here it is. It's a brief Memorandum.

(To General Council)

You'll find when you read it the miners get more
    Than you ever expected to stand 'em.
I thought of the things that'd please you and them,
    I wrote 'em all down quite at random.
No pledges, of course, but if you will say yes,
    I think I can say one can fairly well guess
You can trust Mr. Baldwin to clear up the mess.
I cannot say more, (aside) and I couldn't say less.
    It's a gem of a brief Memorandum.

During the second verse Thomas and Citrine have been reading the
Memorandum with every sign of delight.

Citrine: Ah! The strike's as good as over. Thank God, my reputa-
                tion is saved. In the nick of time. They'd have all gone
                back tomorrow.
Thomas: So now we can call off the strike.
Citrine: Just a minute. What do the miners say? (shouting) Mr.
                Cook!

Enter Cook and Smith.

Citrine: We have just received the Memorandum from Sir Herbert
                Samuel. What do you say to it?
Cook &
Smith: Not a penny off the pay,
                Not a second on the day . . .
Thomas & Citrine (together):
                Positively scandalous!
Citrine: We must call off the strike at once. It's a glorious victory.
Thomas: The community has triumphed.
Citrine: It all comes of having me for a Strike Committee. (To
                Samuel) By the way, you're quite sure the Government
                accepts this?
Samuel: Of course, you must quite understand — I have just come
                from the Prime Minister. There can be no pledges. It is
                impossible for the Government to pledge itself, but . . .
Citrine: Oh, of course. It wouldn't do for the Government to look
                as if it was beaten, would it?
Samuel: But Mr. Baldwin authorises me to say that the matter will
                receive the most careful consideration.
Citrine: Oh come, that's quite as good as we can expect after
                striking against the Constitution, you know. Well, what
                about it? Do we call off the strike?
Thomas: Of course we do — at once. I'll go and tell the Press.
                (Putting hands to mouth) All go back to work at once!

The cry is taken up on all sides and repeated from a distance.

STRIKE'S OFF! ALL GO BACK AT ONCE! GLORIOUS VICTORY!

The stage clears, leaving only Thomas and Citrine, who sing as follows:

Song

('For all the Saints', from Hymns A. & M.)

Thomas:	Peace, perfect peace, in this dark world of Red,
	Thank God, throughout this strike we kept our head,
	Now we can go off home and take to bed.
Both:	Alleluia! Alleluia!
Citrine:	Peace, perfect peace, and peace with honour too,
	In spite of Smith and Cook we've pulled it through,
	Just when the strike had almost gone napoo.
Both:	Alleluia! Alleluia!
Thomas:	Peace, perfect peace, the Constitution's sound,
	Statesmen like us are never wanting found,
	Praise to Saint Baldwin, with his halo crowned,
Both:	Alleluia! Alleluia!
Citrine:	Peace, perfect peace, we always feared the worst,
	Red revolution might from this have burst,
	This is the end we worked for from the first .
Both:	Alleluia! Alleluia!

CURTAIN

ACT III   Low Life -- Heaven

The scene shows the gates of heaven. At the back are two doors, one labelled 'Heaven' and the other 'Jugs and Bottles'. Signposts to left and right indicate the way to Hell and the London School of Economics respectively. The stage is empty as the curtain rises. Enter the ghost of Karl Marx.

Marx: The way is long, the wind is cold,
I feel infirm and very old;
But I am doomed to trudge it till I come
In the last volume to Elysium. (Looks round)
Is this the place that I so long have sought?
Can I at last enjoy rest dearly bought?
Where am I? (Sees notice on door) Heaven?
There's no such place.
'Tis a mere superstition of man's race,
Discarded since the eternal truth I proved
All things are by material forces moved
(With growing eloquence)
To one predestined end — the end of classes,
The final triumph of the exploited masses.
If this be heaven I must be dead or drunk;
I can't stop here — I think I'll do a bunk. (Impressively)
By heaven, I swear this place does not exist.
My whole conception is materialist.

The door labelled 'Heaven' opens, and St. Peter steps out and sits down at his post by the entrance. He sees Marx's ghost.

Peter: Are you seeking admission?
Marx: Good sir, my position compels me to say you're a myth.
You aren't there, you're nowhere, I won't see you, so
        there!
Peter: Your remarks to me seem to lack pith.
What has flustered you so? Are you anxious to know
        whether this way or that way you're destined to go?

(He points to Hell and Heaven)

Marx: I am seeking a land where the masses were fanned by
                    reading my works to rebel,
               And to throw off the yoke which my prophecies broke
                    into pieces.

Peter: You surely mean Hell. You must turn to the right and go
               on till you're quite enveloped in endless and absolute
               night.

Marx: Can't I stay here awhile? I am sick and senile;
               Mayn't I lie down and rest till the day?

Peter: Can you lie upon air? Can you rest on nowhere?
               If you do not believe go away.
               There are places in Hell where they do one quite well.
               I am sure you'll find Kapital lodgings in Hell.

Marx: But I cannot go there, for you must be aware it has no
               more existence than you.

Peter: Well, you must go away. You can't stop here all day.
               I'm busy, be off with you, do.

Marx: Oh for somewhere more cool! (He hobbles off towards
               Hell).

Peter: 'Tother way, you old fool! And ask Beveridge for
               Cannan's[19] old job at the School.

Marx shuffles away, dropping *Das Kapital* out of his pocket as he goes.
Peter picks it up and begins to read it with every sign of interest. Sacred
music is heard off; enter the Archbishop of Canterbury and attendant
clerics.

Song

('Rio Grande')

Archbishop: Come, brethren, we march to the promised land,
Chorus: On to heaven.
Archbishop: Our place is reserved in the heavenly band,
Chorus: And we're bound for the promised land.
               So it's on, on to heaven,
               On to heaven.
           Our place is reserved in the heavenly band,
           And we're bound for the promised land.

Archbishop (To Peter, who is deep in Marx):
          My man. (Peter makes no answer) My man! (Peter looks
          up) Open the gate, we're coming in.
Peter: Who are you?
Archbishop: I'm the Archbishop of Canterbury.
Peter: What did you do in the Great Strike, daddy?
Archbishop: I worked for compromise and called it peace.
Peter: Right turn!
Archbishop: But, my good man, I am God's vice-regent on earth.
Peter: Right turn.
Archbishop: Oh, if you don't want me here, I am sure I have no desire
          to come in. I shall be much better appreciated elsewhere.
Peter: Yes. The road to Hell is paved with compromises.

Song

('I don't want to play in your yard')

Archbishop: I don't want to go to heaven,
          I won't join the angel band.
          You'll be sorry when you see me
          On the devil's own right hand.
Peter: You shan't have a harp or winglets.
Archbishop: No, the other path I choose.
          I don't want to be an angel.
          I am going to the deuce.

(To his followers) Come, dearly beloved brethren, I think this is the
          way for us.

(Exeunt towards Hell).

More music is heard off. Enter the Liberal Party, reduced to two.

Peter (counting them):
          Only two of you? There must have been a by-election.

Song

('From Greenland's Icy Mountains')

Liberals: We are the Liberal Party,
          Our nonconformity

> Of our admission to this place
>> Is ample guarantee.
> We shut the pubs on Sundays,
>> We don't let people swear,
> We keep the public conscience
>> In our especial care.
>
> We are the Lib. . .

Peter (loudly):
> Go away!

Liberals:
> But you can't have heard what we said!
> We are the Liberal Party,
>> We are the chosen few . . .

Peter (louder):
> I said GO AWAY.

The Liberals look blank for a minute and then steal off. Peter resumes his reading of Marx. More music off. Enter Thomas and Citrine.

Song

('Dear Little Buttercup', from *H.M.S. Pinafore*)

Citrine:
> We are called leaders, Yes, we are called leaders, although we can never tell why,
>> For the last thing we do is to lead anybody, and mostly we don't even try.

Thomas:
> Now these last nine days we've been all in a maze, and we're sadly in need of a rest,
>> For a General Strike is a thing we don't like, though of course we did all for the best.

Citrine:
> In calling it on we'd a dreadful respon-sibility that's broken our nerve;
>> But for calling it off, though the rank and file scoff, the best thanks of the gods we deserve.

Thomas:
> So we've come here to claim our reward for the same, and to join the celestial choir;
>> For, thank Heaven, up here not a strike we need fear, and we're safe from both censure and ire.

Both:
> So, Peter, admit us and cunningly fit us with heavenly harps and with wings;

And we'll flutter around, and all heaven shall resound
    when the General Council psalm-sings.
Rank & File (appearing suddenly):
    Yah, fakers!
Peter (to Rank & File):
    Hullo, Charlie, come in and have a drink. (They go in
    together by the 'Jug and Bottle' entrance, leaving Thomas
    and Citrine outside. The door slams behind them. Thomas
    and Citrine look at each other in dismay.)

Thomas: That low fellow — gone to heaven!
Citrine: And we left outside.
Thomas: After all we've done for him.
Citrine: After this, it'll be their own fault if they have a strike
    among the angels.
Thomas: Well, it's no good hanging about here. Which way shall we
    go?
Citrine (looking at the notices):
    Hell, or the London School of Economics. Not much in it.
Thomas: No, it's a bit of a come-down either way. Well, which shall
    it be? Let's toss for it. Heads, Hell; tails, the School.
    (Tosses) Heads it is; this way. (Exeunt)

Elgar's music is heard off. Enter Baldwin, Churchill, Jix and others
marching.

Song

('Land of Hope and Glory')

Jix: By our firmness Tory
        Britain is set free
    From the plottings gory
        Of Bolsheviki.
    Firmer still and firmer
        Chains on Labour fix,
    If they dare to murmur
        Pass them on to Jix.
Chorus: If they dare to murmur
        Pass them on to Jix.
Jix: Now we come to glory,
        Honours sure to meet —
    For we need no mercy
        At the Mercy Seat.

There is left in heaven
   Room for five or six —
Austen, Winston, Stanley,
   Birkenhead and Jix.

Chorus: Austen, Winston, Stanley,
   Birkenhead and Jix.

Churchill: Go on, Stanley. We rely on you to get us in. This isn't my
          job.

Baldwin (clearing his throat):
          Chrrm! Chrrm! (To the others) There appears to be no
          one here.

Churchill raps at the door, which opens. There emerge St. Peter and the
Rank and File, holding glasses, and rather the worse for drink.

Baldwin: Chrrm! Chrrm!

Song

('Barcarolle', from *Tales of Hoffman*)

I did not cease to strive for peace
   Through life with all my powers;
To save men's souls I cut down doles
   And lengthened miners' hours.
To teach the fools I shut the schools
   And stopped the children's milk;
And all the time my tongue did wag
   As sleek and soft as silk.

So now from you I ask my due —
   A seat at God's right hand.
I claim the right to dress in white
   And join th' angelic band.
And with me too my colleagues true
   With angel hosts must mix —
Austen, F.E., must angels be,
   And Winston too and Jix.

In plain prose, we're coming in.

Peter (To Rank and File, waving his glass):
                Hic! D'you know these chaps?
Rank & F.:   Not 'arf.
Peter: Shall we 'ave 'em in?
Rank & F.:   No, 'tother place. They bloody well roasted us on earth,
                and it's abaht time someone bloody well roasted them in
                'ell.
Peter: Y'hear what he says. Y' can't come in.
Churchill: But this is monstrous. Do you know who I am? I'm
                Winston Churchill. If you won't have Baldwin here, have
                me. You need me; I'll organise Heaven. I lay all odds there
                isn't a paper up here like the *British Gazette*.

Song

('When I go out of doors', from *Patience*)

When I rule the Promised Land
I'll have you understand
All burkers and shirkers and devilment workers
    will soon be well in hand.

My manners may not be bland,
But my intellect is grand,
And with me for cunning no man's in the running,
    especially when I'm canned.

I am a burning brand,
I live on monkey gland;
Poor Stanley's a moron, but when there's a war on I
    quickly take command.

I'm Mussolini and
Napoleon and Alexand-
er rolled into one of me. Back me for bonhomie.
    Yes, I beat the band.
And now I'm coming in. (He makes for the door)

Peter: He's stronger than me, Charlie.
Rank & F.:   Out you go! (Exit Churchill bumpily) What ho, she
                bumps! Who's next?
(Jix runs out in fear. Baldwin backs out slowly, singing)

Song

('Yoho, yoho', from *Peter Pan*)

Oh dear, oh dear, I greatly fear I am not wanted here.
For all my services to man I've no reward, 'tis clear.
I did my best with all my zest a middle course to steer,
But in the end I have no friend. Good gracious me, how
    queer!

Rank & File (drinking):
    This is a little bit of all right, eh, Pete?

Music off. Enter Cook and Smith, accompanied by the ghost of Karl
Marx.

Cook &
Smith: Not a penny off the pay,
          Not a second on the day.
          Right through Earth and Hell and Heaven we shall keep
             on saying that.
          We have nothing else to say,
          For we never found the way
          To unlearn our pretty slogan when we'd got it off so pat.

Rank & F.:   Hullo, old pals! Come inside and have a drink.

Peter, Cook, Smith, Marx and the Rank and File line up and sing. By a
stage convention, the rest of the company swarms on to the stage and
joins in. The verse is sung by whoever has the best voice. All sing the
chorus.

Song

('The Red Flag')

The angels' flag is deepest red,
As Conrad Noel[20] always said;
And while the wicked squirm and roast
We give you all this parting toast:

Chorus: Then raise the scarlet standard high,
          O'er heaven it waves in empery,

To pay off every earthly debt
We give you GOD'S OWN SOVIET!

CURTAIN

Notes

1. The Workers' Educational Association (WEA) and the National Council of Labour Colleges (NCLC) were at that time rivals in providing adult education classes for workers. The WEA was recognised and partly financed by universities and the Board of Education: the NCLC, which was stoutly Marxist, refused such 'tainted money'. Some unions supported one; some the other.
2. David Amyas Ross, WEA Staff Tutor. Educated at Repton (where he came under the influence of a master named Victor Gollancz); he became a socialist early in life, and in the summer of 1918 appeared in the office of the Labour Research Department enquiring, on behalf of the sixth form at Repton, what they could do to help spread the Russian Revolution. After graduating at Oxford he became, first, an unorthodox but very popular WEA tutor, a Labour candidate in the 1929 election, the founder (with Peggy Norgate) of the Soho Gallery for selling fine art reproductions, and a wartime civil servant in the Ministry of Supply. His death at forty, as the result of a road accident, was a great loss.
3. Arthur James Cook, the eloquent and passionate secretary of the MFGB, who succeeded Frank Hodges after Black Friday. He died of cancer in 1931. Herbert Smith, of the Yorkshire Miners, had succeeded Robert Smillie as President of the MFGB.
4. The franc was at a very low level at this time.
5. It was commonly believed that the Astors and their 'Cliveden Set' had a great influence on J.H. Thomas.
6. Frank Varley represented the Nottinghamshire miners on the MFGB Executive; but was not a very influential character.
7. The Organisation for the Maintenance of Supplies (OMS) was a private volunteer body formed to help maintain supplies and vital services in the event of a General Strike.
8. When an appeal was made for the miners' wives and children, the Prince of Wales — the future Edward VIII — sent a contribution out of the income voted to him by Parliament.
9. Edward VIII was popularly known in his youth as Prince Charming.
10. Jix was Joynson-Hicks, Home Secretary. Winston Churchill was Chancellor of the Exchequer; a year previously he had forced on the nation the return to the gold standard — which was part-cause of the crisis.
11. This refers to the 'Red Letter', signed by Zinoviev and afterward generally held to be a forgery, whose publication in the 1924 election, combined with MacDonald's inept handling of the resultant situation, largely accounted for the Labour Party's heavy defeat.
12. Sir Alfred Mond, later Lord Melchett, the industrial magnate in the chemical industry; after the strike was over he initiated with the trade unionist Ben Turner the 'Mond-Turner' talks, which finally led nowhere. He was lampooned by the socialist song which began:

My name it is Alfred and English I vos
Of all dis great country I vos der boss:
Mit synthetical chemical products of coal
Over living and dyeing I give de control.

13. The National Society of Operative Printers and Assistants: their branch in the *Daily Mail* offices had refused to print a leader fiercely attacking the unions.

14. This is a reference to wartime posters in which George V disclaimed any responsibility for the war.

15. The Archbishop of Canterbury was Randall Davidson, who was forbidden by Sir John Reith to broadcast an appeal for peace.

16. J.L. Garvin, editor of the *Observer* and noted for enormously long, lecturing editorials.

17. Commander J.C. Kenworthy, Liberal MP for Central Hull and later Lord Strabolgi. He was at first a strong supporter of the Russian revolution, and once in 1918 turned up in the Labour Research Department offering his services in its support.

18. W.M.R. Pringle was left-wing Liberal MP for Lanarkshire during the war: his persistent questioning was a great thorn in the side of the Coalition government.

19. Edwin Cannan, economist, became a lecturer at LSE in 1897, and from 1907 to 1926 was Professor of Political Economy there.

20. Conrad Noel. The Red Vicar of Thaxted in Essex, placed there by his patron, the 'Red Countess of Warwick'. Noel displayed the Red Flag and the flag of Sinn Fein alongside the Union Jack in his church, which was more than once raided by students from Cambridge. See *Dictionary of Labour Biography*, Vol. 2 (1974), pp. 276-86.

4 COLLECTIVE BARGAINING IN THE STEEL INDUSTRY IN THE 1920s*

Frank Wilkinson

Introduction

Historically, the development of the iron and steel industry's collective bargaining system was marked by an unusual degree of industrial peace. The methods for peacefully resolving disputes over wages and conditions of work which had been widely adopted after 1860 proved more successful and persisted longer in iron and steel than in other industries. The joint boards of arbitration and conciliation established in the iron industry in the 1860s were still operating successfully fifty years later, long after most of those in other industries had broken down. Similarly sliding scales, by which wage rates fluctuated automatically with changes in product prices, continued in operation and extended their coverage in iron and steel well into the twentieth century, while those in coal and other industries, established in the same period, were soon abandoned. This commitment to industrial peace is well illustrated by an exchange between the employers and the union leaders at their meeting to discuss the participation of the Iron and Steel Trades Confederation (ISTC) in the 1926 General Strike. John Gregorson, for the employers, said:

> If there is one industry in this country in which no one would have expected such an event to occur, it is the iron and steel industry. It has been the pride — mutual boast, indeed — that no strike, no lock out, no serious dispute of any kind has taken place in the industry during the past half century.

John Hodge, president of the ISTC, agreed and admitted 'that the action of our Confederation was absolutely legally wrong, nay it was morally wrong.'[1]

* I would like to thank Laurie Handy, Ajit Singh, Bob Rowthorn and Jo Bradley for their help in preparing this paper and Professor H.A. Turner who commented on an earlier draft.

Despite this lapse during the General Strike the industry maintained its reputation for peacefully resolving its own wage disputes during the 1920s. But this was not because the problems faced by iron and steel were in any sense less serious than those of other industries. Iron and steel were severely depressed throughout the decade: by 1929 prices had fallen to 30 per cent of the peak 1920 level, few firms paid any dividends after 1921 and the unemployment of insured workers scarcely fell below 20 per cent from 1923 onwards. One consequence of the recession was a reduction of the real wage of the lowest-paid workers below their 1914 level. These grades were newly organised and not firmly established in the bargaining system, but the erosion of their living standards in the 1920s led to demands for wage increases from them. The employers were reluctant to concede any wage increases without compensating concessions on wages and working conditions from the higher-paid. Negotiations on these questions went on throughout the 1920s before agreement was finally reached in 1929.

This paper considers these negotiations in the context of the historical development of collective bargaining. It shows how successive groups of less skilled workers established themselves in the formalised industrial relations system and how this modified collective bargaining and redistributed the industry's wage fund in favour of the newly organised groups. It is argued that production techniques and related skills, industrial organisation and economic forces determined the framework within which collective bargaining could operate peacefully. Within this framework, however, the conflicting interests of sections of the labour force as well as those of labour and capital determined the nature of the bargaining institutions, methods of wage determination and the wage structure.

The paper is divided into two main sections. The first considers the historical development of industrial relations in iron and steel in the second half of the nineteenth century and contrasts various explanations of these developments. The second section considers the main issues in collective bargaining in the 1920s and describes the negotiations and their outcome in some detail.

The development of collective bargaining before the First World War

Formalised collective bargaining began in the industry in the mid-nineteenth century and its main features developed during the following fifty or sixty years. This development had elements of both continuity and change. Skilled process workers were the first to unionise and, although unions were not formally recognised, a system of wage regulations by joint boards of arbitration and conciliation was established in which the unions played an important informal role. Product prices were the main influence on general wage rates and this relationship was made automatic by the introduction of sliding scales linking wage rates with the price of iron. Organisation among semi-skilled process workers was the second phase of trade union organisation. These unions preferred direct negotiation to informal relations with the joint boards and this reduced the relative importance of the joint boards. Nevertheless, the new unions became committed to arbitration and also, eventually, adopted sliding scales. This section considers these developments as an essential first step in understanding the changes in steel's industrial system in the 1920s and emphasises the importance of the underlying economic and technical factors in explaining the industry's collective bargaining system.

Wrought iron making and finishing consisted of a series of linked processes. Iron was refined in puddling furnaces, beaten under shingling hammers to remove the slag, shaped between rolls in semi-finishing mills into puddled bars and finally rolled in finishing mills to produce rails, plates, construction shapes, etc. The change-over from wrought iron to mass-produced steel, which began in the 1870s, saw the replacement of the puddling furnace by the Bessemer and open-hearth steel furnaces, but the semi-finishing and finishing processes remained relatively unchanged. The various stages of production were controlled by process workers, whose skills were specific to the industry – puddlers, shinglers, shearers, rollermen, etc. – and who combined manual skills and metallurgical know-how in an era before the development of scientific quality control. They also had important managerial functions. It was general practice for the employers to contract out the operation of the individual processes at a rate per ton to skilled workers, who then organised production and hired and paid their own underhands.

The first permanent union of iron-workers, The National Amalgamated Association of Ironworkers (the Ironworkers' Union), was formed in 1868 and consisted almost entirely of contractors. The underhands were eligible for membership but had few rights and were afforded little protection against the contractors who employed them.[2] Other sections of the iron industry labour force also found membership of the Ironworkers' Union to be of little value to them. The blast-furnacemen, who were generally considered unskilled, did not feel that there was much to be gained from membership of a union whose 'main concern was to protect the interests of the puddler', so that 'the interests of the labourers and especially the lower-paid blastfurnacemen were entirely neglected'; they broke away and formed their own organisation.[3]

The industry's reputation for industrial peace began with the successful operation of the joint boards of arbitration and conciliation, which regulated bargaining between the organised contractors and the ironmasters. The first of these, the Board of Conciliation for the Manufactured Iron Trade of the North of England, was established in 1869, and a second was operating successfully in South Staffordshire by 1876. These boards consisted of one employer's and one operatives' representative from each member works. Their rules gave no formal status to the Ironworkers' Union. Operative representatives were elected by works' ballots of subscribing members, whether unionist or not, and the operatives' half-share of the boards' expenses was financed by a regular levy of all members and did not come from union funds. But, despite the lack of formal recognition, the union played a very important part in the successful operation of the boards. John Kane, the General Secretary of the Ironworkers' Union, was a keen advocate of arbitration and played a major role in setting up the Northern Board. Moreover, operatives' representatives were generally union members and national union officials acted as secretaries for the operatives' side of the main boards.

The arbitration and conciliation boards operated at two levels. Changes in the general level of tonnage rates were negotiated at full board meetings. The puddlers' tonnage rate was the key rate in these deliberations. This rate was standardised[4] and other rates linked to it, so that when puddling rates changed by 1 shilling per ton the rates for other processes were changed 10 per cent in the same direction. The rates for processes other than puddling were determined by local bargaining. Secondly, the boards provided procedures for resolving local wage rate disputes. Failures to agree at this level were referred to a standing committee of the arbitration board, which consisted of two employers' and two operatives' representatives. If either the full board or the standing committee failed to reach a settlement the question was referred to arbitration, the findings of which were binding on both sides.

Movements in product prices were the main determinant of changes in the general wage level under the arbitration and conciliation boards. Even before the advent of the arbitration board — as early as 1846 — the Thorneycroft sliding scale had automatically linked contractors' tonnage rates to the price of iron in South Staffordshire. This scale, agreed after a strike of puddlers at the Thorneycroft ironworks, established the

principle that the rate for puddling was 1 shilling per ton for every £1
of the price of puddled bars. The 'shillings for pounds' formula continued to play a major role in the determination of the general wage
level in the Midlands after the formation of arbitration boards, although premiums on these base rates were sometimes agreed. The
Northern Board made several attempts in the early years of its operation to establish a permanent relationship between wages and prices,
but these scales were short-lived. Nevertheless, despite the lack of
formality in the wage-price relationship, changes in product prices were
the main determinant of wage changes, even in the North.[5] Finally,
in 1889, a permanent sliding scale was established by the Northern
Board; subsequently the general wage level was automatically regulated
by the price of iron products, although the basis of this relationship
was changed periodically.

The effective unionisation of the contractors' underhands did not
begin until the 1880s. The first permanent organisations were established in the rapidly growing Scottish steel industry with the setting up
in 1886 of the British Smelters' Association (the Smelters' Union) for
open-hearth smelting furnace underhands, and the formation in 1888
of the Associated Society of Millmen for underhands in rolling mills.
These unions were opposed to contracting and adopted a policy aimed
at replacing it with the direct employment of all process workers —
skilled workers and underhands — by the firm. The underhands' resistance to contracting centred around the wage payment system. The
contractors' pay was based on output and they paid their underhands
time rates. Thus all the benefits of increased productivity accrued to
the contractors. The new unions, and especially the Smelters , grew
rapidly, and wherever they secured recognition an end to contracting
was soon negotiated.[6] When this happened the contract rate was
divided in agreed proportions between the ex-contractors —who
generally became the leading hands — and the rest of the mill or furnace
team. Thus the tonnage payment was extended to cover all process
workers, and, in effect, individual contracting was replaced by group
contracting.

Despite the ending of contracting, differentials remained wide. To
resolve the difficulties this caused and to guarantee promotion of
branch members to the highest paid jobs, rules for promotion by
seniority were introduced at the insistence of the branches. These
effectively eliminated inter-plant mobility of skilled workers because
each move meant beginning again at the bottom of the promotion line.
By insisting on promotion by seniority, based on service in a single

plant, the branch members virtually guaranteed access to a limited range of jobs at the cost of severely limiting opportunities outside the plant.

The growth of the Smelters' Union reduced the relative importance of arbitration boards. In 1890 the Smelters refused to agree to the establishment of an arbitration board on the same lines as those in the iron industry on the grounds that this would weaken the union.[7] Nevertheless, occasional meetings between the union and employers continued throughout the 1890s, with a gradual move toward centralised, direct negotiations.[8] The Smelters were also originally opposed to sliding scales,[9] but in 1905 they signed the North of England Sliding Scale Agreement with the newly formed Steel Ingot Makers Association. This was the first national agreement in the steel industry and the sliding scale continued in operation until it was frozen as a wartime measure in 1940.

Despite the Smelters' Union's preference for direct negotiations, the procedures adopted for these negotiations were curiously reminiscent of those followed by the conciliation and arbitration boards. The Smelters developed a procedure for resolving local disputes, under which failures to agree at plant level were submitted to a 'neutral committee' consisting of two union and two employers' representatives from works not directly involved in the dispute.[10] Neutral committees had the power to reach binding settlement, or, if agreement proved impossible, to refer the matter to arbitration. These committees, therefore, had a similar composition, and a similar function, to the standing committees of the arbitration boards. For central negotiations the Smelters met the employers in joint conferences, consisting of representatives of each employer and of each trade union branch (branches were works-based). Thus the composition of the joint conferences resembled that of the arbitration and conciliation boards.

The development of formal collective bargaining in the iron and steel industry in the nineteenth century, therefore, had elements of both change and continuity. The unionisation of the underhands and the ending of the contract system extended the coverage of collective bargaining, from its exclusive concern with the relations between the contractors and their employers, to include all process workers. But this did not dramatically alter either the character of the collective bargaining institutions or the method of wage determination. The relations between organised workers and employers became more formal as a result of the Smelters insistence on direct negotiations. But the presence of a delegate from each branch meant that the bargaining procedure retained

much of the representative character of the arbitration boards. Methods
of wage payment characteristic of the contract system – tonnage payments and sliding scales – were extended downwards to include all
the workers newly involved in collective bargaining. Moreover, despite
the changes in the composition of the bargaining group, the industry
retained its attachment to arbitration and maintained its reputation for
industrial peace.

Some explanations of industrial peace

Labour historians and industrial relations specialists have generally
offered one or more of three main explanations for the successful
avoidance of strikes and lock-outs in the iron and steel industry.
Firstly, it has been suggested that control of the unions by an aristocracy of process workers guaranteed industrial peace. In the wrought
iron industry and in the steel industry in its early days this group consisted of contractors. The contractors were very highly paid and were
consequently cushioned against the fluctuations in wage rates resulting
from their close association with product prices. In addition, as employers and controllers of promotion to their ranks, they were well
placed to discipline their underhands.[11] Peaceful industrial relations
outlived the contract system. However, it is argued that, even after contracting was replaced by direct employment, the high pay of certain
process workers placed them in a position analogous to that of the contractors, which enabled them to control the unions.[12]

The second main explanation for the prevalence of industrial peace
in iron and steel is that the union leadership was committed to an
avoidance of strikes and had sufficient power over the membership to
enforce this policy. The Webbs regarded the introduction of arbitration
boards and sliding scales as evidence that union leaders had accepted
the 'capitalists' axiom that wages must necessarily fluctuate according
to capitalists' profits, and even with every variation in market price'.[13]
Clegg, Fox and Thompson have been critical of this view and regard the
acceptance of such forms of wage determination as necessary if the
unions were to survive. But these commentators emphasise the disciplinary powers of the union leadership as an explanation for the continued success of the wage boards and sliding scale. They argue that, as
the Secretary of the Ironworkers' Association was the Secretary of the
North of England Board of Arbitration and Conciliation and the President of the union was the Secretary of the Staffordshire Board, both
receiving salaries for their services, they were to a large degree independent of their members. The union leaders also had the disciplinary

powers of the boards at their disposal, with which to coerce union members into compliance with board decisions. The unions' authority was further reinforced, suggest Clegg, Fox and Thompson, by the vulnerability of the contractors to replacement from among the ranks of the underhands.[14] One weakness in this argument is that commitment to sliding scales and arbitration persisted after wage boards had given way to direct negotiations between unions and employers. But Clegg, Fox and Thompson overcome the difficulty by suggesting that the union leaders' control of promotion by seniority placed a powerful disciplinary weapon in their hands.[15]

There seems little doubt that the successful operation of arbitration and sliding scales owed much to the enthusiastic support of the union leaders. But this does not necessarily imply that they required extraordinary powers of discipline to ensure membership compliance. In fact, there is some doubt as to whether the union leaders had the disciplinary powers attributed to them. The officials were the secretaries of the *operatives' side* of arbitration boards, and not of the boards themselves, and their salaries were paid from a levy on operative members of the board. There is, therefore, no reason to believe that this position gave them any more independence from their members than they already enjoyed as union leaders. The interpretation of the nature of promotion by seniority is also mistaken. Control over promotion is, and always has been, vested in the union branch rather than in the union executive, and is not therefore available to the leadership as a disciplinary weapon.

The evidence of the union leaders' success in securing compliance with wage board decisions and adherence to sliding scales is, at best, ambiguous. Much of it suggests that the industry was not sufficiently well organised, or that the union leaders were insufficiently strong relative to the branches, to be the principal factor guaranteeing industrial peace. The Ironworkers' Association was given formal recognition by the first arbitration board in Staffordshire, but this board failed because many ironworkers were unorganised and therefore the union could not accept responsibility for ensuring compliance with the board's decisions. When it was reformed, the Staffordshire board followed the Northern example by not formally recognising the union. Similarly, when the Northern Board had difficulty with discipline the employers proposed a joint employer/union committee to guarantee acceptance of the board's decisions. The unions rejected this proposal on the grounds that they were not sufficiently well organised for such a role.[16] Moreover the Ironworkers' leaders could not always guarantee their membership's loyalty to the board. In 1886, for example, when a decision by the Northern Board met with widespread opposition, the Ironworkers' Association was obliged to call a delegates' meeting to decide further policy on arbitration boards.[17] There is even less evidence to support the contention that the disciplinary power of the Smelters' Union leaders was a major factor guaranteeing the peaceful operation of sliding scales and arbitration. Clegg, Fox and Thompson show that, although John Hodge signed the 1905 North of England Melters' Sliding Scale Agreement, it had to be countersigned by a delegate of each branch, and some at first refused to do so. They seem to interpret this as a victory for the employers; but it is also a clear example of union branch opposition to executive policy.[18] There is other important evidence of the power of the branches relative to the executives. In 1902 the Bell Brothers, Port Clarence, branch of the Smelters refused to submit a dispute to arbitration and the union executive decided to appoint an arbitrator. The branch then exercised its right to appeal to the trade and the matter was submitted to a vote of all branches. Although the vote went against it, this form of appeal demonstrates the importance of local control in the union.[19]

The economic conditions of the industry provide the third main explanation for the successful avoidance of industrial conflict in iron and steel. In his study of wage policy and industrial fluctuation, Professor A.G. Pool argued that it would be wrong, on the evidence of the successful operation of sliding scales and the long history of industrial peace, to conclude that the latter necessarily stemmed from the former. It could be 'that the successful avoidance of industrial disputes and the acceptance of sliding scales stemmed from other factors peculiar to the iron and steel industry'.[20] These were the coincidence of payment by results and a large steady increase in production, which gave an upward bias to earnings independent of the effect of sliding scales. Professor Pool also took into account the conciliatory attitude of the union and leaders and concluded:

> But whether the leadership of an industry is conciliatory or militant in character must depend not on whether the industry is blessed with more or less than the fair share of men of good will, but on its underlying economic characteristics. And economic circumstances have certainly enabled the leaders of the iron and steel workers to obtain their ends by the pursuit of a conciliatory policy.[21]

There is little doubt of the importance of economic factors in explaining industrial harmony in the iron and steel industry. But this in itself could be regarded as being unusual: economic prosperity is not necessarily, or even usually, associated with industrial peace. Furthermore, one would have thought that the exposure of the iron and steel industry to the full rigours of the trade cycle and to world market forces, which resulted in wide fluctuations in both price and output, hardly provided a suitable background to a successful industrial relations policy. To explain why, in spite of this, industrial strife was avoided required a consideration of the institutional arrangements which allowed the benefits of increasing productivity to accrue to the organised workers without recourse to militant action. And this requires further examination of the role of the skilled workers, both in the process of production and in collective bargaining institutions.

The contract system is of central importance in such a discussion. The high level and specific nature of the contractors' skills and their semi-managerial status brought about an important element of mutual dependence in the relationship between the contractors and the ironmasters. This view is shared by Katherine Stone who, in a recent analysis of the contract system in the USA iron and steel industry (which, like the British system, was characterised by tonnage payments and sliding scales) regards contracting as a form of co-operative production.[22] In this position, and with their wage closely linked to the industry's prosperity with respect to both prices and output, the contractors had as great an interest in industrial peace as their employers. This could explain the informality of the operations of the arbitration boards and, because many contractors regarded arbitration boards as an alternative to trade unions, the weakness of trade union organisation. Thus the union leaders' attitudes reflected the underlying harmony in worker/employer relationships.

The extension of collective bargaining to cover the less skilled underhands reduced the degree of mutual dependence and increased the importance of collective strength. With this polarisation relations between the employees and employers became more and more formal. In the branches, however, the replacement of individual by group contracting and control of entry by promotion rules preserved much of the status and bargaining power of the individual contractors for the process workers as a group. Therefore, despite important changes in the composition of the bargaining group and the methods of bargaining, the underlying reasons for industrial peace remained.

But while these factors were necessary for industrial peace they were not sufficient to maintain it. It is unlikely that the methods of wage determination adopted would have been tolerated long if they had produced a continuous decline in real wages. This was avoided by the combined effect of the tonnage payment system, the increase in productivity and the workers' ability to resist reductions in the base (i.e. before sliding scale additions) tonnage rates. It became custom and practice that, once agreed, base rates could only be changed if techniques or working conditions changed. But as much of the change came piecemeal it was often difficult for the employers to establish the basis for rate changes and so earnings drifted upwards. However, productivity changes did not affect the earnings of all plants to the same extent and thus wide inter-plant wage variations existed. Statistics produced before a Northern Board arbitrator in 1879 showed a range of net payments (i.e. after paying underhands' wages) of from 19s. to 38s. per shift.[23] The high earnings were explained by the operatives' representatives in terms of effort, skill and responsibility, but the employers argued that the high earnings had resulted from the effect of improved machinery and mill management on output.[24] Edward Trow (General Secretary of the Ironworkers' Association) told the 1892 Royal Commission on Labour of differences of 100 per cent in the earnings of contractors employed on different mills in the *same* works and he explained this by differences in mill output rather than by differences in workers' ability. Trow also demonstrated the process by which such wage differentials developed:

> A may be as fully competent as B, but A's machinery is not equal to B's, B gets the lesser rate when he commences in order to put him on a par with A, but B continues to improve. A remains stationary, and the improvements of B increase his wages so that while he may have commenced equal with A he sometimes reaches 100 per cent higher wages.[25]

It became clearer from subsequent answers that Mr Trow meant that B's advantage lay 'not in himself, but in his mill'. This, then, is an early example of what has since been called 'wage drift'. The principal ingredients were: loose rates and worker resistance to rate reductions, technical progress, and the 'learning effect' whereby output increased sharply after the 'running in' period and after rates had been fixed. Union branches coped with the resulting problem of large differences in earnings between members by imposing promotion by seniority rules on the transfer of workers from low- to high-paid mills. This maintained wage differentials and kept the relatively low-paid junior process worker happy in the knowledge that eventually the high-paid mill would be his; it thus helped to prevent wage claims based on comparisons which could 'spoil the job'.[26] Promotion rules also maintained inter-plant wage differentials by limiting entry to the job hierarchy to the lowest skill level.

Both the high wages and the wage variation help to explain the success of the iron and steel industry's industrial relations system. The high pay of process workers explains their satisfaction with the system and their ability to 'ride out' earnings fluctuation related to output and price variations. The inter-plant wage differences help to explain the difficulties in co-ordinating branch opposition to executive policy. The branches were works-based and, even if the low pay of certain branches brought them into opposition to wage board or union policy, the high pay of other branches helped prevent this from being general. Promotion by seniority further reinforced branch separatism. The process worker skills were specific to the iron and steel industry and therefore not transferable between industries. Moreover, promotion rules made them equally non-transferable within the iron and steel industry. Thus process workers were effectively 'locked into' a single plant and this encouraged them to protect their own relatively small job clusters from outside competition.

A final reason for the good relations between the organised process workers and their employers was the partial coverage of collective bargaining. The existence of a large unorganised section of the labour force with a limited ability to increase, or even maintain, its share of the wage fund provided a cushion to profits from the claims of organised workers. Before 1886 the semi-skilled underhands were included in the unorganised group. Their unionisation into the Smelters and local recognition ended the contract system and the division of the contract rate amongst the underhands improved their relative wage position at the expense of the contractors rather than impinging further on profits. Thus the Smelters' success in securing local recognition rested largely on their ability to improve the underhands' wage position without affecting profits by increasing wage costs. Their complete recognition at industry level had to await their acceptance of the sliding scale principle and the profits/wage ratio this implied.

Summary

The period before 1914 saw the development of collective bargaining from the original concern with the relationship of the skilled contractors and employers to include semi-skilled process workers. This transition was accomplished without any substantial change in wage bargaining and methods of wage determination and, moreover, without harming the industry's reputation for industrial harmony. There are both economic and institutional explanations for this.

The basis for industrial harmony lay in the employers' and key bargaining groups' mutual interest in the industry's prosperity which led to the acceptance of arbitration and sliding scales as means of avoiding strikes. Local control of tonnage rates secured for organised workers a share in the benefits of increasing productivity and this helped to offset any reduction in living standards that might have resulted from the effects of product price fluctuations on the general wage level. Thus market conditions and increasing productivity which, other things being equal, determined the industry's capacity to pay, established the conditions for industrial peace. On the other hand, collective bargaining institutions ensured that organised workers shared in the prosperity and this was also of major importance in the avoidance of strikes.

But by 1914 the coverage of collective bargaining was still, at best, only partial and it remained the exclusive preserve of the skilled and semi-skilled process workers. Low-paid ancillary workers and labourers had so far failed to secure any significant measure of recognition from the employers, despite the growth of trade union organisations amongst their ranks. They were, with few exceptions, paid time rates and were excluded from sliding scale arrangements.[27] During the First World War the previously unrecognised groups were awarded national war bonus increases and in the early twenties their wages were made subject to sliding scale fluctuations by national agreement. But steel prices fell sharply and the low-paid workers' real earnings, unprotected by any links with productivity, were seriously eroded. This raised major industrial relations problems in a decade of severe recession in steel. These difficulties were only resolved after major concessions by the relatively highly paid process workers. We now examine these developments and their effect on collective bargaining, the wage structure and location of power in the union.

National bargaining during the 1920s

By the early 1920s the institutional framework for national bargaining was complete. Competing unions had, in 1917, amalgamated to form the Iron and Steel Trades Confederation (ISTC). This brought most of the iron and steel process workers into a single union: only the blast-furnacemen remained outside. The ISTC was much more broadly based than either the Ironworkers or the Smelters, and included in its membership large numbers of ancillary workers and labourers. The employers responded to union amalgamation by tightening up their own organisation. In 1922 the employer associations in heavy steel came together to form the Iron and Steel Trades Employers Association (ISTEA) to 'present a united front to organised labour'.[28] The ISTEA and the ISTC adopted the joint conference negotiating procedure of the Smelters' Union and the Steel Ingot Makers' Association. This provided the procedural framework for the prolonged and detailed bargaining of the decade.

Negotiation in the nineteen twenties revolved around a claim by the ISTC for an increase in the base rates of the lowest-paid workers. The ISTEA opposed this demand so long as the union was not prepared to concede a wage rate reduction for the highest-paid process workers and the relaxation of restrictions on weekend working. Bargaining continued throughout the period and before agreement on all issues was finally reached in 1929 it proved necessary to modify the bargaining procedure to reduce the direct influence of the trade union branches. In analysing these events we shall first consider the background and the content of both the union's and the employers' case, and then the course of the negotiations.

Low pay

During the First World War, and in the post-war boom, iron and steel prices rose sharply, substantially benefiting workers covered by sliding scales. But workers excluded from sliding scale agreements received no wage increases until August 1917, when they were awarded the war bonuses first negotiated in the engineering industry. After 1917 non-scale men received fairly frequent wage advances, which by 1921 had added as much as 170 per cent to pre-war rates. In late 1920 iron and steel prices began to fall sharply and by December 1921 the selling price regulating the melters' sliding scale had fallen to just over £11 per ton, from a peak of more than £24 in December 1920. This reduction caused a precipitous fall in the sliding scale addition.[29] But the war bonuses were not price-linked, and their value rose sharply in terms of steel prices. The Secretary of the ISTEA noted that 'as no action was being taken by other industries . . . ways and means had to be found to obtain reductions in the war bonuses of this large body of work people'.[30] The ways and means were found in agreements signed with the Iron and Steel Trades Confederation in April 1921, and with the National Union of General Workers and the National Amalgamated Union of Labour in July of the same year (called the Brown Booklet and the Grey Booklet Agreements respectively, although they were identical in content). The terms of these agreements subjected the wages of all labourers and ancillary workers to the fluctuation of the melters' sliding scale. The pre-war wage level of each grade was taken, with only slight modifications, as the base rate. Actual rates were calculated by adding to, or subtracting from, the base rate percentages given by a sliding scale determined by variations of steel prices around a standard price. Thus if the sliding scale gave a 50 per cent addition, actual shift rates would be base rate plus 50 per cent of that rate.

The Brown and Grey Booklet Agreements became effective on 1 May 1921 and on that day the melters' sliding scale was reduced from an all time high of 190 per cent addition to 166.25 per cent. Prices continued to fall and in 1923 the sliding scale averaged approximately 40 per cent. These automatic wage reductions caused by the collapse of steel prices reduced the real wages of the time-rated, lower-paid workers below their 1914 level.[31] Pre war rates formed the basis for the calculation of wage rates under the terms of the Brown and Grey Booklet Agreements, so that in 1923 the money wages of workers covered by these Agreements were not much more than 40 per cent higher than their 1914 level. Over the same period the Ministry of Labour Index of Retail Prices rose by 74 per cent. The resulting real wage reduction created a serious situation for a group of workers whose normal earnings were very low, ranging from 30s. to 50s. for a 47-hour week in 1923.

This caused considerable difficulties for the ISTC from sections of its own membership and from the general unions, which were organising very actively in the industry, particularly in Yorkshire, Scotland and the North of England, and were recruiting dissident ISTC members. The general unions refused to accept any responsibility for the effects of the Grey Booklet Agreement, as a spokesman made clear when he told the ISTEA

and you must not forget that our people had a grievance at the beginning. They did not volunteer to come within the ambit of the Grey Booklet Agreement . . . we do not forget, and our members do not allow us to forget, that during a depression in your trade you changed the basis on which we were paid. That basis was changed before ever we discussed it with you. When we first met you the predominant organization [i.e. the ISTC] had come to an agreement on the matter, and we were told in no unmeasurable terms that either we had to take that or no other system would be offered us, and we accepted it. Some of us have never been allowed to forget it.[32]

The general unions' subordinate bargaining position was reaffirmed in 1925 after they had cancelled the Grey Booklet Agreement and attempted to negotiate separate wage agreements. An unsuccessful strike in Yorkshire was followed by negotiations between the newly formed National Union of General and Municipal Workers and the ISTEA. Settlement was only reached after the NUGMW agreed to reinstate the Grey Booklet Agreement, to accept the industry's negotiating procedures and to grant its negotiators in iron and steel the power to settle without referring back to the executive.[33] But although the NUGMW was given full recognition, its collective bargaining position in the industry remained precarious. The ISTC continually refused to co-operate with it in a joint approach to management and negotiations carried out by the NUGMW at national level merely amounted to 'meeting the employers to discuss the application to its members of agreements already under discussion between the employers and the ISTC.'[34]

Despite the general unions' failure to establish separate bargaining arrangements for the lower-paid iron and steel workers, the pay position of these grades continued to be a major issue in industrial relations. Before the First World War, the ancillary workers and labourers had been excluded from collective bargaining and were generally paid the local labour market rate. But the war bonuses and post-war agreements created rates of pay exclusive to the iron and steel industry, which could only be negotiated in that industry. Moreover, the conditions that made possible the successful operation of the sliding scales for process workers — high basic wages and the semi-automatic increase in wages as rising productivity increased tonnage payments — were absent in the case of the ancillary workers and labourers. The low basic rates meant that wages were soon reduced to an intolerably low level as the sliding scales moved downwards, and, as the workers were time-rated, there was no compensating direct link between their earnings and productivity. Finally, the lower-paid workers were by now well organised and the desperation resulting from the rapid erosion of their living standards made them a force to be reckoned with, both inside and outside the ISTC.

Weekend working

In the severely depressed conditions of the 1920s the employers would not, and probably could not, increase the wages of the low-paid without some compensating concessions from the unions. The ISTEA's claim against the union had two main parts. Firstly the employers wanted the removal of restrictions on hours of work and on weekend working. The 1919 Newcastle Eight Hours Day Agreement had reduced the working day from 12 to 8 hours and had restricted weekend working by establishing agreed starting and finishing time for the production week. Weekend working was further limited by customary restrictions on recharging furnaces after a certain time on Friday nights and on furnace-charging before the official start of the working week. The employers were anxious to relax these restrictions so as to increase furnace production and reduce overhead charges by using plant more fully.

With these intentions, the ISTEA called a meeting in 1922 to discuss 'the state of the industry and the ways and means, if possible, to assist towards the rehabilitation of the trade'.[35] After negotiation the union side agreed to a temporary lifting of some of its weekend working restrictions. The production week was extended by one hour on Saturday and by eight hours on Sunday (with *no* overtime premium paid on the extra hours) and the union agreed to abandon customary restriction on weekend working. This agreement, called the Ways and Means Agreement, was made for a period of twelve months, after which it was to be reviewed. In August 1923 the ISTEA approached the union about renewal, but, after a vote by ISTC branches and a joint central conference, attended by a representative of every union branch affected, the union decided to terminate the agreement.

High pay

The employers' main counter-proposal to the union's wage claims for the low-paid was for a reduction in the earnings of highly paid workers, particularly those of melters on certain types of open-hearth furnaces. Melters' tonnage rates had been standardised when furnaces were very small and had not been reduced as technical progress had increased furnace size. Therefore, as output is closely and directly related to furnace size, melters' earnings were very high on large furnaces. Table 1 shows the average, and the dispersion, of open-hearth melters' earnings on basic, fixed machine-charged furnaces in 1926.

Table 1: Distribution of Open-Hearth Melters[a] by Levels of Earnings, 1925

Weekly Earnings (£)	1st Hand Melter	2nd Hand Melter	3rd Hand Melter	All Melters
More than 15	5			5
13-14.99	19			19
11 - 12.99	17	5		22
9 - 10.99	25	19	5	49
7 - 8.99	15	31	14	60
5 - 6.99	3	29	53	85
3 - 4.99			12	12
Total	84	84	84	252
Average weekly Earnings	£11.37	£7.83	£6.46	£8.56

[a]Working fixed, basic, cold metal and machine-charged open-hearth furnaces.
Source: ISTEA, *Survey of Melters' Earnings*, 1926.

The figures for average weekly earnings in the table are misleadingly high, because they show melters' earnings only for the time their furnaces were in production. But open-hearth furnaces did not produce continuously; their linings frequently needed repairs and they were periodically taken out of service for a complete relining. When the furnace was out of commission the melters were paid relatively low time-rates. However, it is unlikely that, even if non-productive time were included in calculating melters' weekly earnings, they would be more than 25 per cent less than those shown in the table. The earnings of third hand melters would then average around £5, a level some £2 a week higher than average earnings in steelmaking and rolling in 1925.[36]

Table 1 also shows that average earnings hide very wide inter-furnace wage variations. In each grade the highest paid enjoyed earnings 100 per cent higher than the lowest paid, and in the case of the first hand this difference was almost threefold. The range of earnings in each grade was much larger than the difference between the average earnings of first and third hand, but the highest paid first hand earned four times more than the lowest paid third hand. This extremely wide inter-furnace wage variation was almost entirely accounted for by differences in output. The range of tonnage rates was very narrow, from 2s.1d. to 1s.9½d. (the variation was due entirely to the adjustment of rates when the eight-hour day was introduced) but furnace output varied from 300 to almost 1000 tons per week.[37]

The procedure for revising wage rates to reduce the high melters' earnings was, as we have seen, traditionally based at the plant level. When new equipment was installed, or existing equipment was modified, new rates were agreed by local negotiations. If agreement was impossible the question was referred to a neutral committee and if no settlement was reached at this level the matter went to arbitration. The employers had used this procedure to vary the tonnage rate according to productive capacity in plants employing such advanced techniques as hot metal charging and tilting furnaces. But the majority of furnaces were the older fixed, cold metal, machine-charged types. Before rates could be revised it was necessary to demonstrate a change in practice or working conditions and in 1906 this customary principle had been enshrined in the Melters' Sliding Scale Agreement.[38] The employers failed to establish increases in furnace size and productivity as changes in practice and therefore could not revise the tonnage rate through the normal procedure.

When, in the 1920s, the ISTEA raised the question of the high earnings of open-hearth melters at national level, and proposed radical revisions of rates, they were clearly in breach of established bargaining procedure, custom and practice, and of existing national agreements. The ISTC executive initially opposed national negotiations about tonnage rates on these grounds. But, even when it showed a willingness to consider the employers' claim, it was hindered by the union's decision-making process and its political structure. Despite the amalgamations and its increase in size, the Iron and Steel Trades Confederation had retained much of the federal character and the democratic methods of decision-making of its constituent parts. As we have seen, in the early days each branch of the Smelters' Union sent a delegate to central joint conferences. However, as the union grew, this method of representation became less and less practical. Eventually, divisional committees, elected by the branches, were established, from which representatives to central conferences were selected. These representatives had the authority to agree a settlement with the employers or could delegate this power to a small group. Nevertheless, the union's side of the joint conference remained a lay body directly responsible to the branches and tended to refer difficult questions back to branches for decision. The branches were then, as now, plant-based and dominated by the tonnage paid workers. We have already seen how they asserted their authority by voting against the continuance of the Ways and Means Agreement, and that the joint conferences called to discuss this decision reverted to earlier practice by including representatives of all branches affected by the agreement. The importance of local power in the union also soon became apparent when the employers' national claim against the melters' earnings challenged branch autonomy in the determination of tonnage rates.

To summarise: the bargaining in the 1920s revolved around the union's claim for an increase in the wages of the lowest-paid steel workers and the employers' counter-proposals for a reduction in the wage rates for the highest paid and an end to restrictions on hours of work and weekend working. However, the employers' claim against the open-hearth tonnage rates cut across the established procedure for resolving such disputes, contributing an additional strand to the complex negotiations which lasted from 1924 to 1929.

National negotiations 1924-1929

On 19 March 1924 the ISTC met the ISTEA to discuss the union's claim for an increase in the base rates of lower-paid workers. The employers were only prepared to negotiate if the unions were willing to make concessions. Their case was summed up by John Gregorson, who said to the unions,

> you ask for stability and permanency in the increase you claim on behalf of the lower paid men. We ask for permanence and stability in some relief with regard to the hours which we hastily agreed at Newcastle in February 1919 . . . we ask that you combine with us to shorten the gap between the stopping time Saturday and the starting time Sunday. We also ask for relief in regard to the anomalies of the higher paid men.[39]

No agreement was reached at this conference, but Arthur Pugh (General Secretary of the ISTC in the 1920s) later recalled that

> the employers' side had, however, faced the men's side with a poser and placed on the Confederation the responsibility of deciding whether the low paid workers should get an advance or not.[40]

Subsequently the ISTEA and ISTC met in joint sub-committee and reached a draft settlement, by which the employers agreed to increase the earnings of the lower-paid in exchange for the restoration of the Ways and Means Agreement. But this was rejected by a union delegates' meeting. The ISTEA reacted to this by attempting, without success, to secure an agreement whereby the union's side of the joint conference had the power to settle. Eventually, however, the employers proposed a wage settlement which the union executive decided to put to a branch delegates' meeting. In August 1924 such a meeting empowered the ISTC's side of the joint central conference to get the best possible deal for the lower-paid in exchange for a temporary reintroduction of the Ways and Means Agreement. A settlement soon followed, which gave special bonus increases (not subject to sliding scale or overtime premium) ranging from 1s.2d. per shift on base shift earnings of 4 shillings and less to 2d. on base shift earnings of from 6s.6d. to 7s.6d. and restored the Ways and Means Agreement for a two-year period.

Despite the special bonuses, the wage position of the lower-paid deteriorated further as sliding scales continued to fall. In September 1925 the ISTC again approached the employers, in an attempt to persuade them to exempt the lower-paid from that month's 5 per cent scale reduction. The ISTEA reiterated its unwillingness to limit the discussion to the low pay question and suggested that a joint subcommittee should be set up to discuss much wider issues. But the Confederation refused to allow such a committee a 'roving commission',[41] and insisted that any matter other than the sliding scale question had to go to a full delegate conference. This was held in February 1926, and the ISTEA proposed the establishment of a joint committee to consider, among other things, the position of the lower paid, greater flexibility of working under the eight-hour day agreement, the disparity in earnings between the higher- and lower-paid workers, and possible revisions of rates in melting shops and mills to take account of technical progress. The union agreed to discuss the first and third of these items, as long as clause 8 of the Melters' Sliding Scale Agreement was not prejudiced, but flatly refused to consider negotiating either the eight-hour day or tonnage bonus rates. Consequently the employers withdrew all their proposals.

After this breakdown both sides made repeated attempts to re-open discussions. Eventually, in early 1927, the ISTC forced the issue by giving notice of its intention to terminate the Ways and Means Agreement; it claimed an increase in base rates for the lower-paid workers to replace the special bonuses and the *ex gratia* scale concessions (in February 1926 the employers had voluntarily frozen the sliding scale at 32½ per cent for workers receiving the special bonuses), and demanded the introduction of tonnage bonus rates for workers on time rates. A conference, convened to discuss the union's claim, set up a joint subcommittee to give detailed consideration to the proposals. But it soon became clear that the ISTEA was giving nothing away. It agreed to increase the base rate of the lower-paid by merging the special bonuses and the scale concessions, but was not prepared to give any additional increases. Nor would it agree to the introduction of tonnage bonuses, unless this was compensated for by a reduction in the time rate. The employers also insisted on widening the discussion to include the pro- posals they had made in the previous February. After two meetings, the second lasting three days, the union's side of the subcommittee decided to refer back to joint conference. The employers responded by raising the whole question of the authority of the union's represen- tatives on the committee and, after withdrawing all their proposals, made the power to settle at joint subcommittee level a condition for resuming discussions. The issue was not resolved until May 1928, when it was agreed that both sides of joint central conferences had full plenary powers; to make this more effective the unions accepted a reduction in the size of their delegation to conferences.

Meanwhile the ISTEA had been carefully preparing its case for a revision of tonnage rates. It had carried out a detailed survey of melters' earnings and, in addition, had gathered information on all possible claims against established tonnage rates in both melting shops and rolling mills.[42] On the basis of this study the ISTEA decided to rely on local procedure for claims against rolling mill rates, but to press at national level for a general revision of melting shop rates. The executive of the ISTC accepted that

the employers were on reasonable grounds in arguing that if they were to make concessions by a variation of the agreements in the case of the lower paid men, a contribution to the cost should be made by men in the higher and better paid grades,[43]

but they were very much concerned at the nature of the new claim. When they met the employers the unions refused to discuss the sub- stance of the claim and concentrated instead on the matters of principle which it raised. They were concerned about the extent to which the employers' initiative both breached the 1906 Melters' Sliding Scale Agreement and also was contrary to custom and practice.

The union's executive was clearly in an extremely difficult position. On one hand they were faced with the progressively worsening position of the low-paid members and on the other by a challenge to the tradi- tional method of wage rate determination. This challenge was all the more critical for the union leadership, because the power to fix wage rates rested with the branches. Any concession by the ISTC leaders on open-hearth melting rates could have led to a mass revolt of the union's most powerfully placed and influential members. The executive was therefore obliged to call a national meeting of all open-hearth melting shop delegates. The decision reached at this meeting provided the basis for negotiations with the employers. The delegates accepted the principle of a reduction in tonnage rates on output above an agreed level, providing a satisfactory settlement could be reached on claims for an improvement in the wages of the low-paid. They also resolved to suspend the Ways and Means Agreement.

A direct result of this historic delegates' meeting was an agreement between the ISTEA and the ISTC, on 14 August 1928, to set up a joint committee, both sides of which were given the power to settle without referring back. This committee was empowered to negotiate permanent agreements on: lower-paid workers' rates; tonnage bonus for time-rated workers; the Ways and Means Agreement; and arrangements for automatically varying the open-hearth melters' base rates with respect to output. Both sides accepted that a failure to agree on one of these items meant failure to agree on all of them.

Negotiations began on 12 September 1928 on the lower-paid workers' rates, the tonnage bonuses of time-rated workers and the Ways and Means Agreement. Agreement was reached on 11 October. The employers had attempted to extend provisions for weekend working beyond those in the Ways and Means Agreement and to modify the eight-hour day agreement to allow two ten-hour shifts in some mills. The union agreed to allow workers not on the three shift system to work 47 hours a week net of mealtimes, but refused to make any further concessions, and with these modifications the provisions of the Ways and Means Agreement were incorporated into a permanent agreement. Lower-paid workers' base rates were increased by the consolidation of special bonuses and the *ex gratia* scale concessions and this increased earnings by the extent of the Sliding Scale addition on the consolidated amount. Wage increases were also agreed for workers with a base rate of between 7s. and 8s. per shift (who had been excluded from the provisions of the special bonus agreement), so that more of the ISTC's members could benefit. Workers on time rates in process departments also benefited from the introduction of tonnage bonus payments for 'all grades of workmen in occupations which directly influenced or controlled output'.[44] Part of this bonus was financed out of a reduction in time rates, but the rest was a net addition to earnings.

With these long-standing issues resolved, the negotiation over melting rates began in earnest. After protracted and very hard bargaining, settlement was eventually reached in May 1929. The agreement, which came to be called the Brown Book Agreement, established the principle that (and the method by which) as furnace output increased, the melting rate was automatically reduced. Time rates for certain non-productive maintenance jobs on open-hearth furnaces were standardised and increased and the share of the melting rates going to each grade of melter was regularised.

The national negotiations during the years 1924-9 produced substantial benefits for the lower-paid. Table 2 shows the percentage increases to various base rate levels resulting from these negotiations. The lowest-paid received increases of 37 per cent, and the smallest increase was 3 per cent on base shift rates of 7s.9d. However, the increases shown are the minimum increases, because no account is taken of the provision in the 1928 Agreement for the introduction of tonnage bonuses for the lower-paid, an unspecified amount of which was to be 'new money'.

Table 2: Effect of Collective Bargaining in the Period 1924-9 on the Base Shift Rates of the Lower-Paid

Old base rates	New base rates	% increase
s. d.	s . d.	
3 10	5 2	37
4 0	5 4	35
5 0	6 0	20
6 0	6 10	13
7 0	7 8	9
7 9	8 0	3

Source: Memorandum of Agreement between the ISTEA and ISTC, 20 September 1928.

The costs of the 1924-9 negotiations were borne by the highest-paid. Control of weekend working was relaxed and the Brown Book Agreement reduced melters' tonnage rates on the most productive open-hearth furnaces. The effect of the Brown Book Agreement on the melting rates for basic, stationary, machine-charged, cold metal practice open-hearth furnaces is shown in Table 3. This table gives tonnage rates on furnaces with different output levels taken from the 1926 survey of melters' earnings and compares them with the Brown Book rates for the same furnace output. The average reduction in the tonnage rate was 13 per cent, but this hides variations in change from an 8 per cent increase on the least productive furnace to a 30 per cent reduction on the most productive. However, Table 3 presents a very static picture of the gains to the employers from the Brown Book Agreement. Furnace output was increasing steadily as furnace size increased and as the process was improved, so that the gains to the employers from the agreement increased progressively with technical advance.

Table 3: The Effect of the Brown Book Agreement on Melting Rates at Various Levels of Furnace Output*

Range of Furnace Outputs	Tonnage Output	Melting Rate 1926[a]	Brown Book[b]	% Change in Melting Rate
		s. d.	s. d.	
Lowest	340	2 0	2 2	+ 8
Lower Quartile	529	2 1	1 10	−12
Median	595	2 0	1 9	−13
Upper Quartile	698	2 0	1 8	−17
Highest	980	1 11	1 4	−30
Mean	596	2 0	1 9	−13

* Basic, fixed, machine charged, cold metal practice open-hearth furnaces.
Sources: [a] ISTEA Survey of Melters' Earnings, 1926
       [b] Memorandum of Agreement between ISTEA and ISTC (Brown Book), 1929, Schedule A.

Summary

The 1920s saw the third major stage in the development of the steel industry's industrial relations system, with the entry of ancillary workers and labourers into formal bargaining relations with the employers. This effectively reduced the homogeneity and the average skill level of the bargaining group and therefore modified collective bargaining in two important respects. Firstly, industrial relations became more formalised with full-time officials of both the unions' and employers' associations playing a much more central role in bargaining. Secondly, the character of national bargaining changed. Previously, centralised bargaining had been mainly concerned with *general* wage movement, whereas *wage rates* were usually determined locally. In the 1920s, however, the wage rates of the lower-paid became subject to national negotiation and this changed the balance between local and national bargaining. The consequent increase in the union leaders' responsibilities for wage rate determination necessitated a relocation of decision-making power within the union away from the branches and towards the executive. But this could only be achieved with the compliance of the branches, which had traditionally been controlled by the high-paid process workers whose earnings and working conditions were threatened by the employers' counter-proposals to the union's low-paid workers' pay claim.

There are several reasons why, despite these difficulties, national bargaining secured agreement on all issues without strikes or lockouts. Firstly, it is not inconceivable that the high-paid felt a genuine concern for the low-paid and were consequently prepared to make sacrifices, provided the low-paid benefited. John Hodge explained the branch delegates' rejection of the draft agreement made at an ISTEA/ISTC joint conference in 1924 partly by the fact that 'a good many of the branches considered that the advance offered to the lower paid men was not worth the extension of hours.'[45] A less altruistic explanation of the eventual acceptances by the branches of the employers' demands is in terms of the change in the balance of power in the branches resulting from the growing importance of ancillary workers, as the steel making and rolling processes became more mechanised and as the new race of machine operators became unionised. One important example of this fairly general process was the development of machine charging in the open-hearth melting shops. In the early days the furnaces were hand-charged by the melters assisted by labourers. But with the growth in the size of furnaces this manhandling was progressively replaced by machine-charging; and the charging machines were driven by ancillary grades who were paid relatively low time rates. Thus with the growing dependence on machines, some of the control of output was transferred from process workers to ancillary grades. It has been suggested that the effect of this on the process workers' control of the union branches was offset by their dominance of the promotion system to their ranks.[46] However, many of the more important of the ancillary workers — charger drivers, crane drivers — had specialised skills and were outside the process workers' recruitment system. In fact, within each branch, promotion lines for ancillary workers were established separately from those of process workers. Thus the change in the unions' composition which, as we have argued, transformed national bargaining, had its impact in the branches. The branches' eventual acceptance of some redistribution of the wage fund probably reflects a coming to terms with this reality.

A third clue to the success of national bargaining is provided by the fragmented nature of the union structure, which made organised opposition to executive policy difficult. The wide inter-plant wage dispersion meant that the very high wages were concentrated in a small proportion of steel works. Moreover, while each works probably had some workers who stood to benefit from the wage rate increases, it seems reasonable to suppose that these were concentrated in low-pay plants. This unequal distribution between branches of the costs and benefits of national bargaining no doubt helped the executive to secure support it needed from the union delegate meetings. Finally, the long tradition of industrial peace meant that bargaining deadlock did not result in strikes or lock-outs. The two sides returned again and again to the bargaining table and the union leaders were given sufficient time to convene and re-convene delegate meetings from which they eventually acquired the necessary power to reach final settlements.

These agreements extended sliding scales and, to a lesser extent, tonnage bonus payments to groups of workers who had previously been excluded from these arrangements. Furthermore, the relative wage position of the newly recognised groups was improved largely at the expense of the process workers who had previously dominated the employees' side of collective bargaining. In these important respects the events of the 1920s resemble those in the late nineteenth century, when the underhands successfully established bargaining rights from which they had previously been excluded by the contractors.

Conclusions

We can conclude by commenting on the economic and institutional factors favourable to industrial harmony. Economic factors set the limits within which the peaceful resolution of wage disputes is possible. Some minimum living standard probably sets the lower limit to the wage levels which workers find acceptable, while the employers' capacity to pay wages is constrained by some minimum profit requirement. If the sum of wages and profits is sufficient to satisfy both constraints, an economic basis for industrial peace exists, and any surplus further reduces the likelihood of conflict. An industry's wage- and profit-paying capacity is, in a static sense, determined by the difference between non-labour costs and prices; dynamically it is determined by the trend in prices relative to the trend in non-labour costs and productivity.

The relative importance of price and productivity constraints varied between levels of bargaining. In the free trade era prices were given by world market forces and therefore acted as a constraint on the industry's wage-paying capacity. On the other hand, productivity levels depended on the circumstances of the individual plant and therefore acted as a further constraint on wage determination at local level. This division helps to explain the two-tiered bargaining system. It was necessary for the employers to control wages relative to prices and this, in the face of organised labour (and possibly to control competition amongst themselves), required centralised bargaining and sliding scales. There was no intrinsic value to workers in sliding scales, but their acceptance reflects the common interest shared by the employers and key bargaining groups in the industry's prosperity. Before peaceful industrial relations could be established, however, organised labour was obliged to recognise its commodity status. Having done so, it found that the price of the product of labour, i.e. iron and steel, determined as it was by free market forces, was as impartial an arbiter of the price of labour as could be found. This did not mean peace at any price however: minimum living standards constrained the long-term downward movement of wages. But in the iron and steel industry local control over wage rates and increasing productivity caused real wages to rise. Differences in plant productivity meant differences in the capacity to pay between works and this explains inter-plant wage variations, the unions' branch structure and methods of controlling entry adopted at local level. Thus industrial peace was achieved by industry-wide agreements to allow product prices to regulate wages and was maintained because local success in securing the benefits of increasing productivity prevented the erosion of living standards which might have resulted from the effect of downward product price movements on money wages.

But, paradoxically, the nature of local bargaining strength prevented the growth of a more cohesive industry-wide union policy, the opportunity for which had been created by the growth of multi-skilled and industrial-based union organisation. With the development of promotion by seniority, the institutionalised horizontal division created by skilled unionism was replaced by institutionalised vertical divisions between plants. The trade union card gave the worker the right to a place on the promotion line and hence the right to the series of jobs which made up the promotion line. Skills, or job opportunities, were transferable neither to other industries, nor within the iron and steel industry, and therefore the iron and steel process workers had the status of unskilled labour outside the plant in which they were employed. If this was a high-productivity, high-pay plant, the worker's economic position was relatively secure. But in a low-pay, low-productivity plant, the worker could only improve his wage position at the risk of closing the works which, because of his unskilled status outside, would have resulted in even lower earnings. This locking in of the economic opportunities of individual workers to a particular works released the union leadership from any industry-wide responsibility for

them. Therefore in everything except 'the most general sense' the union
leadership became divorced from the particular interests of individual
member and irrelevant to the bargaining strength, or lack of it, of
individual branches.

This freeing of the union leadership from direct responsibility for
individual members placed them in a position where their own interests
were closely identified with that of the industry. Providing the work-
force remained unionised, which was guaranteed by the high pay
secured by local organisation in the most productive plants, the composition of the union membership was irrelevant and the union's leaders'
security depended on the industry's viability. Thus the leadership became effectively incorporated, because the membership established
locally-based sectional interests at the expense of more general interest.
Consequently the union was crippled in any attempt to pursue a policy
in the interest of the whole work-force and was forced to trade off the
interests of one group against the interests of another. The trading off
benefited the lower-paid but did nothing to increase the cohesiveness of
organised labour: in fact, by further concentrating power in the hands
of the leadership, it had the opposite effect.

Notes

1. Minutes of a Joint Central Conference between ISTEA and ISTC, 28 May
   1928, quoted in John Hodge, *Workman's Cottage to Windsor Castle* (n.d.),
   p. 366.
2. Clegg, Fox and Thompson, *A History of British Trade Unions Since 1889*
   (Oxford, 1964), p. 204.
3. Jack Owen, *Iron Men* (Middlesbrough, 1953), p. 9.
4. Puddling furnaces produced a single product by a standardised process
   which changed little between its invention in 1798 and the end of the nineteenth century. By contrast, rolling mills and other semi-finishing and
   finishing equipment varied widely in types, product and productivity. There
   was no basis for standardisation therefore and rates were negotiated plant
   by plant.
5. L.L.F.R. Price, *Industrial Peace* (1887), pp. 62-70.
6. Despite the Smelters' efforts, contracting lingered on in sections of the
   industry until well into the twentieth century. The final major dispute was
   bitterly fought in 1909-10 at Hawarden Bridge, between the Smelters
   representing the underhands and the old Ironworkers representing the contractors. See Clegg *et al.*, op. cit., pp. 446-8.
7. J.C. Carr and W. Taplin, *History of the British Steel Industry* (Oxford,
   1962), p. 142.
8. For example, an agreement was concluded in 1896 which standardised
   open-hearth furnace melting rates in five works. See A. Pugh, *Men of Steel*
   (1951), p. 108.

9. Royal Commission on Labour, *Minutes of Evidence Group A* (1892), Q.16, 404-8.

10. Members of neutral committees were essentially lay members of their organisations and not full-time officials.

11. S. and B. Webb, *History of Trade Unionism* (1920 ed.). p. 735. Clegg *et al.*, op. cit., p. 204.

12. Clegg *et al.*, op. cit., p. 206.

13. S. and B. Webb, op. cit., p. 339.

14. Clegg *et al.*, op. cit., p. 204.

15. Ibid., p. 206.

16. Pugh, op. cit., p. 61.

17. Ibid., pp. 60-1.

18. Clegg *et al.*, op. cit., p. 350.

19. Pugh, op. cit., p. 123.

20. A.G. Pool, *Wage Policy in Relation to Industrial Fluctuations* (1938), p. 173.

21. Ibid., p. 178.

22. Katherine Stone, 'The Origins of Job Structures in the Steel Industry', *The Review of Radical Political Economics*, Vol. 6, No. 2, (1974).

23. *Report of Discussion Before the Arbitrator at Darlington*, 21 August 1879 (Darlington).

24. Ibid.

25. Royal Commission on Labour, op. cit., Q.15,351.

26. Ibid., Q.15,352.

27. Some open-hearth ancillary workers were members of the Smelters' Union and were included in sliding scale provisions. The fluctuation of their wage rates with respect to a given price change was only half that of the melters'. If, for example, the sliding scale gave 2½ per cent increase to melters, it gave a 1¾ per cent increase to ancillary workers. These were called half-scale men.

28. J.A. Gregorson, *Memorandum of Work Done by the ISTEA*, unpublished (1932).

29. The selling price ascertained in December determined the sliding scale addition in February. The sliding scale addition fell from 190 per cent in February 1921 to 60 per cent in February 1922.

30. Gregorson, op. cit.

31. H. Gintz, 'Effect of Technical Change on Labour in Selected Sections of the Iron and Steel Industry', London University Ph.D. Thesis (1954), unpublished, p. 526.

32. Minutes of Proceedings at a Joint Sub-Committee between the ISTEA and the National Union of General Workers . . ., *5 May 1924*.

33. Memorandum of Agreement between ISTEA and NUGMW, 3 March 1925.

34. H.A. Clegg, *General Union*, (Oxford, 1954), p. 278.

35. Pugh, op. cit., p. 342.

36. H. Gintz, op. cit., p. 522.

37. The relationship between earnings and output is given by the equation:
$$y = 7.0 + 0.09x$$
$$(0.938) \ (0.002)$$

$$\overline{R}^2 = 0.924$$

where y = total weekly earnings of each gang of melters in £s
x = average weekly output per furnace.

This equation suggests that variations in output explain more than 90 per cent of the inter-furnace variations in melters' earnings.

38. See Pugh, op. cit., p. 602.
39. *Minutes of Proceedings of a Joint Central Conference between ISTEA and the ISTC,* 19 March 1924.
40. Pugh, op. cit., p. 375.
41. Ibid.
42. ISTEA, Memorandum of Cases Received . . . May 1927 (unpublished).
43. Pugh, op. cit., p. 425.
44. Memorandum of Agreement between ISTEA and ISTC, 19 September 1928.
45. Minutes of Proceedings of a Joint Central Conference between ISTEA and the ISTC, 3 July 1924.
46. H.A. Turner, 'Trade Unions, Differentials and the Levelling of Wages', *The Manchester School*, Vol. XX, 1952, p. 261.

5 THE NON-POLITICAL TRADE UNION MOVEMENT

A.R. and C.P. Griffin

Introduction

Prior to World War I, Liberalism remained the dominant ideology of the labour movement, including the mining trade unions.[1] Nevertheless, the growth of political consciousness among the working class evoked a combative response from those who feared socialism as an insidious disease; hence the formation of organisations like the Liberty and Property Defence League (LPDL) founded in 1882 and the Anti-Socialist Union (ASU) founded in 1908.[2] The swing to the left which developed throughout the labour movement during the war gave impetus to such bodies and stimulated the creation of new ones with broadly similar aims. Of these, the British Workers' League (BWL) was particularly connected with the development of so-called non-political trade unionism. Lord Milner (1854-1925), who financed it, saw it as a platform for his ideas on Empire preference and related subjects.[3] The National Democratic Party (NDP), which was the political counterpart of the BWL, aimed to recruit working class anti-German patriots in support of Lloyd George's coalition. Twenty NDP candidates stood for Parliament on Lloyd George's coupon in December 1918 and ten were successful; but the party disappeared in 1922. The BWL remained, advocating industrial peace and non-political unionism through its paper, *Empire Citizen*, and public meetings in working-class districts.[4]

The Vice-President of the BWL was J. Havelock Wilson of the Seamen's Union. During the war his union entered into an arrangement with the shipping companies which effectively guaranteed industrial peace in exchange for a closed shop. During the miners' lock-out of 1921, his members acted as strike-breakers, loading ships with European coal for Britain which continental dockers had refused to handle.[5]

Sycophantic trade union leaders were found at local level to advocate the 'non-political' cause. In Nottinghamshire, at least, there were some who spoke both for the BWL and for the Economic League which was founded in 1919 'to preserve personal freedom and free enterprise and actively to oppose all subversive forces . . . [in] British industry in particular'.[6]

The Nottinghamshire coalfield should have provided fertile ground for these organisations following the 1921 lockout. Nottinghamshire

miners knew that their wages were depressed by their being grouped
with less prosperous districts.[7] Also, the Nottinghamshire Miners'
Association (NMA) ended the dispute heavily in debt, so was forced to
impose substantial levies on its members and restrict unemployment
pay. Many members left the union, the fully paid-up membership
falling from 43,901 in August 1921 to 23,764 a year later.[8] Four of its
five Agents sat in Parliament for varying terms and were thus only available for union business during recesses and at weekends in a period
when local disputes were constantly occurring. This caused frustration
at branch level.[9] Then, the 'butties' (subcontractors), particularly at
the Bolsover and Barber Walker pits, were intent on protecting their
privileged positions. Meetings at which local officials of the NMA
attacked its political affiliation and advocated industrial peace were
held under BWL auspices throughout Nottinghamshire and Derbyshire.
In 1922 the NMA Council instructed the Financial Secretary to assess
the amounts received from the union's political and general funds by
the two principal BWL speakers, Joseph Birkin and William Holland,
and considered taking legal action against them and others.[10]

At the Barber Walker pits, Joseph Birkin established a central committee representing the interests of the 'butties', whilst at the Bolsover
pits an organisation calling itself the Midland Counties Industrial Protection Society, obviously inspired by the BWL, was established in
1923.[11] When George Spencer MP asked at a public meeting at
Mansfield who was at the back of this organisation, a member of the
audience replied 'The Bolsover Colliery Company'.[12]

However, the BWL attracted little support among the rank and file
but the organisations established by its supporters were to provide the
nucleus of the Spencer Union in 1926.

The 1926 lockout and the splits in the Nottinghamshire and Leicestershire Miners' Associations

The 1921 lock-out and the depression which followed had weakened
the district miners' associations, especially Nottinghamshire. Despite a
vigorous membership campaign organised by a left-wing pressure group
called the Mansfield District Committee, many men remained outside
the union. Then, when the 1926 lock-out started, Frank Varley and
George Spencer made it clear that they were in favour of a compromise
settlement, whilst the veteran Lib-Lab official J.G. Hancock took no
part in the dispute at all. Further, the long tradition of co-operation
between NMA officials and the owners manifested itself in a tacit
understanding that three new collieries which were being developed

could continue to work;[13] whilst from the beginning of the lock-out many men worked outcrop coal.

The NMA was unable to support its members financially and local Boards of Guardians were unsympathetic. Again, many Nottingham-shire miners lived in urban communities and so lacked the cohesive spirit of the close-knit mining village characteristic of most districts.[14]

During August, the fourth month of the lock-out, the Bolsover Colliery Company met delegates representing the BWL-inspired butties' organisation (whom the men nick-named 'the black hundred'.) Knowing this, the NMA leaders sought authority from the Miners' Federation of Great Britain (MFGB) Conference to meet the Notting-hamshire coal-owners, but this was refused. The Bolsover Company then concluded an agreement with 'the black hundred', and most of their men went back to work. All the owners in Nottinghamshire and Derbyshire then re-opened their pits on the same terms. The Digby Colliery Company reported to the owners' association on 20 August that copies of the new terms were displayed for men to see as they signed on, 'but our managers state that the majority of the men do not appear to take any notice of the details'.[15]

Complete demoralisation set in among the men, who found strangers taking their jobs. Spencer and Varley were now in a quandary. They could not negotiate a return to work but were helpless to stem the flow of men going back. This was the situation at Digby and New London on 5 October when Spencer agreed to arrange for the few still out to return to work. Seventy per cent of the NMA's 34,000 members were by then back at work in the county. Following his expulsion from the MFGB conference Spencer was offered and accepted leadership of the 'breakaway'. After failing to carry the rest of the NMA Council with them, the Spencer group decided to form a separate union, which the owners recognised.[16]

The events in Leicestershire ran parallel to those in Nottinghamshire. From the outset, at Ibstock colliery more than the proper number of safety men were at work. Then, in July the owners twice invited the Leicestershire Miners' Association (LMA) leaders to meet them, following which they offered to re-open their pits on the pre-stoppage conditions, but these moves were rejected.[17]

By 13 September the LMA Council reacted to the spread of out-cropping and to men returning to work in substantial numbers by requesting the MFGB's permission to meet the Leicestershire coal-owners, but this was refused. Instead, after a visit from A.J. Cook, General Secretary of the MFGB, they resolved 'to stand firm by

Federation policy' although eighty per cent of their members were then back at work.[18]

During the first week of October, the Leicestershire owners publicised terms on which their pits were open for work on billboards, in newspaper and cinema advertisements, and in letters mailed to their employees. On 9 October the LMA Council resolved to write to Cook

> explaining that we as a Council have not officially called off the lockout as stated in the press and that district terms have not been accepted or agreed between us and Leicestershire colliery owners. But in the view of the fact that 90 per cent of the men are back at work we could not ask our members to stay out any longer and the Council itself will sign on at their respective collieries by 13 October.[19]

Jack Smith, the left-wing Agent of the LMA, wrote to his Council in these terms:

> I am desirous of serving an organisation that is loyal to the Miners' Federation. If the Council cannot see its way clear to give the lead to the men then I shall be compelled to refuse to obey its dictates and work only on behalf of Federation members and in support of its policy.

An attempt to demand Smith's resignation was defeated and instead, after a joint meeting with the MFGB Executive, the Council members resolved to cease work again and to urge their members to do the same. This move had no chance of succeeding. Indeed, a meeting of branch committee men suggested that the Federation's propaganda sheet should be put to 'a suitable purpose'. Council itself was so demoralised that a motion to secede from the MFGB was only narrowly defeated.[20]

Jack Smith told the MFGB Conference on 13 November that his duty was to his loyal members even if there were only two of them, and by this time there were undoubtedly very few.[21] Within a week, the Federation had authorised an organised resumption of work in all districts, but the Leicestershire owners now refused to accept Smith as a member of the LMA deputation. At first, Council supported Smith but on 18 January 1927 agreed to send a deputation without him. Meantime, several branches had demanded a ballot vote to test whether Smith retained the confidence of his members; whilst T. Growdridge the Secretary, and W. Blower the President, subjected him to humiliating treatment. On 1 February Smith wrote offering his resignation because he could not 'stand the mental strain any longer' and excused his absence from the Council meeting saying it was impossible for him 'to attend any meeting until the men have expressed their opinions on the matter'. However, Council did not give the men any opportunity to express their opinions. They simply decided to accept the resignation.[22] The minority of Council members who thought the matter should go to ballot were quickly silenced.

Trouble between Smith and the LMA Council was not new. In a district traditionally Lib-Lab in outlook, he belonged to the left wing and at times acted in a somewhat flamboyant manner; (for example, some years earlier when working as a miner in Nottinghamshire, he threw a brick through the window of the Miners' Offices in protest against the NMA's policies.)[23] He had been in dispute with Council regarding his salary, which he considered inadequate, and his expense claims, which they considered excessive, and had annoyed them intensely by appealing to the MFGB Executive over this domestic issue and also by holding public meetings without their authority. Then, during the 1926 dispute, he had spent much time touring the country with A.J. Cook and in Russia on a fund-raising mission instead of concentrating on the situation in Leicestershire. Finally, he had become an embarrassment to them by making himself *persona non grata* with the district coal-owners' association with whom the LMA had long had a warm relationship.[24]

Smith reacted by forming a 'breakaway' union with an office near Whitwick Colliery where most of his support lay. He claimed that his was the legitimate union. Supporting Smith at public meetings, Richard Hatton, a Whitwick miner and member of Coalville UDC, said the LMA Council had acted unconstitutionally and thus forfeited the right to speak for the miners. The MFGB Executive tried to heal the breach but the LMA refused to discuss the matter with them and Smith's union soon collapsed. Its minimal support may be judged by its first month's contributions of £25.10s. representing perhaps 250 members.[25]

Then, in March 1927, a delegate to Council and ex-Vice President of the LMA, G.J. Brooks, proposed that the Association should form itself into a non-political union like Spencer's. He suggested that members should vote for delegates pledged 'to free the Association from politics and amend the rules to that effect'.[26] So it is not surprising that Growdridge was questioned about Leicestershire's attitude to Brooks and non-political unionism at the MFGB Conference on 2 June 1927. The President of the MFGB, Herbert Smith, in defending Growdridge said :

> We have got to take our Leicester friends as they are and try to
> bring them into the fold. They may not be moving like us . . . I
> have been . . . there and I had to smile on two men.[27]

The Whitwick branch later made an unsuccessful attempt to have
Smith appointed as an agent to build up the membership which had
fallen from about 6,000 to about 2,500. For many years thereafter
Smith had difficulty in earning a living and suffered considerable personal hardship. His last move in connection with LMA affairs was made in
1931 when he tried to influence elections of branch delegates by
making derogatory allegations regarding various officials of the union
and was threatened with legal action if he persisted.

Summarising, it seems that Thomas Growdridge, with the backing of
the overwhelming majority of his Council and branch officials, achieved
in Leicestershire what Spencer tried to achieve in Nottinghamshire: a
tacit agreement on a return to work on compromise terms. The LMA
subsequently pursued the same sort of collaborationist policy with the
Leicester owners as Spencer did with those in Nottinghamshire, although the owners refused to maintain the long-standing closed shop.
We may conclude that a separate 'industrial' union would have been an
embarrassment to the owners in Leicestershire because they obtained
the relationship they wanted with the official union. The MFGB's
attitude is more difficult to understand. In effect, they accepted the
legitimacy of a Spencer-type organisation and allowed Jack Smith, who
had tried to uphold the policy of the MFGB, to sink. Smith's error was
to absent himself from the County during much of the dispute, leaving
Growdridge, the Secretary, ably supported by the President, in undisputed charge of the organisational machine so that he was always on
the defensive. They called the meetings to which he was summoned;
and Growdridge, as Secretary, was the Association's official correspondent. One can only conclude that the MFGB Executive recognised that,
however they might dislike what Growdridge had done, his position was
impregnable.

Having Liberal sympathies, Growdridge opposed payment of the
political levy, and Leicestershire made no contribution to the MFGB's
Parliamentary Fund between July 1928 and December 1934. After a
derisory payment from capital in 1935, they failed to pay again in 1936,
and in September 1937 the MFGB instructed their President and Secretary to meet the LMA Executive to try to induce them to support the
political fund.[28] So, in this respect also, the LMA acted as a Spencer-
type union.

Wilson, Hodges and Spencer

Among the Spencer papers is a pile of letter headings of the 'Non-Political Trade Union Movement' founded by Havelock Wilson. This Movement clearly had its antecedents in the British Workers' League.

During the War, Wilson's members bore the brunt of Germany's U-boat campaign, so it is perhaps natural that he, as well as shipowners, should have shared the anti-German sentiment of the British Empire Union (BEU) with which the BWL was associated and that he should have been antagonistic to those left-wing labour people who opposed Britain's participation in the war. At the same time, he and the shipowners struck a deal which provided his union with a virtual closed shop in return for industrial peace. His prominent role in the BWL can therefore be well understood. Besides strike-breaking during the 1921 lock-out his union refused to support the General Strike in 1926.

When George Spencer broke with the MFGB on 8 October he was not convinced of the wisdom of forming a non-political union, but hoped for some weeks to be able to win legitimacy for his group and continue to be a Labour MP. The Spencer group continued to meet at the Miners' Offices until 1 November and a meeting they held on that day was attended by three of the other four officials for part of the time,[29] but Spencer was the only permanent official to attend the negotiations with the owners which commenced on 16 November. The new union was inaugurated a few days later.[30]

Spencer had some support from Frank Hodges who was then secretary of the Miners' International. Three weeks before the 1926 lock-out began, Hodges had said at Nottingham that it would be better for the miners to accept a temporary lengthening of the shift 'up to the extent of half-an-hour rather than submit to the depressing and devastating influence of the low wage'. Then, on 19 May, he accused miners' leaders of a 'noticeable disposition to fly-away from economic facts'. Ten days later, he asserted that if the MFGB's campaign for the maintenance of existing wages and hours were successful, 'it would be a victory only for some men, a minority of men fortunate enough to be working in the best districts, or even the best mines within those districts.'[31] More fundamental, perhaps, was his assertion reported on 11 October:

> The Federation is crumbling up. The district associations alone remain intact and virile. The district leaders have now to consider, not district versus national settlements, but district versus unauthorised pit settlements . . . The problem for the present . . . is how to get

the best possible terms for the men, not what we would like to get, not our ideal agreement, but the very maximum which the industry, plus able negotiations, can now yield.

He also said: 'The one man, who, in recent Parliamentary debates, has made the most practical and constructive speeches on behalf of the miners is Mr George Spencer MP.'[32]

Spencer no doubt welcomed speeches such as these, but Hodges gave little practical help. After all, he had no wish to give up the secretaryship of the Miners' International for which he was paid £500 a year plus perquisites and expenses, although he was forced to relinquish it in July 1927 following his appointment as a member of the Electricity Board.[33] Subsequently, he accepted various company directorships including the lucrative chairmanship of the Leicestershire Colliery and Pipe Company Ltd, and when he died in 1947 he left £132,959.[34]

By December 1926, 'breakaway' unions on the Spencer pattern had been formed in several districts from among men who had returned to work before the lock-out ended. In Yorkshire, the support for Spencerism was concentrated mainly at Bentley and Askern. Some 80 members of the Spencer Union moved into Yorkshire from Harworth but were quickly induced to join the Yorkshire Miners' Association.[35] The Northumberland and Durham union had considerable help and encouragement from some colliery owners (e.g. Lord Londonderry).[36]

Havelock Wilson openly promoted the miners' breakaway. On 7 July 1927 a deputation from miners' non-political unions in Scotland, Durham, the Midlands and South Wales was received by the Executive Committee of the National Union of Seamen (NUS) and the following motion was carried:

That this Council resolves in the best interests of the National Union of Seamen to give financial support in the way of a loan to the Non-Political Association, the loan not to be less than £10,000, free of interest.

Bill Davies, the General Secretary, was asked to sign a cheque for £10,000, but refused. On 1 August, a special conference of the NUS endorsed the decision to make the loan, but payment was held up for some time because Davies and others sought an injunction to prevent it. Wilson took his revenge by having them expelled from the union.[37]

At a dinner held at NUS Headquarters on 8 July attended by leaders of the NUS and the miners' industrial unions, including Spencer and

Hodges, Wilson said:

> They had decided to establish an industrial union for the miners, in
> which politics would be debarred . . . he intended to back the miners
> up to the hilt, and in that he would go 'the whole hog'.[38]

At about the same time, Hodges was invited to accept the presidency of
a Federation of Miners' Industrial Unions but declined, though he gave
it his blessing:

> That there is a movement among the men for new leaders is apparent
> from the fact that these organisations have grown up in spite of the
> opposition of the Miners' Federation. My own view is that as long as
> the present leaders are there the lot of the miners will not improve.

Spencer was appointed President instead.[39]

The NUS sent 'three or four motor cars and three or four fully paid
agents for the services of the non-political movement in South Wales',
whilst a paper calling itself *The Non-Political Miners' Journal* had its
editorial office at NUS Headquarters, which was also the address of the
Non-Political Union itself.

One public meeting in support of the new union held at Newcastle-
upon-Tyne was addressed by Wilson, Hodges and Spencer. The MFGB
reported that 'Special invitations were issued to employers. Free omni-
bus and railway tickets were issued by the colliery employers' officials
and motor rides given to encourage men to attend.'[40]

In June 1927, Wilson issued a circular in the North-East in which he
appealed for £30,000 to establish nine district non-political unions.
Lord Londonderry gave £50, but asked that his subscription should not
be publicised for fear of antagonising the Durham Miners' Association.
Small amounts were also subscribed by various businessmen, merchants,
shopkeepers and gentry.[41]

The secretary of the Northumberland and Durham Miners' Industrial
Union (N&DMIU) was J. Edmondson, who had been lodge secretary
and check-weighman at St. Hilda Colliery since 1916, with John
Duncan as full-time organiser. They sought recognition, but the owners'
associations said they could only negotiate with the organisation representing the majority of the men. However, branch officials of the
N&DMIU were generally allowed to represent their members with
individual grievances, and two companies (Stella and the Consett Iron
Company) recognised the Industrial Union for the negotiation of pit

price lists until the end of 1928.[42]

The legitimate Northumberland and Durham unions employed every weapon they could to crush the non-politicals: strikes, legal action, propaganda and ostracism. By April 1930, the remaining members of the N&DMIU were demoralised and dissolution was decided on.[43]

The desire of Welsh colliery owners for a client union is understandable in view of that coalfield's troubled industrial relations. But the South Wales Miners' Federation (SWMF) was too strong to offend throughout much of the district, so when the South Wales Miners Industrial Union (SWMIU) applied for recognition to the owners' association, it was turned down. Some owners did agree to recognise it, however, the principal one being the Ocean and United National Collieries Ltd. Two others, each with one colliery, were Taff-Merthyr (a joint subsidiary of Ocean and Powell Duffryn) and Bedwas. Taff-Merthyr was a new colliery which had never had a SWMF lodge whilst Bedwas was a re-opened colliery, so in both cases the owners were able to hand-pick their men. There were other pits where both unions were recognised.[44]

The original secretary of the SWMIU was a Conservative, W.A. Williams, with William Gregory as full-time organiser and M. Lewis as Vice-President, but after internal dissensions, in August 1928 Gregory emerged as the undisputed leader with the style of Agent and Secretary. His President was W. Gooding, although when the union was under particularly heavy attack from the SWMF in April 1935, George Spencer accepted the presidency.[45]

In 1934, the SWMF began a determined campaign to squash its rival. At Taff-Merthyr, many men were recruited by the SWMF and ten of them were dismissed. The SWMF brought their members out in support of the dismissed men, but the SWMIU continued to work the pit successfully.

The SWMF suggested that the men should be ballotted on which union they wanted to represent them, and when the company refused they threatened a coalfield strike. The Coal Owners' Association intervened, and work was resumed on a compromise formula. The dismissed men were reinstated and the company conceded the principle of a ballot at a future date. Meantime, both unions were recognised but in practice the SWMIU were favoured. A sit-down strike of SWMF members failed through insufficient support. Eventually, in September 1937, a ballot vote of the 917 men revealed a majority of five for the SWMIU.[46]

'Stay down' strikes were dramatically successful elsewhere in 1935-6, the classic case being Nine Mile Point. There is no doubt that the strategists of the stay-down strike campaign were the Communists. Typically, (as at Dare for example) the SWMF ranks were strengthened by activists who took up employment there in contemplation of a dispute.

But the most significant victory for the SWMF was Bedwas. This colliery was owned by the Bedwas Navigation Colliery Company (1921) Ltd., a subsidiary of S. Instone and Company, who also owned the Askern Coal and Iron Company, Yorkshire, besides being involved in coal exporting, shipowning (J. Instone & Co. Ltd.), coal distillation (Doncaster Coalite Ltd.) and civil aviation (Instone Air Line).[47] In 1933, the company gave the SWMIU sole negotiating rights because the strike policies of the SWMF had caused a temporary closure of the colliery. The SWMF tried unsuccessfully to prevent the resumption of production. Thereafter for three years the company claimed that industrial relations were ideal.

In July 1936, the SWMF demanded recognition and threatened strike action, but the owners were not impressed. The Federation then asked that the men should be ballotted on which union they wanted to represent them. The SWMIU said they would boycott any ballot because:

> A ballot can only prove effective if it can be agreed beforehand, regardless of results, that the losing organisation would withdraw from the colliery and cease all connections with the men thereat. As it is, inter-union hatred is at fever-pitch . . . How can the Industrial Union risk losing when they know their members will be victimised? We believe that the owners will not desert us and agree on a peace ballot.

The SWMF threatened a coalfield strike, and in order to avoid this the coal-owners' association prevailed on the company to agree to a ballot. The result was a resounding victory for the SWMF: 1,177 votes to 309 for the industrial union.[48]

At the beginning of 1936, the SWMIU had 5,991 members but because of its defeat at Bedwas and collieries in the Ocean group, membership fell to 443 by the end of the year. Following its success in the Taff-Merthyr ballot, membership increased slightly to 589. But by this time, the Spencer Union in Nottinghamshire had amalgamated with the NMA and George Spencer was under an obligation to bring about the amalgamation of the SWMIU with the SWMF. This occurred on 7

June 1939, following visits to Cardiff by Spencer with two colleagues
to wind up the affairs of the organisation. Curiously, in the process,
Spencer and Arthur Horner, the Communist leader of the SWMF,
appear to have developed a grudging respect for each other.[49]

Company unionism, the non-political trade union movement and Mondism

To refer to one of the miners' industrial unions as a company union,
as David Smith does of the SWMIU, is understandable but misleading.[50]
In the 1920s and later, many firms tried to head off bona fide trade
unions by encouraging their employees to enrol in house unions whose
policies were guided by the companies themselves. A company union
may have all the trappings of a democratic organisation of employees,
with elections for officers and committees, branch meetings, annual
conferences, audited accounts; organising welfare and educational
activities, consulting with management and engaging in formal negotiations on wages and conditions of employment, but it lacks genuine
independence. Its primary purpose is to serve the interests of the firm
rather than of its members, so it is unlikely to have any provision in its
rules for strikes.

The Ocean and United National Collieries derived the same sort of
benefit from the SWMIU as it might have done from a company union.
In particular, it expected to enjoy peaceful industrial relations. But the
SWMIU was not just the creature of one firm, it was part of what aimed
to be a wide trade union movement.

The firms which formed company unions were inward-looking.
Those which supported the non-political trade union movement were
outward-looking. They were concerned not just to ensure industrial
peace for themselves but to promote peaceful industrial relations in the
nation at large; they worked to preserve the capitalist system and not
just their own place within it. The creation of a 'non-political' trade
union movement in opposition to the TUC was one way of promoting
industrial peace.

Havelock Wilson circulated an appeal to employers and 'all those
who value peace and goodwill in industry' to subscribe funds for a
'Non-Political Trade Union Movement' designed to counteract 'foreign-
controlled Communist domination' by co-ordinating and organising the
'forces opposed to this political bias in the Trade Union movement'.[51]
Among the individual subscribers were twelve peers, eight Knights, or
baronets and one relative by marriage of the royal family. In addition,
93 firms covering almost every industry and service responded to the

appeal. Prominent among them were thirty shipowners and shipbrokers and nine coal-owners and merchants. A pamphlet issued by the Labour Research Department (LRD) said, 'there is little doubt that a ready response will be forthcoming' to the appeal for more funds. But however successful the appeal for funds, the Movement was a dismal failure. The only unions of any size to join it were the NUS and the miners' industrial unions. The only registered non-political unions outside the mining industry in 1928 were these:

Table1: Non-political Unions Outside Mining

Register No.	Name and Address	Members	Funds £
T1778	Industrial Union of Engineering Workers (Melton House, Durand Gardens, Clapham Road, SW9)	10	1
T1859	Shipbuilding, Shiprepairing and Engineering Industrial Union (15 Goree Piazzas, Pier Head, Liverpool)	683	1,150
T1953	Railways Salaried Staff (non-Political) Association		Formed 1928
T1493	National Union of Seamen (St. Georges Hall, Westminster Bridge Road, SE1)	73,782	310,764
T1951	Government Workers' Industrial Union (85 Plumstead Road, SE18)		Formed 1928

Source: Annual Report of Chief Registrar of Friendly Societies, 1928.

Apart from the NUS, the only one of these bodies to be mentioned in the Registrar of Friendly Societies' *Report* for 1929 was the Railways Salaried Staff Association, which was in course of dissolution; and in the 1930 *Report* none are mentioned. After Havelock Wilson's death in 1929, the NUS severed its connection with the non-political movement preparatory to rejoining the TUC in 1930, which it was allowed to do on undertaking not to give any future support of any sort to 'non-political' unions.[52] Thereafter, the Movement was confined to the mining industry, and it may not be without significance that the address on its letter-heads (3 London Wall Buildings) was the same as that of the Mining Club, to which many coalowners belonged.

Several subscribers to the Non-Political Trade Union Movement were among the sponsors of the Mond-Turner talks of 1928-9, including the coal royalty owner, Lord Londonderry, and Sir Hugo Hirst of the

General Electric Co Ltd. The LRD pamphlet drew this conclusion:

> The non-political movement cannot be considered by itself. It is not
> without significance that its list of subscribers contains names
> associated personally or through directorships with signatories of
> the Mond invitation which was accepted by the General Council of
> the TUC. The full drive of the capitalist attack on wages and con-
> ditions can only be realised when it is seen in its various forms. The
> State machinery has been brought to bear through the Trade Union
> Act, the Unemployment Act of 1927, the cutting down of relief
> rates and the removal of elected Labour Guardians in favour of
> capitalist-controlled officials. The publicity machinery has been
> brought to bear through the Press and the 'educational work' of the
> Economic League, the Industrial Peace Union, and similar bodies.
> The machinery to undermine the resistance of the workers has been
> brought to bear through co-partnership and welfare schemes, and
> collaboration and 'industrial peace' conferences of all kinds, local
> and national. And definite employers' organisations have been set
> up in the Company Unions on a small scale and the Spencer Unions
> on an industrial scale; they are now to be followed by the creation
> of further 'non-political' unions in other industries, culminating in
> a national body of employers' men which will be recognised 'in the
> Councils of the Nation'.[53]

The Mond-Turner talks demonstrated the determination of large employers and leaders of the TUC to collaborate rather than to collide.
Employers became more willing to give full recognition to trade unions,
and the unions responded by seeking to settle disputes peacefully and
by co-operating in the introduction of rationalisation schemes to improve industrial efficiency, from which employers and workers could
both hope to benefit. From this time, too, comes the acceptance that
political and industrial questions should be kept separate: that direct
industrial action should not be used for political ends. These hallmarks
of 'Mondism' are virtually the same as those of 'Spencerism'; and in
retrospect it seems more sensible to see the two as alternative, rather
than as complementary, approaches to the problems of British capitalism in the post-General Strike period.[54]

The Nottinghamshire and District Miners' Industrial Union

The Nottinghamshire and District Miners' Industrial Union, popularly
called 'Spencer's Union' had the appearance, and some of the reality, of

a genuinely independent union. Its objects included the negotiation and enforcement of agreements, protection of members unjustly treated, securing the true weight of mineral gotten and:

> 2(f) To provide a weekly allowance for the support of members and their families who may be locked out, victimised, or on strike, in accordance with the rules of the Union . . .

The right to strike was, however, hedged about by restrictive rules similar to those which had long been in force in the NMA. Thus,

> 19 Strikes and Lockouts
> No Branch, portion of a Branch or member having a grievance or dispute must strike or leave off work with a view to causing the works to stand unless and until the grievance or dispute has been thoroughly investigated and the sanction of Council obtained for such a strike or cessation of work, but such sanction shall not be given until every available means of settling the grievance or dispute by negotiation has been exhausted . . .

A Joint Wages Board was established which provided conciliation machinery for settling disputes peacefully. The effect of Rule 19 and the Wages Board Agreement taken together was to make an official strike impossible.

The special character of the Spencer Union emerges in these rules:

> 2(g) The Union is an Industrial Organisation and no funds of the Union shall be used for any Political purpose whatever.[55]
> 16(b) Communists, and members of the Minority, or any similar revolutionary movement shall not be eligible for membership or entitled to benefit and the Council of the Union reserves to itself the right to expel any member found to be in membership with any such movement or advocating its policy.[56]

Another unusual rule facilitated undemocratic control of the union's affairs:

> 22 Branch Meetings
> The holding of Branch meetings shall be left to the discretion of the Branch Committee.[57]

The only branch meeting which had to be held was the annual general meeting at which officials and committee elections were held. Now, the basis of the democratic control of a district miners' union was the mandating of delegates by their branches. In Spencer's union, this system was watered down.

Rule 28 sought to limit the right of workmen's inspectors appointed under Section 16 of the Coal Mines Act of 1911. The workmen employed in a mine were empowered to appoint two experienced miners to inspect the workings 'once at least in every month'. However, NMIU Rule 28 reads:

> Pit inspections shall only take place in case of a fatality or any other emergency that may arise, except when ordered by the Council.

Of course, where the men appointed NMA members as inspectors this restriction did not affect them, but there were many pits where NMA workmen's inspectors would not have kept their jobs for long.

One other clause in the NMIU rules is worth noting:

> 31 Dissolution
> The Union may at any time be dissolved by a Resolution passed at a special meeting duly convened and held of the Council of the Union provided that due notice shall be given of the purpose for which such meeting is to be held and that such Resolution shall be passed by a majority of not less than two thirds of the members present and entitled to vote at such meeting.

This simple procedure, making reference to the membership unnecessary, was as deliberate as everything else Spencer did.

The owners' association gave Spencer's Union sole recognition, but assured the TUC in 1928 that:

> The Nottinghamshire Coal Owners' Association intend loyally to carry out the agreement made with representatives of their workmen, and cannot recognise any other organised body of workmen than that with which they are now dealing. The Nottinghamshire Coal Owners' Association however, make no inquiry or discrimination in regard to a man's trade union.[58]

That this was the position of some owners is attested by the negative response of the Sherwood Colliery Company to requests from Spencer

for help in recruiting members.[59] Generally, the older companies of the
Leen and Erewash Valleys, especially those with a liberal background
(Sherwood, Babbington, Digby) were least antagonistic to the NMA;
and one family firm, James Oakes and Company, allowed NMA officials
to collect subscriptions on colliery premises. At some collieries, pit
inspections by NMA members were tolerated and NMA men, acting as
checkweighmen or representatives of contractors, took part in price list
deputations. Again, firms like Bestwood and the Stanton Ironworks
Company would reply to letters from the NMA concerning individual
workmen; and where, as at Selston, NMA officials were secretaries of
Miners' Welfare Schemes, they were able to confer informally with the
owners.

On the other hand the Bolsover, Barber-Walker and New Hucknall
Companies were bitterly antagonistic to the NMA. The Bolsover and
New Hucknall Companies engineered the dismissal of several NMA
checkweighmen, at Annesley 200 men were given notice for refusing
to join the Spencer Union in 1929, and at Welbeck all the men were
locked out in 1928 and membership of the NMIU was made a condition
of employment. The victimisation of individual NMA members was
widespread.[60]

In 1928, the TUC arranged for a ballot to determine which union
the men wanted to represent them. Some 32,277 voted for the NMA
and 2,253 for the NMIU. Spencer was not impressed; he said he knew
men who had cast three votes: 'If our opponents could have shown the
owners 32,000 men on their books it might have made a difference, but
32,000 ballot papers were no good . . .'[61] This point did not escape the
TUC leaders themselves. The NMA branches at Kirkby and Newstead,
which had 2,000 and 920 members respectively at the beginning of
1932 compared with 2,687 and 1,525 respectively at the beginning of
1926, showed that generally a determined branch could hold its ground
reasonably well.[62]

However, even under the same company, it was much easier for the
NMA to retain the loyalty of its members in the settled mining
communities attached to older pits than in the new mining villages. This
is best illustrated by reference to the Barber-Walker pits. (See Table 2.)

There was a rapid turnover of labour at Harworth, and applicants for
employment (most of whom came from other districts) were told that
they were expected to join the NMIU though they were not compelled
to do so. During 1928 the Spencer Union helped to recruit from Leicestershire and Yorkshire 100 face-workers who were non-political union
supporters, for Harworth.[63]

Table 2: Membership of NMA at Barber-Walker pits

		1926	1932
Old Mines	Moor Green	662	480
	Underwood	584	160
	Watnall	520	210
New Mine	Harworth	671	35

Source: N.M.A. Minute Books, 1926 and 1932

On the other hand, the fluidity of the labour force facilitated the introduction of men determined to undermine the NMIU. A Communist-inspired cyclostyled newsheet, *The Harworth Spark*, was being 'printed and published by the militant miners at Harworth pit' as early as 1930. Its first issue attacked not merely the coal-owners but also the MFGB, the Labour government and 'the renegade Cook'.[64] It announced:

> The local grievances which we feature on the back page are only a
> few of many which exist in the Harworth pit, and this paper of
> miners in Harworth will be a medium through which the workers in
> the pit can voice their grievances and the *Spark* will give a lead on all
> important issues. To accomplish this, the *Spark* must become the
> voice the leader and organiser of the workers on the job.

Readers were urged to 'READ THE DAILY WORKER for news of the Miners Struggle.'[65]

During 1935, the NMA increased its membership from 8,500 to 9,869. A new branch had been formed at Harworth and membership there shot up from seven in January to 157 in December.[66] Six months later with membership up to 302, the founder-President of the Branch, J. Pickering, was outvoted by Mick Kane, a Communist militant who had started work at Harworth on 28 March 1935. His engagement is surprising in view of the fact that he had been dismissed a few years earlier from Langwith Colliery in Derbyshire for reasons which the Harworth management could easily have established.

Early in 1935, the MFGB had assumed responsibility for achieving unity in the Nottinghamshire coalfield, but there was a stumbling block. From 1929 to 1930, talks arranged by A.J. Cook under the auspices of the Secretary for Mines, Emmanuel (now Lord) Shinwell, to negotiate fusion of the two unions, were frustrated by the refusal of many in the NMA to have any truck with Spencer.[67] In 1935, the MFGB leaders believed that fusion was the only practicable way to bring the split to an end, but most of the leading members of the NMA still wanted to see the NMIU crushed. In the two years which followed, the MFGB, with the reluctant assent of the NMA, tried to negotiate terms for fusion through the national coal-owners' organisation and the Mines Department; but the alternative policy aimed at crushing Spencerism was being pursued at Harworth. Spencer wrote to *The Times* about a speech in which Mr J. McGurk, a member of the MFGB Executive, spoke of smashing Spencerism at Bedwas and Harworth at the same time as the MFGB were negotiating for fusion:

> . . . it appears they are offering one hand of friendship and in the other hold a weapon of violence . . . How is it possible with such a spirit prevailing to enter into any form of negotiation? We have been willing to listen to the voice of reason and to co-operate if there is a real spirit which would make for peace and prosperity in the industry, but we will not be intimidated by violent language into abandoning our rights to organise.[68]

Spencer had always realised that he could not hope to maintain a permanently schismatic union, which is the real significance of Rule 31. He was willing to consider fusion with the NMA but he expected it to be on his terms.

The bitter dispute at Harworth between 1936 and 1937, in which the 2,200 odd men were evenly divided,[69] delayed the final settlement, which was reached in May 1937 after the MFGB had threatened a national strike. The terms were virtually dictated by Spencer. They provided for him to be appointed President of the amalgamated union; for political business to be discussed only at special meetings called for the purpose; for the existing district wages agreement to be continued for five years during which time Nottinghamshire was to be immune from strikes; and for Spencer to be the Nottinghamshire representative on the MFGB Executive Committee for the following year.[70] Spencer also pressed on the owners and his colleagues the need for a new pension scheme. One of the features of the Spencer Union had been a pension fund jointly financed by owners and union. After an initial contribution of £10,000 followed shortly after by one of £2,500, the owners regularly subsidised the fund, which was administered by a joint committee.[71] The new scheme (the Notts. and District Miners' Pension Fund) was to be financed directly from wages as part of the 'ascertainment' process.[72]

An assessment

There are some trade unions, particularly covering white-collar workers in the public sector, which have traditionally held aloof from political affiliation. But the Non-Political Trade Union Movement was not non-political in that sense at all. It was opposed to the use of the industrial weapon for political ends; and it was fostered by employers who were bitterly anti-socialist.

Many of its supporters were unprincipled sycophants but others sincerely wished to return to the style of industrial relations which existed before World War I. In July 1927, Spencer said:

> Non-political trade unionism is not a new movement as is often supposed . . . it is seeking to return to the line of action and modes of expression which characterised the movement before the Communist elements got hold of it.[73]

Similarly, in August 1927, he told Herbert Smith, President of the MFGB that if he

> was prepared to build up again an organisation upon the lines and for the purpose which the distinguished leaders of the old conciliation boards pursued which gave such long periods of peace and prosperity, he would find that men were prepared to co-operate with him.[74]

A delegate at an SWMIU meeting at Pontypridd in February 1927 said that men

> can only get out of an industry what they have put into it and it is the duty of every workman to produce fully and then claim his share for the labour he has given.[75]

This is how Spencer expressed it:

> In my view there can be no improvement in the lot of the worker unless and until there is co-operation between the two, but while I am co-operating with the owners, I shall see to it that the workers get their share of the wealth that the joint efforts create.[76]

Similarly, W. Gooding, President of the SWMIU, said, '. . . we have as our ultimate object the advancement of our members not by strikes and revolution, but by peaceful co-operation with the employers.'[77]

As A.J. Cook pointed out, there was no great difference between these objects and those which emerged from the Mond-Turner conferences. The separation of industrial and political matters; co-operation in maximising profits by schemes of rationalisation; settling disputes by negotiation and compromise rather than by strikes and conflict, all these became the official policy of the TUC in the period following the general strike. It is also no coincidence that, of the seven industrialists on the Mond-Turner committee, two had been sponsors of the Non-Political Trade Union Movement.[78]

George Spencer also equated the new policy of the TUC with that of his union:

> The TUC who had turned war on the Communists ought to support the new union instead of crushing it . . . the only reason they were not with the Industrial Union was that there were no politics in their organisation. That was their only offence.[79]

The Non-Political Trade Union Movement was therefore an anachronism established to combat a syndicalism which had already been abandoned; and, after the first flush, financial support from employers appears to have dried up. There is certainly no evidence in the accounts of the miners' industrial unions of any large subventions.

There is another reason for the failure of the Non-Political Movement: the nature of its leadership. Frank Hodges, after a preliminary flirtation, dropped out and Havelock Wilson died in 1929. This left George Spencer.

Spencer was too parochial in outlook to offer effective leadership to a national movement. He was always opposed to national wage agreements, he opposed all schemes for subsidising less profitable districts from the earnings of the more profitable, and he opposed the formation of a national union as distinct from a national federation. For him, non-political unions in other districts, or in other industries, were important only to the extent that they helped to preserve his position in Nottinghamshire; the more of them there were, the less isolated would he be.

Spencerism took root in the Nottinghamshire coalfield largely because of historical factors. In its heyday, Nottinghamshire's Leen Valley was the most prosperous mining district in Britain and this was reflected in its superior wages and conditions of employment. After the 1893 lock-out, when it was the owners' association which split, a special relationship was built up between the Liberal coal-owners and Liberal union officials like J.G. Hancock.[80]

The leaders of the NMIU at area and pit level included many respected Liberal and right-wing Labour figures. Its first President was a Labour County Councillor and magistrate, its first Agent a Labour MP and its Treasurer a Liberal ex-MP. Also, the Derbyshire, Nottinghamshire and Midland Counties Colliery Enginemen, Firemen and Motormen's Union (E&FU) a well-established body affiliated to the MFGB for many years, with 2,323 members in 1928, accepted a seat on the District Wages Board set up by Spencer and the owners, conferring on it an air of legitimacy, and co-operated with the NMIU on the District Miners' Welfare Committee.[81]

Some men were coerced into the NMIU, and many more who joined it for 'bread and butter' reasons still had an 'affection' for the old union.[82] Nevertheless, there was a general if grudging acknowledgement that the NMIU was reasonably effective in representing members; it was not as tame as its detractors alleged. Spencer certainly did his best to avoid strikes, but he was not averse to claiming that a failure to settle on terms acceptable to the men could cause them to strike in spite of his efforts to dissuade them. Also, he used the NMA as a 'bogey': a failure to settle a dispute quietly and generously would allow the NMA to make capital out of the situation. Spencer also had an enviable reputation in connection with personal injury claims.[83] At pit level, branch officials who failed to represent members very well could be, and sometimes were, defeated in the annual elections.

Among those who had special cause to support Spencer, because he helped them to maintain their privileged positions, were the 'butties', especially at the Bolsover pits where the system was still firmly entrenched. The General Secretary of the NMIU from 1930, Horace Cooper, was formerly employed by the Bolsover Company who had financed his recruiting missions in the early days of the Union. Thereafter, he retained a special relationship with Bolsover, and in its dealings with that firm, the NMIU's role was very close to that of a company union.[84]

Finally, Spencer's chauvinistic advocacy of the doctrine that the earnings in each district should be determined by that district's profitability, whilst it unfitted him to be a national leader, evoked a sympathetic response in Nottinghamshire which stood to gain most from it.[85] This particular aspect of Spencerism lives on. It was shown, for example, in the debate at the NUM conference in 1966 on the National Power Loading Agreement where the Nottinghamshire delegates were alone in opposing the Agreement because it would be to the detriment of the highly-paid districts. More recently, Nottinghamshire was the only large Area which returned a majority for a reintroduction of incentive payments in 1974.[86]

Apart from the temporary adherence to it of the NUS which died with Havelock Wilson, the Non-Political Trade Union Movement was a failure in every industry except coal-mining. In coal-mining, support for the movement was confined largely to Nottinghamshire and its success there was due to special factors which existed nowhere else except, perhaps, in Leicestershire. In the case of Leicestershire, the MFGB chose to tolerate non-political unionism within its own ranks knowing that the alternative course would have driven the LMA into alliance with Spencer and it is, perhaps not without significance that one of Leicestershire's leading coal-owners in this period was Frank Hodges. The NMIU lasted for almost eleven years; but the wider Non-Political Trade Union Movement, which is now no more than a title on an old letterhead, was never very much else.

APPENDIX

Table 1: Miners' Industrial Unions

(i) Funds at the end of each year

Year	NMIU £	SWMIU £	N&DMNPTU £	YMITU £	S&CMITU £	CCITU £	F&KMITU £	CONDUIT £
1927	3,904	78	36	76	8			
1928	2,480	123	- 649	49	Dissolved			
1929	3,471	237	47	121				
1930	2,074	NA	Dissolved				212	1,724
1931	985	NA						
1932	3,884	NA						
1933	7,566	NA						
1934	12,257	NA						
1935	17,601	NA						
1936	21,870	903						
1937	22,041	617						

(ii) Membership at end of each year

Year	NMIU	SWMIU	N&DMNPTU	YMITU	S&CMITU	CCITU	F&KMITU	CONDUIT
1927	12,853	6,435	3,911	1,300				
1928	15,086	7,635	4,081		94	400		
1929	10,774	7,116	4,068	780				
1930	11,467	6,450		750			76	89
1931	11,182	NA						
1932	12,945	NA						
1933	14,524	NA						
1934	15,046	NA						
1935	16,644	5,991						
1936	16,948	443						
1937	17,179	589						

NMIU   Notts. & District Miners' Industrial Union
SWMIU   South Wales Miners' Industrial Union
N&DMNPTU   Northumberland and Durham Miners' Non-Political Trade Union
YMITU   Yorkshire Miners' Industrial Trade Union
S&CMITU   Stirling & Clackmannan Miners' Industrial Trade Union
CCITU   Cannock Chase Industrial Trade Union
F&KMITU   Fife and Kinross Miners' Industrial Trade Union
CONDUIT   Conduit Colliery Industrial Trade Union (Staffordshire)

Source: *Annual Reports of Chief Registrar of Friendly Societies;* Letter from Registry of Trade Unions & Employers' Associations to C.P. Griffin dated 5 February 1974 (in respect of SWMIU).

Table 2: Nottinghamshire Miners' Association Membership and Income and Expenditure 1927-37

Year	No. of Members	INCOME From Members	From other Sources	Total	EXPENDITURE Unemp. Pay	Pensions	Grants To Other Bodies	Admin.	Other	Total	Funds
		£	£	£	£	£	£	£	£	£	£
1927	16,624	13,367	5,105	18,472	4,810	4,656	723	8,673		18,862	14,095
1928	13,950	9,870	433	10,303	–	76	553	8,393		9,022	15,376
1929	13,934	8,889	638	9,527	2,240	–	721	8,386		11,347	13,556
1930	13,475	9,776	703	10,479	1,791	–	322	7,290		9,403	14,625
1931	12,295	9,130	1,092	10,222	4,325	–	307	6,915		11,547	13,300
1932	11,065	8,771	598	9,369	4,000	–	320	6,826		11,146	11,523
1933	10,125	7,516	324	7,840	3,817	–	403	4,507	873	9,600	9,763
1934	8,500	7,233	260	7,493	2,482	–	401	4,345	206	7,434	9,822
1935	9,869	7,187	998	8,185	2,323	–	370	5,099	745	8,537	9,669
1936	11,146	9,227	7,442	16,669	3,034	–	394	5,699	6,549*	15,676	11,062
1937	9,700										8,149

* Includes £6,176 dispute pay at Harworth.
Source: Annual Reports of Chief Registrar of Friendly Societies.

TABLE 3: Nottinghamshire & District Miners' Industrial Union Membership and Income and Expenditure 1927-37

Year	No. of Members	INCOME From Members	Other Sources	Total	EXPENDITURE Unemp. Pay	Pensions	Grants to Fed. Pol. Parties etc.	Admin.	Other	Total	Funds
		£	£	£	£	£	£	£	£	£	£
1927	12,853	14,136	4,046	18,182	1,883	5,513	26	5,942	914	14,278	3,904
1928	15,086	19,304	3,484	22,788	10,254	5,332		7,835	791	24,212	2,480
1929	10,774	15,224	3,792	19,016	2,934	7,403		7,152	556	18,045	3,471
1930	11,467	11,282	4,530	15,812	985	8,915		6,723	687	17,310	2,074
1931	11,182	12,105	4,436	16,541	4,290	6,428		6,081	831	17,630	985
1932	12,945	13,928	2,557	16,485	2,625	4,444		5,499	1,018	13,586	3,884
1933	14,524	17,767	1,855	19,622	2,329	3,883		5,465	1,263	12,940	7,566
1934	15,046	16,190	1,931	18,121	2,526	3,686		5,813	1,405	13,430	12,257
1935	16,644	16,540	2,629	19,169	2,770	3,259		6,710	1,086	13,825	17,601
1936	16,948	17,444	2,502	19,946	4,327	2,896		7,021	1,433	15,677	21,870
1937	17,179										22,041

Source: Annual Reports of Chief Registrar of Friendly Socieites.

Table 4: South Wales Miners' Industrial Union Income & Expenditure 1936-7

Year	INCOME From Members £	Other £	Total £	EXPENDITURE Total £	Funds £
1936	1,245	—	1,245	2,213	903
1937	180	142	322	755	617

Source: Letter from Registry of Trade Unions and Employers' Associations to C.P. Griffin, dated 5 February 1974.

Table 5: Pattern of Expenditure of NMA and NMIU Compared

(i) Benefits as a percentage of total expenditure

1927-36

	NMA				NMIU						
	A Total Expend. £	B Unemployment Benefit Amt. £	As a % of Col. A	Avg. per Member £	A Total Expend. £	B Unemployment Benefit Amt. £	As a % of Col. A	Avg. per Member £	C Pensions Amt. £	As a % of Col. A	Avg. Amt. per Member £
	112,574*	28,522	25.3	2.4	160,933	34,713	21.5	2.6	51,759	32	3.9

* Includes: £6,176 Dispute Pay 1936
£4,732 Pension Payments 1927-8.

(ii) Administration costs as a percentage of total expenditure

	NMA			NMIU			
	A Total Expend. £	B Admin. Costs £	'B' as a % of 'A' £	A Total Expend. £	B Admin. Costs £	'B' as a % of 'A' £	Avg. Amt. per Member £
	112,574	66,142	58.8	160,933	64,341	40	4.7

Table 6: Membership of Industrial Unions Compared with 'Official' Unions

Year	Northumberland & Durham			South Wales			Nottinghamshire		
	Numbers Employed	Percentage in: Official Unions*	Ind. Union	Numbers Employed	Percentage in: Official Union	Ind. Union	Numbers Employed	Percentage in: Official Union	Ind. Union
1927	181,306	95.3	2.2	194,100	42.0	3.3	57,955	28.7	22.1
1928	177,077	90.7	2.3	168,269	43.4	4.5	52,114	26.8	28.9
1929	188,323	88.3	2.2	178,315	33.6	4.0	52,702	26.4	20.4
1930	180,747	90.8		172,870	43.1	3.7	52,393	25.7	21.9
1931						N.A.	51,307	24.0	21.8
1932						N.A.	49,499	22.4	26.2
1933						N.A.	46,909	21.6	31.0
1934						N.A.	46,852	18.1	32.1
1935				138,720	79.7	4.3	43,923	21.5	36.2
1936							45,538	24.5	37.2
1937							45,579	21.3	37.7

Sources: (a) Numbers employed (including salaried persons): *Annual Reports of Chief Inspectors of Mines and Secretary for Mines*.
(b) Membership Figures: *Annual Reports of Chief Registrar of Friendly Societies*.
* These percentages are not comparable with those in other columns. The Durham Miners' Association figures are often considerably in excess of numbers employed in this period, probably because unemployed miners were still reckoned as members.

Notes

1. J. Saville, 'Notes on Ideology and the Miners Before World War I', *Bulletin of the Society for the Study of Labour History* (subsequently *BSSLH*), No. 23 (Autumn 1971); K.O. Morgan, *The Age of Lloyd George: The Liberal Party and British Politics 1890-1929* (1971), pp. 38-57; R. Gregory, *The Miners and British Politics* (1968), passim; P.F. Clarke, *Lancashire and the New Liberalism*, (1971), *passim*.
2. N. Seldon, 'Laissez Faire as Dogma: The Liberty and Property Defence League, 1882-1914', *Essays in Anti-Labour History*, K.D. Brown (ed.) (1974), pp. 208-33; K.D. Brown, 'The Anti-Socialist Union', ibid., pp. 234-61.
3. Ibid., p. 255, C. Cook (ed.), *Sources in British Political History 1900-1951*, I (1975), pp. 25, 31-2, 86, 219 (subsequently *Sources I*); R. Douglas, 'The National Democratic Party and the British Workers' League', *Historical Journal* 15, No. 3 (1972) (subsequently Douglas).
4. Cook, *Sources I; Douglas.*
5. A.R. Griffin, *The Miners of Nottinghamshire 1914-1944.* (1962) (subsequently Notts. Miners II), pp. 221-2; H. Pelling, *A History of British Trade Unionism* (Harmondsworth, 1963), p. 158.
6. Cook, *Sources I.* (It is interesting to note that when the ASU was wound up in 1949 its assets were given to the Economic League – Brown, 'Anti Socialist Union', p. 257).
7. *Notts. Miners II*, pp. 91-2, 112-13.
8. Ibid., p. 109.
9. Ibid., pp. 238-9.
10. Ibid., p. 117.
11. Ibid., p. 7; J.E Williams, *The Derbyshire Miners* (1962), p. 676 (subsequently *Williams*).
12. *Derbyshire Times*, 19 May 1923, cited *Williams*, p. 677.
13. The SWMF similarly allowed Taff-Merthyr to work during the stoppage. See *Notts. Miners II*, p. 165; A.R. Griffin, *Mining in the East Midlands, 1550-1947* (1971), pp. 239-40 (subsequently *East Mids.*).
14. *Miners' Federation of Great Britain Minute Book* (subsequently *MFGB*) (1926), pp. 859-62, 891-2.
15. *Notts. Miners II*, p. 202.
16. Ibid., pp. 193-220; *East Mids.*, pp. 243-7; *NMIU Minute Book* (1926) (Spencer MSS, in A.R. Griffin's possession).
17. *Leicestershire Miners' Association Minute Book* (subsequently *LMAMB*), 18 June and 12 July 1926; *MFGB* (1926), p. 664. (It should be remembered that the owners in Leicestershire, as in Derbyshire, Nottinghamshire and Cannock Chase, did not give their men notice for a reduction in wages. In those districts the dispute was, strictly speaking, a sympathetic strike rather than a lock-out – *MFGB* (1926), p. 665.
18. *LMAMB*, 13, 18 and 20 September 1926.
19. Ibid., 11 October 1926; *Coalville Times*, 15 October 1926; *MFGB* (1926), p. 940.
20. *LMAMB*, 18 October 1926.
21. *MFGB* (1926), pp. 1025-6.
22. *LMAMB*, 29 November 1926; 18 January and 3 February 1927.
23. *Notts. Miners II*, p. 174.
24. *Colliery Guardian*, 24 April 1925 and 4 February 1927; *Coalville Times*, 4 and 11 February 1927; *LMAMB*, 24 September 1925 and 10 March 1926.
25. *Coalville Times*, 18 February, 25 February and 4 March 1927; *LMAMB*, 9 March, 2 May and 10 June 1927; *MFGB* (1927-8), pp. 18, 36, 74-5. (The

present General Secretary of the Leicestershire Area of the NUM, Mr Frank Smith, was a member of Jack Smith's union.)

26. *Coalville Times*, 3 December 1926; *Colliery Guardian*, 11 March 1927.
27. *MFGB* (1927-8), p. 143.
28. *LMAMB*, 14 February 1927, 10 June 1927 and 31 July 1931; *Coalville Times*, 11 November 1927; *MFGB* (1936), pp. 326-8; ibid. (1937), pp. 75, 402 and 410.
29. *Nottingham Journal*, 2 November 1927.
30. *Notts. Miners II*, pp. 207-20.
31. *Times*, 10 April, 19 May and 29 May 1926; cited *MFGB* (1927-8), pp. 595-6. (Unlike Hodges, Spencer and Varley would have preferred a wage reduction to an increase in hours.)
32. *Times*, 11 October 1926, cited ibid., pp. 600-2.
33. *MFGB* (1927-8), pp. 587-93.
34. R.P. Arnot, *The Miners: Years of Struggle* (1953), p. 523.
35. *MFGB* (1927-8), pp. 156-7. Bentley and Harworth were both owned by Barber Walker.
36. Ibid., pp. 148-9.
37. Ibid., pp. 344-8. K.G.J.C. Knowles, *Strikes — a Study in Industrial Conflict* (1952), p. 85.
38. *MFGB* (1927-8), p. 499.
39. *Colliery Guardian*, 10 June 1927.
40. *MFGB* (1927-8), pp. 499-500.
41. R. Mason 'The Miners' Unions of Northumberland and Durham 1918-31 with special reference to the General Strike of 1926' (unpublished Ph.D. thesis, Hull, 1967), pp. 453-4.
42. *Colliery Guardian*, 28 April 1927 and 4 January 1929; W.R. Garside, *The Durham Miners 1919-60* (1971), pp. 232-4; *MFGB* (1927-8), p. 499. (Duncan's organisational duties covered other districts, too.)
43. *Garside*, op. cit., pp. 231-4; *Colliery Guardian*, 14 December 1928, 4 April and 18 April 1929. (After its formal dissolution, the union survived for a time as The North of England Mine Workers Protective Association — *Colliery Guardian*, 31 October 1930 and 21 April 1933).
44. D. Smith, 'The Struggle Against Company Unionism in the South Wales Coalfield 1926-1939', *BSSLH*, No. 23 (Autumn 1971); also article with same title in *Welsh Historical Review* (subsequently *WHR*), VI (1973). *Colliery Guardian*, 18 October 1929, 17 April 1930 and 19 October 1934.
45. *Colliery Guardian*, 30 September 1927, 17 August 1928 and 9 April 1935; D. Smith, 'Company Unionism', *WHR*.
46. *Colliery Guardian*, 19 and 26 October 1934 and 17 May 1935; D. Smith, 'Company Unionism', *WHR* (under the compromise formula, the officials, as distinct from the branches, of neither union were recognised.)
47. *Colliery Year Book and Coal Trades Directory* (1951 edn.), p. 462.
48. *Colliery Guardian*, 17 July, 21 August, 4 September, 18 September and 30 October.
49. Letter from Registry of Trade Unions and Employers' Associations to C.P. Griffin, dated 5 February 1974; letter from H.W. Booth to A.R. Griffin (n.d.), and conversation with G.A. Spencer (1954). David Smith is incorrect in stating 'Company Unionism', *WHR*, p. 359, that there are no records available for membership and finances of the SWMIU. There are the annual returns to the Chief Registrar of Friendly Societies.
50. David Smith, loc. cit.; Knowles, *Strikes*, pp. 83-8.
51. Labour Research Department, *The Non-Politicals* (1928), 15 pp.
52. Ibid., also Knowles, op. cit., p. 85.

53. *The Non-Politicals*, p. 14.
54. F. Williams, *Magnificent Journey (1954)*, pp. 398-414.
55. Notts. and District Miners' Industrial Union (MMIU), *Rules* 2(b) to 2(g) (1927).
56. Ibid., 16(b) (1933).
57. Ibid., 22 (1933).
58. *Notts. Miners II*, p. 224.
59. Sherwood Colliery Deputation Book (NCB North Notts Area), cited B. Taylor, *Uphill All the Way: A Miner's Struggle* (1972), pp. 190-3.
60. *Notts. Miners II*, pp. 210-11, 223-6; *Nottinghamshire Miners' Association Minute Books* (subsequently *NMA*); *MFGB* (1935), pp. 9-13.
61. *Colliery Guardian*, 11 May 1928 (The *Colliery Guardian* around this time has much to say about a 'gunman on the move' who was threatening to assassinate Spencer.)
62. *Notts. Miners II*, pp. 223-4, also *NMA*.
63. *Colliery Guardian*, 3 February 1928 and 11 January 1929. (A Mr Phillpot of Tunbridge Wells offered £100 towards their removal expenses.)
64. A.J. Cook, general secretary of the MFGB.
65. *Harworth Spark*, No. 1, 12 December 1930.
66. *NMA* (1934 and 1935).
67. Private communications from H.W. Booth and E. Shinwell and conversations with G.A. Spencer.
68. *Notts. Miners II*, pp. 256-7, 266-70.
69. Ibid., pp. 255-78; *East Mids.*, p. 310; *Harworth Colliery Time Book* for 1936-7 (NCB North Notts. Area).
70. *Notts. Miners II*, pp. 267-8. (Similarly, part of the South Wales settlement was that Taff-Merthyr should be strike-free for five years, and that SWMIU men should join the branch committee.)
71. *NMIU* Rule 13(b).
72. *Notts, Miners II*, pp. 284-6.
73. *Colliery Guardian*, 8 July 1927.
74. Ibid., 5 August 1927.
75. Ibid., 11 February 1927.
76. *East Mids.*, p. 302.
77. *Colliery Guardian*, 30 September 1927.
78. F. Williams, *Magnificent Journey*, p. 401; *The Non-Politicals*.
79. *Derbyshire Times*, 28 April 1928, cited Williams, op. cit., p. 741.
80. *East Mids.*, pp. 150-1, 156-7, 303-4; *Notts. Miners II*, pp. 24-31, 85, 290-306.
81. George Annable, Secretary of the E&FU, was joint secretary of the Notts. Wages Board and was also a workman's representative on the parallel Derbyshire Board alongside the leaders of the DMA, and also joint secretary of the Notts. District Welfare Committee.
82. *Colliery Gardian*, 11 May 1928. (Some men paid into both unions.)
83. *Notts. Miners II*, pp. 251-2, 286-8.
84. Letter H.W. Booth to A.R. Griffin (n.d.), and conversation with W.V. Sheppard.
85. *Notts. Miners II*, pp. 291-306.
86. *East Mids.*, pp. 314-5. In the ballot on the proposed incentive scheme in the autumn of 1974, there were 79,078 in favour and 133,110 against. The areas in favour were: Notts. Leics., South Derbys., Cokemen, Durham Mechanics, Durham Enginemen, Northumberland Mechanics, Yorkshire Enginemen, Colliery Officials & Staffs, Power Group No. 1, Power Group No. 2.

6 TOWARDS REVISION AND RECONCILIATION: H.N. BRAILSFORD AND GERMANY, 1914-1949

F.M. Leventhal

Among the radical critics of British foreign policy whom A.J.P. Taylor disparages so affectionately in *The Trouble Makers*, few are less remembered or more deserving of reconsideration than the author and journalist Henry Noel Brailsford. Born in 1873, the son of a Methodist preacher, Brailsford studied classics and philosophy at Glasgow University and briefly at Oxford and Berlin with the intention of pursuing an academic career. He was, however, to make his reputation not as a scholar, but as a leader-writer and foreign correspondent for a succession of Liberal periodicals, most notably the *Manchester Guardian*, the *Daily News*, and the *Nation*. A member of the Independent Labour Party from 1907 to 1932, he became increasingly identified in the public mind as a socialist and edited the ILP weekly *New Leader* from 1922 to 1926.[1] During the First World War he began to contribute regularly to the *Herald*, and in the thirties and forties he was best known for his articles in the *New Statesman* and *Reynolds News*. By the time he retired, more than fifty years after he had begun to write professionally, he was widely regarded as the most astute and eloquent socialist journalist of his time. In addition, Brailsford was the author of more than twenty books, most of which dealt with international affairs or with his impressions during travels abroad. Like most 'dissenters', to adopt Taylor's term, he generally found himself in fundamental disagreement with the aims and methods of British foreign policy. His idealism expressed itself in an alternative approach to international relations, based on the repudiation of national self-aggrandisement and the advocacy of disarmament and economic co-operation: the themes not only of much of his journalism, but of books like *The War of Steel and Gold* (1914), *A League of Nations* (1917), and *Property or Peace?* (1934). Inevitably his concern with reconciliation among the powers forced him repeatedly to consider the place of Germany in European affairs. From his earliest days on the *Daily News* until his withdrawal from active journalism after the Second World War he sought to instill in the minds of his readers a greater tolerance towards Germany, to dissipate the hostility and misunderstanding that twice erupted in war. Although one would scarcely attribute infallibility of

163

judgement to a writer who tended to err on the side of generosity in interpreting the motives of others, a stronger case can be made for Brailsford than emerges from the derisive remarks of *The Trouble Makers*. Seen in context, his pronouncements reflect a far more coherent and carefully reasoned viewpoint than Taylor's scattered quotations suggest.[2]

Brailsford's experiences as a student in Berlin in 1895 and the cultural affinity which once led him to describe Bach, Beethoven, Goethe and Kant as 'four intimate German friends' may have inspired a sentimental attachment, but they never blinded him to the militaristic and undemocratic aspects of Imperial Germany.[3] If he seemed to endorse its claims before 1914, it was out of sympathy for mistreatment suffered at the hands of rivals determined to thwart its expansion overseas. Menaced by diplomatic encirclement, excluded from the exploitation of Morocco by devious Anglo-French arrangements, an aggrieved Germany could retaliate only by arming militarily, cowing its antagonists into belatedly conceding a place in the sun. To Brailsford, the motive behind these sordid conflicts was economic: the desire of capitalist nations to carve out areas for exclusive financial penetration. Their competition for markets and investment opportunities had engulfed Europe in an armaments race, a potentially explosive war of steel and gold.[4]

Until Europe was prepared to unite, mutual concessions and the appeasement of Germany were a necessary first step towards general reconciliation. Since national boundaries were no longer in dispute, or so Brailsford believed, it would be possible to compensate Germany without sacrificing vital interests. Convinced that the points of friction were all overseas, he was prepared to argue that 'the frontiers of our modern national states are finally drawn', and that there would be 'no more wars among the six Great Powers'. Not even Alsace-Lorraine posed insuperable obstacles to accord, having 'entered irrevocably into the German network of commerce and finance'.[5] The French would not attempt to recover the lost provinces by force, and Alsatians might be disposed to acquiesce in their status if Germany were to apply 'an ungrudging policy of conciliation', in particular, a measure of local autonomy. In return the French should open their money market to German enterprise and the English cease to regard a German-sponsored Bagdad railway with disfavor. Anglo-German collaboration, which, in fact, seemed on the verge of implementation in June 1914, would have the additional advantage of restoring Turkish prosperity. In order to reinforce this accommodation, an African settlement should be devised to augment German holdings.[6]

Europe's headlong plunge into war did not cause Brailsford to dis-
card his diagnosis, merely to revise his estimation that the leaders of
finance capitalism were too rational to permit the outbreak of actual
fighting. Much as he castigated Germany for violating Belgian neutrality,
he doubted whether any 'nation save innocent Belgium can come forward with clean hands to boast that it is in the right'.[7] Distrust of
Russia, not hostility towards England (about whose intentions there had
been much confusion in Berlin), precipitated German belligerence, through
fear that pan-slavist pressures would succeed in destroying the Austro-
Hungarian empire. As a prominent member of the Union of Democratic
Control, Brailsford refused to succumb to the obsession with war
guilt, to which not even his own *Nation* was immune. Instead of appor-
tioning blame, he believed that those in favour of a negotiated peace
should strive to eliminate the sources of conflict. Even if Russian
mobilisation had afforded a pretext for war, its underlying causes
related to the growth of German population and the restraints on
export of capital, a desire for *Lebensraum* expressed in terms of
imperial ambitions. Short of the ideal solution of co-operative international development of the world's resources, some equitable allot-
ment had to be devised to prevent

> such an obvious anomaly as the assignment of an area like Morocco
> to a Power like France, with a dwindling population, possessed
> already of two good colonies of the same type (Algeria and Tunis),
> while Germany with a teeming population has none.[8]

Brailsford's writings during the war touched on both these themes
simultaneously. On the one hand, he advocated a league of nations with
sweeping military and economic powers to enforce peace and allocate
resources. At the same time, until the league concept became a reality,
he insisted that 'we must make room for German ambitions beside our
own in the world.'[9] German predominance in Turkey, so assiduously
pursued by Berlin before 1914, would mean 'the recovery of a wasted
and unhappy region for civilisation'.[10] Nor was there any reason to
believe that 'a German Turkey would be a graver menace to the world's
liberty than a British India. The chief menace to the world's liberty
today is an unsatisfied Germany.'[11] If the Allies restored Germany's
African colonies or compensated her with comparable territory (at the
expense of the Belgians or Portuguese), a contented Germany would no
longer refuse concessions to wronged nationalities — like the Alsatians

and the Poles — whose claims had too long been neglected.[12] That it was somehow inconsistent for a staunch critic of imperialism to propose that Germany be given a share of the spoils appropriate to her power seems never to have troubled him. As long as imperialism was the name of the game, Germany had a claim to be included among the players. Magnanimity on the part of the victors would not just make restitution for past injuries: it was the only antidote to militarism. A dictated peace, particularly one which deprived Germany of territory, would prolong the war and unite its people to eradicate the humiliation. He predicted that

> A settlement which left eighty millions of Germans angry, embittered, and cherishing revenge, might last for five, or ten, or twenty years. But it would perpetuate, even while it lasted, the armed peace, and so far from crushing militarism in Germany, it would impose it also on ourselves.[13]

While the enemy was to escape punishment, the Allies were expected to forgo the rewards of victory in the interests of a durable peace. Whatever the sentiment in France, its reoccupation of Alsace could be justified only if the Alsatians so determined by means of plebiscite. Brailsford, convinced that German-speaking districts would be reluctant to change their affiliation, favoured the establishment of a neutral buffer state in the area economically linked with Germany.[14] Self-restraint was not to be imposed on the French alone: England was urged to resist the temptation to use naval supremacy to complete Germany's economic ruin. Any settlement which 'failed to give Germany access to the world's store of raw materials would be the most disastrous of all possible defeats'.[15]

In later lamenting the onerous peace and the folly of indemnities, Brailsford was hardly unique among writers on the left. Nor did any of his works achieve the singular notoriety of Keynes' *Economic Consequences of the Peace*, many of whose insights his own articles anticipated. What is notable about Brailsford's writings at the end of the war, apart from the compassionate indignation they can still evoke, is their logical consistency; the outcome had merely confirmed his forecast of what would happen if the wrong policies were followed. His prescription for a lasting settlement seemed even more relevant once the mistake against which he had protested in vain were enshrined in a treaty. Tirelessly, although somewhat more stridently, he renewed his appeal for reconciliation after 1918: by appeasing Germany, England, at least, might rectify the injuries perpetrated at Versailles. In dozens of articles and several books over the next two decades he was to re-iterate his plea for treaty revision, often condoning German violations as justified attempts to break free of unwarranted restraints.

Brailsford's illusions about the 'cool reasoning power' of British voters suffered a rude awakening when, as a Labour candidate in the 1918 election, he contested Montrose Burghs and received less than a quarter of the vote. Braving virulent anti-German sentiment, he branded the clamour for indemnities as 'an appeal to the irrational instincts of the mob'.[16] So far from benefiting the British economy, an indemnity, he asserted, could be paid only by the export of goods for which nothing was taken in exchange. An economic transfer of this kind would represent 'the most colossal, most wanton, most suicidal organisa-tion of dumping that the world had ever known'.[17] But its most perni-cious effect was that it was 'strangling German democracy in its cradle. We are visiting the sins of the Kaiser and his Junkers on the people which has cast off their yoke.'[18]

Touring Central Europe early in 1919 on assignment for the *Nation* and the *Herald* and as a member of an economic commission sent to Poland by the Peace Conference, he had the opportunity to witness the devastation at close quarters. Hardly a dispassionate observer, even he had not anticipated the extent of suffering that the continuing Allied blockade had provoked. His reports documented shortages of coal and food, the deteriorating physical condition of the people, the gnawing shame of middle classes reduced to penury and unemployed workers rescued from starvation only by makeshift relief programmes. Industry was at a standstill. Malnutrition sapped the energy of working people, who had little incentive to work, since goods were either unavailable or beyond their means.[19] Poverty had not merely shaken the social struc-ture: it had begun to erode the moral fabric of society.

> We are pleased to talk of Huns, [he wrote] but when history tells the whole story of the working of this blockade from the Urals to the Rhine, in the hospitals that lack drugs, linen, and anaesthetics, in the garrets where dying children call to unemployed fathers, in the streets where desperate mobs pillage under the fire of brutalized troops, the next generation will ask with probing curiosity what devastation it was that Attila wrought to compare with this achieve-ment of ours.[20]

To compound the savagery of the blockade with a 'peace of strangulation' was to add insult to injury. Rather than encourage the infant republic, struggling to win approval, the Allies seemed bent on ensuring its disgrace by compelling the anti-militarist régime to acknowledge war guilt. 'No German government', he wrote from Berlin, 'however ruthless, no Allied pressure, however overwhelming, could ensure the tranquility of this nation under these burdens and humiliations'.[21] Only the threat of starvation and the hope of future revision would induce the German leaders to yield. Even so, the signatories would find themselves branded as traitors, and the government, discredited as well as disarmed, would be incapable of coping with *revanchist* militarism or revolutionary strikes. For all the lofty hopes aroused by Wilsonian idealism, in Germany no less than in England, the treaty bore the imprint of 'the mind of the ruling class', its terms providing 'an accurate mirror of capitalist Imperialism'.[22] Stripped of its colonies, its mercantile fleet, its footholds abroad, its access to raw materials, how could a prostrate Germany, saddled with huge indemnities, recuperate sufficiently to pay them, much less to feed its people? Whatever reparation might appropriately have been exacted to compensate France and Belgium for damage, this extortionate scheme could only be viewed as a 'cold-blooded project for the destruction of a commercial competitor'.[23]

Brailsford reserved his sharpest condemnation for the territorial changes, especially the cynical dismemberment of the former empires under the guise of self-determination. Although he now admitted that the loss of Alsace-Lorraine and Posen were inevitable, he rebelled against the subjection of the Saar to French military and economic surveillance. While such arrangements were ostensibly provisional, they might well foreshadow the permanent detachment of the region from Germany. Already the French were recruiting Polish miners, presumably with the intention of displacing native workers so that when the plebiscite ultimately took place, the whole district would fall to the French.[24] As recently as 1917 Brailsford had regarded German absorption of Alsace-Lorraine with equanimity, but the prospect of even temporary French control over the Saar was intolerable. Still worse was the manner in which Germany's eastern boundaries had been redrawn, blatantly disregarding lines of ethnic demarcation. Districts with solidly German population had been turned over to Poland for the sake of an effective strategic frontier. According to his calculations, some two and a half million Germans in Posen, Silesia, West Prussia and Danzig had been subjected to Polish rule without any consideration of their wishes. So large an alien component, incapable of peaceful assimilation, would create a serious irredentist problem.[25] When he visited

Vienna in February 1919, popular sentiment seemed to favour union
with Germany as the only alternative to economic atrophy. Although
the Allies hastened to gratify the nationalist longings of Czechs, Serbs
and Poles, they prohibited union between Austria and Germany in 'flat
defiance of any honest reading of the principle of self-determination'.
To compound the travesty, three and a half million Sudeten Germans,
inhabiting an area that could be detached easily from Czechoslovakia,
were placed under 'foreign rule'. Whatever its deficiencies — and they
were too glaring to be denied — the old Habsburg empire was, in
Brailsford's view, a workable economic entity whose size and geographical diversity made sense. In its place a galaxy of small, contentious
states, no less heterogeneous in composition and far less viable economically, had been created. These succession states, with their artificial
borders, were the result of a deliberate French plan to encircle its
former enemy with military satellites, whom fear of Germany and
mutual antipathy would compel to lean on French arms for protection.[26]

The dislocated post-war economy and the ineffectual clamour for
treaty revision filled Brailsford with foreboding about the future. That
paradoxical faith in the innate reasonableness of liberal societies, a
curious corollary of his socialist critique of capitalism, now seemed to
desert him. Nowhere in *After the Peace*, published in September 1920,
can one find even the glimmer of optimism that marked The *War of
Steel and Gold*. Appearing two years before Spengler's *Decline of the
West*, his gloomy analysis prefigured its recognition of the breakdown
of civilisation and the triumph of primitive values. Now that the smoke
of battle had cleared, he had begun to wonder whether the war, the
blockade, and the peace did not reflect some suicidal element in capitalism, whether, in fact, it could survive at all in view of its failure to produce goods and feed the people. The blockade had paralysed Central
European industry, while the structure of debt spelled 'the economic
death of half a Continent'. Versailles had deprived a defeated nation of
hope:

Millions of men of the German race . . . are beaten today into the
acceptance of passivity . . . and they know that for a generation their
lot is to obey . . . A defeat so catastrophic, an abasement so deep as
this, shatters not merely the power of the State, but the conventions
and social morality of its members.[27]

The impossibility of enforcing the peace except by policing meant the

perpetuation of alliances and armaments. 'The image of the future
which presents itself', he prophesied, 'is that of all Central Europe
reduced to the condition of a camp of prisoners of war, kept at work
for the benefit of their gaolers, by a system of calculated intimidation.'[28]

At the same time he began to ponder the wider ramifications of the
settlement, especially the 'world shortage, the dwindling of populations,
the decay of industries, the twilight of civilisation'.[29] So keen had the
Allies been to crush their enemies that they had closed their eyes to the
contribution that Germany had made in the past and must make again
if Europe were to recover economic and cultural vitality. It was almost
as though triumphant capitalism had lost the instinct of self-preservation. Instead of channelling German energies in a constructive direction,
it

> showered its favours on Poles, Roumanians and Jugo-Slavs, primitive
> unschooled races, not indeed without their own charm and emotional
> genius, who never, even after generations of experience, are likely to
> replace the Germans as industrial or intellectual workers.[30]

Out of the ashes of a productive, cosmopolitan civilisation, a provincial,
peasant society was emerging, a portent of retrogression and decay. It
was patently absurd to imagine that Europe could prosper without full
German participation, or that the succession states could fill the role
that Austria had once played. Conversations with Georg Lukacs, the
Marxist critic and Hungarian Commissioner of Education under Bela
Kun, convinced Brailsford that 'culture, in the sense of an activity
which creates and conquers new fields, is dying because the leisured
class itself is sinking to a proletarian level'.[31] But the problem hit close
to home more directly: impoverished consumers on the Continent, unable to buy British goods, meant fewer jobs in England. As Brailsford
explained in a 1921 memorandum for the Labour Party's Advisory
Committee on International Questions, 'The decline of our trade with
Germany, Russia and Austria would alone account for the whole
volume of our present unemployment'. The swollen indemnity could
'only be paid by the export virtually of prison-made goods, produced
under the threat of invasion, by sweated workers'. Savage exploitation
of this kind would ultimately destroy 'the most productive and the
most advanced civilisation of the Continent'. Since German workers
were receiving, according to his figures, less than one-third of British
wages, competitive pressure would, before long, reduce the standard of

living of workers at home to Continental levels. Only by securing the revision of the treaty could England save herself from the impending disaster. A Germany restored to world markets and given access to raw materials on an equitable basis might willingly pay a substantial indemnity to restore shattered districts. If England agreed to forgo its own share of payments, a larger proportion could be allotted to the French as an inducement to moderate their demands.[32]

When Brailsford next visited Germany, during the summer of 1922, unemployment had virtually disappeared, the shops were full, and the factories were humming with activity. But first impressions were deceptive: under the pressure of inflation workers remained poorly nourished, and the middle class was suffering a decline in living standards, its savings wiped out and its meagre incomes failing to keep pace with rising prices. 'The show of busy prosperity', he concluded, 'is only a show. The fact is deep poverty.'[33] Since he was disposed to blame the inflation on the demand for reparations, he was outraged when the French marched into the Ruhr after a German default on the deliveries of coal. It proved once again the 'blind folly' of disarming Germany while France remained an 'omnipotent military power'.[34] The Foreign Office had been a willing accomplice in the 'enslavement' of Germany in order to obtain French support for its own ambitions in Turkey and Mosul. 'It is because Downing Street is grabbing oil', he declared in the *New Leader*, 'that it dare not stop the French from grabbing coal.'[35] By 1923 Brailsford had come to regard French militarism as 'the worst menace to our common culture'. Its goal was 'a new Napoleonic Europe, using the control of iron and coal and the backing of the French army to dominate the whole Continent'.[36] Even a peaceful Germany could not be expected to endure indefinitely such relentless persecution:

> What one fears is the rapid growth in Germany of an inflamed militarist patriotism, which will one day attempt the overthrow of the Republic, because it alone stands in the way of a policy of revenge . . . The fact is that every violence, every insult, every unreason exercised on the prone body of Germany is a blow to the Republic . . . One day all Europe will pay for this insanity.[37]

Although Brailsford continued to proclaim the iniquities of French policy and to invite the English to renounce their share of reparations, the sense of urgency, of imminent catastrophe, disappeared from his writing in the period between Locarno and the end of the Rhineland occupation in 1930. The stridency so characteristic of his post-war style gave way to a quieter, sceptical tone, and his focus shifted to domestic issues, like the Living Wage programme, which he helped to draft for the ILP. It was not that the injustices had been corrected, but rather that foreign relations seemed, inexplicably, to be evolving towards accommodation. His articles and books like *Olives of Endless Age* (1928) were too realistic to ignore the survival of militarism and economic nationalism, but even he was not immune to post-Locarno euphoria. For all its warnings against false optimism, *Olives of Endless Age* conjures up an entirely different mood from *After the Peace*. Despite a prophecy that civilisation would 'not survive a second war' in that generation, he believed that 'the intolerable tension of competing nationalisms, the weariness engendered by the fruitless strife' were at last awakening men to the need for international unity. But unless steps were taken quickly, the book warned, 'our fate will overtake us in our sleep.'[38]

Events soon overtook this cautious optimism. The economic slump and the emergence of the Nazis as a major force in the 1930 Reichstag elections made the need for revision seem even more pressing to Brailsford. By subordinating the interests of peace to the designs of the Powers, the League of Nations was courting disaster, delaying 'the disarmament of the victors, until Germany rises up against the hypocrisy which keeps her disarmed, while her neighbours ring her round with steel'.[39] Once again his chief target was the French, whose ban on arms equality and on the projected Austro-German customs union prompted him to exclaim that 'if one cannot influence the French by plain speaking, then one must frankly isolate them.'[40] By the summer of 1932 he recognised that the Weimar Republic was no longer a functioning parliamentary democracy. Since the end of the war he had been prone to blame the victors for Germany's misfortunes, accusing them of having conspired to discredit the republic by crippling it with ruinous obligations. But as Germany floundered in the morass of economic chaos, Brailsford began to ponder the question, perhaps for the first time, of 'whether the assumptions of classical liberalism, which Social Democrats swallowed whole, will work at all in an epoch that calls for fundamental change'.[41] The Soviet experience had demonstrated that hostile treatment by the outside world was no bar to social progress and internal unity. In Germany, however, the timorous socialists who assumed control after the war had left the class structure intact, their enemies retaining dominant positions in the army, industry, and the bureaucracy. Too cautious to challenge the traditional ruling class or to incur the displeasure of the Allies, the Social Democratic leadership was

content 'to fortify itself behind a frail political barricade . . . defending
not socialism but liberalism'. Democracy in Germany had turned out to
be not so much a failure as an irrelevance, a sop intended to mollify
the workers, and it was, therefore, hardly surprising that Weimar
inspired so little enthusiasm.[42] These two interpretations — the quasi-
Marxist and the familiar revisionist thesis — were by no means incompatible: Brailsford linked them succinctly when he observed two years
later,

> The Nazi counter-revolution . . . was primarily an episode of the
> class-struggle, precipitated by the slump, but it could never have
> happened, nor could it have developed its pathological nationalism,
> unless Germans had felt themselves humiliated and wronged by the
> Versailles peace.[43]

He was at first inclined to underestimate the actual power that Hitler,
whom he viewed as a pawn of industrial magnates, would wield. Confident that the régime would come to resemble its Hohenzollern prede-
cessors more than its Fascist neighbours, he even doubted, somewhat
startlingly, 'whether there will be fewer Jews in a more Nordic
Germany when Hitler's reign is over'.[44] These sanguine assumptions
he was soon to retract in *The Nazi Terror*, a Socialist League pamphlet,
written later in 1933, which documented attacks on socialists, Communists and Jews and made reference to the machinery of repression,
including concentration camps at Dachau and elsewhere. Yet here, and
later in *Property or Peace?*, he was concerned not so much to condemn
as to explain why Nazism had gained a foothold. He stressed the way
in which Hitler exploited lower-middle-class anxiety about presumed
Jewish competition, the lack of professional opportunities, and the
helplessness of the little man crushed between cartel and trade union.
As the 'conscious enemy of rationalism', the Nazi movement appealed
to the frustrated and the insecure, who had seen their savings vanish
along with their hopes.[45]

   If Nazism was a pathological manifestation, its opponents needed to
discover a cure; punitive measures would merely aggravate the persecution mania on which it had fed. Candid about the evil of Fascism,
Brailsford doggedly urged, at least until 1936, appeasement as the most
effective antidote to the Nazi infection:

> To me it seems axiomatic, that however much one may loathe this
> Nazi movement, the first element of a cure is to remove Germany's

wrongs. It is unfortunate that Europe will have to concede to Hitler what the Allies refused to Rathenau, Stresemann and Brüning. But to persevere in injustice, because our victim has begun to look repulsive in the convulsions of his resentment, is neither right nor wise.[46]

Allied statesmen might balk at the invidious task of submitting to a dictator's ravings, but they had only themselves to blame. An unarmed, law-abiding people had pleaded, under socialist and Liberal ministries, for the removal of the 'fetters forged at Versailles'. It was too late now for recriminations: 'what men would not do at the prompting of justice, they will do at the bidding of fear.'[47] Instead of waiting for the blow to fall, it would be better to seize the initiative; by removing the causes of grievance, the Allies would atone for their sins, showing the German nation that fair treatment was possible without recourse to violence. Unless England and France disarmed to Germany's level, as the peace settlement had stipulated, some degree of German rearmament would have to be tolerated.[48] Sanctions to reaffirm German inferiority would be imprudent as well as immoral; it would rally the nation behind its rulers, making it more difficult to replace the Nazis with an internationally-minded régime. Any French attempt to involve England in reoccupying the Rhineland as a way of intimidating Hitler should be rebuffed, because

> this situation [has] come about only as a result of all the oppressions that the Victors heaped on a pacific and democratic Republic, and, above all, because they broke, and still are breaking, their own promise to disarm.[49]

Aside from renewed appeals for disarmament, Brailsford could only counsel patience until the German people were ready to throw off the Fascist incubus. Although his attitude towards resistance to Hitler's demands stiffened dramatically later in the decade, he held to the view, from 1933 until after the Second World War, that Germans alone could determine their fate and that there were always elements in German society uncontaminated by Nazism. He had faith in the resilience of democratic impulses, especially among the young, and was heartened by contacts with members of 'Neu Beginnen', a socialist underground organisation, although it was the evidence of opposition to Hitler, rather than its particular ideological standpoint, that attracted him. His preface to the English edition of its manifesto affirmed the 'debts of comradeship' that the British labour movement owed to the German

working class and warned that 'until it stands on its feet again, there is
no secure future for us'.[50] To Brailsford, Nazism was a malignancy
which had afflicted a desperately misguided nation, an aberration which
disrupted historical traditions, not their logical outcome. A middle class
demoralised by defeat and economic insecurity, a working class caught
in the internecine quarrels of socialists and Communists were too en-
feebled in 1933 to offer more than token resistance to Hitler, but, given
time, the German spirit would heal itself. The 'good' Germans, among
whom Brailsford included the bulk of ordinary people, would eventually return to the mainstream of liberal civilisation.

As long as Hitler's ambitions did not appear to extend beyond revision of the peace terms, Brailsford was loath to condemn. It was not
the violations of a bankrupt treaty that aroused his misgivings, but the
realisation that making amends meant consigning more innocent victims
to tyranny. This 'hideous dilemma' became all too apparent when the
Saarlanders were subjected to intimidation in the months before the
1935 plebiscite. Although the obligation to hold the plebiscite could
not be evaded, 'one shudders at the thought of placing any additional
millions under this despotism'.[51] But he consoled himself with the
thought that once the Saar issue was resolved, 'a new chapter will open'.
All that remained to achieve conciliation was for the Allies to concede
'equality in arms' and to correct that 'crying wrong − the clauses in the
Treaties that forbade the union of Austria with Germany'.[52] Brailsford
had clearly not yet taken Hitler's full measure. Anticipating a substantial negative vote in the Saar by workers and Catholics, he surmised that
such a result, dealing 'a heavy blow to the prestige of the Nazi régime',
would move Hitler to 'greater caution and moderation'.[53] That he had
misjudged not only Hitler but the Saarlanders as well in no way shook
his confident assumptions. While acknowledging that the return to conscription several months later constituted a violation of the treaty, he
felt that the League should refrain from censure:

> One wishes that the Allies had themselves spontaneously revised this
> miserable Treaty many a year ago. They lacked the wisdom to do it.
> Let us, then, have the frankness to say plainly that the Germans
> were justified in breaking it so soon as they had the will and the
> power.

If there had ever been an opportune moment to halt German rearmament, it would have been as soon as Nazi intentions were revealed in
1933, but, of course, he had been even less disposed to resistance at

that time than two years later.

In 1935 Brailsford was impelled to explain to his audience why he was 'arguing for tolerance and sanity' towards Hitler instead of lining up with the Soviet Union against this 'enemy of the whole working class movement'. What was the alternative? Collective security on British terms at that time, he contended, could only mean an alliance with men like Mussolini and Flandin to fight for 'the sanctity of the Versailles treaty', rather than for the interests of the workers.[54] He would refuse to believe that England was sincere in desiring reconciliation until its representatives boldly offered Tanganyika or South-West Africa to Germany.[55] The Rhineland reoccupation in March 1936 dramatised the issue in all its perplexity: certainly Hitler had been 'violent and unscrupulous', but had he any alternative to a unilateral revocation of the Rhineland clauses? 'If he has broken a treaty', Brailsford commented in typically even-handed style, 'did not the victors break their solemn, written promise to reduce their armaments to the Versailles level?' The difficulty was that if, in the name of equity, Germany were allowed to prosper, its new-found strength would be exploited to torment others.[56]

Brailsford's articles during this period of fervent popular front sentiment suggested that it was the enemy within, the ruling clique of capitalists and militarists, against whom the working class should be on guard, more than a potential external menace. Once a socialist government came to power in England, things would be different, and it might then be possible to speak of national interest, to build a fraternal alliance, including the Soviet Union, against Fascism. In the meantime 'vigilant detachment' seemed the soundest approach, coupled with 'mass resistance to veto this country's participation in any capitalist-imperialist war, even if Geneva should bless it'.[57] His sense of estrangement can be seen at its most extreme in an article entitled 'Resist War: Defend Socialism', in which he asked,

> Will you fight to maintain the right of Czechoslovakia to hold three million German subjects against their will? Will you lead English and French workers to the shambles to maintain a clerical-fascist dictatorship in Vienna? To all these and to many similar questions I answer for myself flatly No . . . The survival of most of these States in their present form does not appear to me to be a Socialist interest, and I would pledge no worker's blood to defend them.

At the same time he argued somewhat contradictorily that if Baldwin continued 'retreating before the Dictators, democracy and Socialism will go down undefended in Europe as they did in Germany'.[58]

This article, cloaking its author's ambivalence in rhetorical invective, appeared just as Brailsford's views were undergoing a rapid reversal. By the autumn of 1936, although no less suspicious of the National government, he was abandoning his faith in the efficacy of concessions to Germany. The time for resistance had come, based on 'a firm alliance of all nations in which the working class is still free'. Had such an alliance existed earlier, the League would never have suffered so stinging a defeat in Abyssinia, 'nor would democracy be fighting for its life against overwhelming odds in Spain'. Here is the key to Brailsford's change of heart. He was more concerned about the survival of the Spanish republic than almost any other question in his lifetime, a concern so profound that he was prepared, at the age of sixty-three, to risk his life in fighting for the Loyalist cause. Only those closest to him could dissuade him from this folly, but the Spanish Civil War did become the major focus of his articles and activities during the next three years. He raised money for Spanish relief, encouraged the recruitment of volunteers for the Republican forces, and chaired the Labour-Spain Committee, which sought to promote a more openly pro-Republican policy within the Labour Party. It was German intervention on the insurgent side, in flagrant violation of the Non-Intervention Agreement, that made him believe, perhaps for the first time, that the democratic powers must exert themselves to stop Hitler. How different from his earlier remarks is this declaration of October 1936:

> Certainly if we always retreat, if we always yield to threats and even to bluff, if we adopt a policy of peace at any price, we shall not get peace and we shall sacrifice all that we hold dear . . . Men who will not fight for what they hold dear deserve to go under.[59]

Once he had discovered a cause worth fighting for, Brailsford began to re-examine his attitude towards Hitler's designs elsewhere. Not that the cause for revision had been nullified by German activities in Spain, only that appeasement must be superseded by a combination of justice and firmness. Reluctant though he was to support rearmament by the National government, whose reactionary policies he found repugnant, the Spanish crisis made him believe that resistance to Fascism must override all other ideological considerations.

Collective security, to which he had become a convert, meant a common defence with France — now restored to his good graces — and

Russia, but a defence of human rights, not of imperial acquisitions. If Hitler was to be checked, the working class would have to be mobilised for the coming struggle:

> An attempt to buy Hitler out by offering him colonies elsewhere would only confirm him in his belief that everything can be won by audacious violence. The more we retreat, the further will he advance. The time to consider concessions will come when the democratic Powers have demonstrated their unity and their will to resist.[60]

Yet, after all he had written during the previous two decades, he found it hard to vent much spleen over the *Anschluss* with Austria. Incapable of economic survival on its own, the republic was hardly worth mourning. The real tragedy was that union between Austria and Germany, harmless, perhaps even beneficial when both were democratic, was now achieved by force as part of a plan to dominate Europe. But if it was too late to salvage Austria, there was still time to curb Hitler's ambitions in Czechoslovakia where the case for resistance was 'dictated by prudence as well as by principle'. An 'unambiguous statement', informing Hitler that an attack on the Czechs would mean war, and a British declaration of solidarity with France and the Soviet Union might forestall precipitate action by Germany. But even as he called for firmness, Brailsford continued to urge the revision of that arrangement which attached several million Germans to 'this Slav state'. His solution was to couple 'a prompt and public promise of British support' for the Czechs with an appeal to them to erase this 'blot' either by ceding territory or cantonal autonomy.[61]

This ambivalence towards the Prague régime diminished as the outlines of Chamberlain's policy became clear. By the end of May, recognising that Sudeten autonomy would pave the way for German expansion, he insisted that the Czechs had granted everything that the Germans 'can reasonably ask' in terms of cultural autonomy.[62] Again and again in these months his articles linked the fate of the Czechs and the Spaniards. Hitler must be halted on both fronts; if Prague fell, the loss of Barcelona would follow inevitably. Indeed it was Brailsford's commitment to the struggle against Fascism in Spain that strengthened his resolve to thwart Hitler on the Danube. On the other hand, as long as the British government connived at Italian intervention in Spain, he opposed any expression of support for Chamberlain: 'That we loathe the record, the spirit and the ambitions of Nazi Germany is no reason for placing ourselves under the banner of British capitalist-imperialism.'[63] Implicit in this argument was a contradiction that Brailsford was reluctant to admit. Until Labour was strong enough politically to supplant the National government, Chamberlain would have to be tolerated, even encouraged, if there were to be a show of solidarity at home and firmness abroad. For Labour to withhold support as a way of undermining the Prime Minister was neither practical nor provident. Brailsford was hardly alone on the left, however, in demanding arms for Spain while refusing to condone rearmament at home. Without resolving the paradox of how a defenceless England could intervene forcefully, he claimed that the most effective deterrent to Nazi aggression would be a 'direct, public and mutual guarantee' to the Czechs by England, France and Russia, a step which Chamberlain repeatedly vetoed. Although he was at times inclined to view the Prime Minister's policy as a deliberate attempt to employ Fascism in the battle against the true class enemy in Moscow, he came increasingly to believe that socialists could no longer be too fastidious about their allies. 'This issue of power', he observed, 'turns out to be a struggle for self-preservation, in which our Western rationalist civilisation will perish, if any of us refuse to defend the common cause.' What stuck in his throat was the fact that the survival of Western civilisation had become entangled in the defence of capitalism. But if British imperialism was more palatable than the Nazi variety, it did not necessarily follow that 'we accept in our free minds, even if it should come to war, the leadership of the class and the Party that brought us to this tragic crisis by its greed, its blindness and its weakness'.[64]

It was Munich, above all, which discredited appeasement, inspiring Brailsford to the sharpest indictment of Chamberlain's policy which appeared in the non-Communist press at the time. The search for justice through revision had been betrayed. He thundered in *Reynolds*:

Two Great Powers flinched from their duty to this little State because they realised that the reckless Nazi Dictator would proceed to the last extremity in order to impose his will on it.

Had they stood firm, in association with the Soviet Union, there would have been 'neither war nor surrender'. Those who found solace in the reprieve should face the fact that 'we have saved our skins and lost our honour. We have gained our ease and jeopardised our safety with our freedom.'[65] Chamberlain's policy was intelligible only on the assumption that he envisaged the Axis leaders as 'his partners of tomorrow.'[66]

In 1939, unlike 1914, Brailsford was an ardent proponent of war against Germany, even to the point of chiding the *New Statesman* for broaching the subject of peace aims. Still clinging to the hope of an ultimate international federation, he now maintained that yielding to Fascism impeded progress towards his goal: 'the more we concede, the longer will these dictatorships endure.'[67] With the loss of Spain, his focus shifted to India as the clearest barometer of British intentions. No longer seeking to placate Hitler with colonies, as he had a few years earlier, he now suggested that England counter Hitler's imperial pretensions by relinquishing its own. 'The first step towards winning this war', he avowed, his tone no longer as belligerent, 'is to complete the liberation of India.' A programme of disarmament, federal defence, economic co-operation, and the break-up of empire would 'do more to win this war than all their bombing planes are likely to effect'. By transferring its colonies to international control and renouncing every vestige of privilege, the raw materials of the underdeveloped world would be accessible to all equally, and Germany would thus receive 'much more than she asks'. In other words, Brailsford was urging upon the British government an updated version of proposals he had formulated as long ago as 1912. The main distinction lay in his attitude towards Hitler. In 1914 — indeed until 1936 — he had held that concession was preferable to war. Now he had become convinced that any peace which implied surrender would be a 'mere truce between one aggression and the next'. Reconciliation must wait 'until Hitlerism breaks under a German revolution'.[68] The *Daily Worker*, hostile to Brailsford since his denunciation of the Soviet purge trials in *Reynolds*, feigned astonishment at the paradox of his desire for war, while at the same time wishing to offer Germany 'much more than she asks'. Its own anti-Hitler line muted to suit the Non-Aggression Pact, the *Worker* criticised Brailsford's failure to perceive that the war would not lead to peace 'so long as British Imperialism enslaves millions of people and fosters reaction and Fascism'. English workers should, continued the leader, be fighting Chamberlain, not Hitler.[69] Brailsford's rejoinder the next week noted somewhat pointedly that resistance to Fascist aggression had once emanated from all parties of the left. He refuted the *Worker*'s contention that this was merely a quarrel between imperialist rivals, insisting that the issue was not federal union, which he certainly endorsed, but self-preservation.[70] As he put it a month later, 'We have to choose between resistance and slavery.'[71]

The central theme of his wartime writings, summarised succinctly in the headline of one of his *Reynolds* articles, 'Destroy Fascism, Not the Germans', was that Hitler and his cohorts were the enemy, not the mass

of the people. In January 1941, while the blitz still raged, he tried to
exonerate the Germans from the charges which Lord Vansittart levied
in his notorious *Black Record*. Far from being congenitally barbarous,
they had, Brailsford claimed, betrayed their own cultural heritage in
succumbing to Hitler's tyranny. Nothing in their past indicated a
greater propensity for aggression or cruelty than other European
nations. Prussian militarism was guilty, not of preparing the way for
Nazism, but of blighting social development: an entrenched aristocracy
exploited the three-class franchise to keep the masses in subjection and
retard effective democracy. But Nazism did not derive from this
military tradition; it represented a new social stratum, drawing support
from the 'riff-raff of all classes', many of whom had 'crawled out of the
sewers'. Hitler succeeded because of Weimar's failures and the world
slump rather than because of some innate wickedness in his subjects,
most of whom did not belong to the Nazi party and bore no responsibility for its crimes. Convinced that opposition to the régime was
mounting and should be encouraged, Brailsford appealed for a sign to
the German people that defeat would not bring humiliation as it had in
1918. The first step in changing their outlook would be to show that
'men may be sincere when they profess goodwill, respect and fellowship towards those of other races.'[72] If the only prospect held out to
the enemy was that of political impotence and territorial dismemberment, they would have little incentive to risk their lives by rising up
against their rulers. The proposed cession of East Prussia, Silesia and
Pomerania, provinces indisputably German in composition, to Poland
at the end of the war would militate against 'a pacific and co-operative
habit of mind'. Instead, such treatment would serve to 'keep the Nazi
temper alive and militant'.[73]

Never content merely to exhort from the sidelines, Brailsford became engrossed in the problems of countless refugees whom he befriended during these years. A critic of internment policies, he worked
tirelessly to reverse unfavourable administrative decisions, writing
letters, signing petitions, addressing meetings, and using his influence
with officials to secure more humane treatment. As a respected socialist,
generally indifferent to ideological distinctions, he was particularly
well-suited to mediate among factions of *émigré* socialists and was
instrumental in getting works like Julius Braunthal's *Need Germany
Survive?* published in order to stimulate interest in their plight.[74]
He was stirred to affirm before Hitler's victims, both in Germany and
in England, that the war had not extinguished socialist ideals and
humanitarian values, but he was at a loss to know how to respond to

requests for a manifesto like the one he had furnished during the First
World War.

> I'm besieged with pleas, which move & disturb me, [he informed a
> friend in June 1943] to write something to help my day and genera-
> tion. But what? I'm so pessimistic about the coming settlement that
> I'm paralysed. Am I just once again to write, as I did in 1916, a book
> of amiable day-dreams, which everyone will ignore? And yet, not to
> fight at all, but just to escape into the past, seems too cowardly.[75]

Yet by the end of that summer his effort to comply with Leonard
Woolf's suggestion of a Fabian pamphlet resulted in a book-length
manuscript, which Allen Lane agreed to publish as a Penguin. The
75,000 copies issued early in 1944 were promptly sold, and an
American edition appeared later in the year. Lane distributed a number
of complimentary copies to MPs, but the book received a cool reception. Its author, who had just turned seventy, lamented that it was

> so much ahead of public opinion that (as usual with my books) it
> might as well not have been written. Ten years hence (when it & I
> are forgotten) people will begin to think on these lines .[76]

Our Settlement With Germany was a compassionate and generous
declaration, far-sighted in its recognition of the need for European
unity, yet strangely oblivious to the depths of anti-German feeling in
Allied countries. To Brailsford, the test of an effective settlement was
whether it would enable the German nation to resume a position of
self-respect within the European community. So convinced was he that
the average German knew little of Nazi misdeeds, that it was vital to
dissipate any fears which might prolong the struggle needlessly, that he
was more concerned to resuscitate Germany than to salve the wounds
it had inflicted on others. Arguing that the enemy should be disarmed,
not dismembered, he called for a return to those Versailles boundaries
he had once attacked so vehemently. If any reparation were exacted, it
must not be in territory or in forced labour (as the Poles and Russians
were demanding), but rather in the provision of machinery and equipment, beneficial alike to its recipients and to the Germans who would
be restored to useful employment.[77] While recognising the inevitability
of military occupation, he hoped that it would be brief and that any
ban on political activity would be lifted without delay. Democracy
could only take root if citizens were permitted to resume participation

in trade unions, political parties, and interest groups.[78] Considerable attention would have to be paid to re-educating the enemy. A decade in which truth had been suppressed had broken down the scruples of civilised men, but numbed intellects could begin to work again once Nazi tyranny had been destroyed. Brailsford insisted that Nazi teachers be identified and purged from the schools, but as soon as this process was completed, Germans themselves should undertake the education of the young. Pending the appointment of a Director of Education, a group of prominent intellectuals, men like Einstein, Tillich and Thomas Mann, might be invited to constitute themselves as an interim council.[79]

The most controversial segment of *Our Settlement With Germany* dealt with the punishment of Nazi criminals. Without denying their heinous offences, Brailsford argued that 'to reverse the moral values of civilised men is not a crime known to international law'.[80] Since it was wrong to create a new code retrospectively, it would be better to exile Hitler and other leading Nazis to some remote island than to bring them to trial. As far as the party faithful were concerned, they should be debarred from holding political office for the remainder of their lives. Those guilty of actual atrocities in the conduct of the war might legitimately be brought before international courts martial. For the SS men, Brailsford proposed exile in undeveloped regions, where they might start life again as pioneers on the soil. Alternatively, they could be set to work, under strict supervision, to rebuild German towns, while being subjected to moral indoctrination.[81]

One of the lessons of Versailles was the importance of separating the problem of punishment from the problem of reconstruction. Whatever penalties were imposed on war criminals, Germany itself should not again be treated as a pariah. The question of devastation was to be dealt with in a European context, not by the extortion of punitive reparation from Germany, but by each nation contributing its special skills and resources. Although Brailsford believed that social revolution in Germany offered the best chance for a lasting peace, he recognised that the British and Americans were disinclined to let it happen. But while German heavy industry should be preserved and its productive skills turned to peaceful uses, the power of the Junkers and industrialists must not be permitted to revive. He personally favoured the internationalisation of the Ruhr, with a single multi-national consortium controlling the region's coal and iron, a plan that would relieve Europe from the fear of German predominance and protect Germany against dismemberment. In some sense, Hitler's achievements had not all been negative: his new European order had transformed much of the Continent into a coherent political and economic unit, the advantages of which were not to be discounted in the repudiation of Hitler's methods.[82]

Brailsford concluded with an impassioned appeal to his readers to 'recover for mankind its obliterated instincts and half-forgotten principles of social morality',[83] but the final months of the war were a tragic reminder of 1918. He was deeply pessimistic about Germany's future under occupation, as he told two young American friends:

> The policy of unconditional surrender is as wicked as it is stupid . . .
> At present Hitler can say he was right all the time: our intention is
> to destroy Germany. And that may be our intention, more or less.
> The result is a suicidal resistance which will wholly ruin Germany
> & half-ruin the rest of Europe, besides rendering any future recovery,
> moral & physical, impossible.[84]

His plea for mercy fell on deaf ears, dismissed by many, even on the left, as sentimental and unrealistic. Kingsley Martin considered Brailsford's post-war attitude as 'excessively pro-German', and their differences, especially about partition, were a factor in hastening Brailsford's retirement from the *New Statesman* after he returned from six months in India in mid-1946.[85]

The sharpest reaction to *Our Settlement With Germany* came from the Communist camp. In February 1945 *Labour Monthly* reprinted a venomous review by Ilya Ehrenburg, who accused Brailsford of defending Himmler and his sadistic SS, of seeking to save Hitler, who no doubt would be sent to some idyllic island to 'write his memoirs on baby-massacre'. In a work 'that might have appeared just as well in Berlin', Brailsford had not concealed 'his tenderness for Fascism' when he conceded that the New Order achieved some good results or that the SS should be employed in rebuilding German cities (rather than Russian ones).[86] Brailsford retorted that it was just this kind of 'mendacity and slander [that] has made cooperation between Socialists and Communists difficult in the past'. He recalled that he had been the first English writer to publish a documented exposure of Nazi terror in 1933, the first journalist on the left to advocate a military alliance against Hitler in 1936, and that alone in the socialist press he had endorsed conscription in the spring of 1939. In answer to Ehrenburg's charges, he insisted that his primary concern had been to render the Nazis harmless for the future and to avoid further bloodshed. In the same issue R. Palme Dutt, reproving Brailsford for this 'suicidal leniency', reminded

Labour Monthly readers of his shameful record of 'vituperation in denouncing the Moscow trials' and attacks on Stalin during the battle against 'Finnish fascism'.[87] Nowhere did Dutt mention that Brailsford supported the war against Hitler at a time when the Communist press dismissed it as an imperialist dispute from which the worker class should remain aloof.

During the summer of 1947 Brailsford returned to Germany for the first time since Hitler's rise, and his impressions were strongly reminiscent of his 1919 visit. Once again he was struck by the contrast between the chastened temper of the German people, eager for renewal, and the bleak conditions. In Hamburg, where only twenty per cent of the houses had survived British bombing intact, there was a scarcity of food and building materials, a rise in the incidence of tuberculosis, and a shortage of labour and fuel which crippled industrial production. Plans for dismantling industries seemed to confirm the view that the British purpose was 'to prevent the restoration of German industry as a possible competitor with our own', an argument which Brailsford himself had propounded in the twenties.[88] As in the Weimar period, any attempt to add economic ruin to military defeat could only stifle the growth of a pacific mentality. Not that Germany in 1947 posed a military threat: 'from this decimated and exhausted population', he wrote in a characteristic underestimation of German recuperative powers, 'no aggressor can arise in our generation.'[89] Still, without a tolerable standard of life and the recovery of national unity, the outlook for democratic institutions was unpromising. If the mood of the apolitical mass 'turns to anger, when dismantling actually begins, their resistance will bring with it a revival of nationalism'.[90]

By 1949 Brailsford had concluded that a nationalist resurgence was no longer the most serious danger. The formation of the East German government foreshadowed the absorption of the zone into the Russian economic and military system, while the West, on the verge of remilitarisation, was turning into an American satellite. The rigidity of post-war divisions, the continued presence of a large occupation force, had made Germany the crucible of the Cold War. 'Until we solve the German problem', he warned, 'the threat of a third world war hangs over us'. In place of these 'intolerable arrangements' he proposed to re-unite Germany as a neutral and permanently disarmed state under the guarantee of the four Powers, who would evacuate their armies. Dismantling of industry would cease, the entire country would receive an infusion of Marshall Plan aid, and a new constitution would be promulgated to ensure civil liberties and free elections. Free elections would satisfy the West, while neutrality would allay Russian fears that the military potential of the Ruhr might be unleashed against them.[91] Although he sent copies of his article to a number of prominent MPs, it aroused little interest. None of those who bothered to reply thought his plan feasible, either because they believed the Russians unlikely to comply with the disengagement stipulations or because they could not imagine Germany outside the Western orbit.[92]

In the end, as for so much of his career, Brailsford found himself a lonely spokesman for sanity and reason, his idealism curiously anachronistic in an era of Cold Warriors and Kremlinologists. His conception of an international community derived from the nineteenth century, and its mingling of Cobdenite non-interventionism with a secularised Christian morality was increasingly out of step with the drift of public opinion. It was only in the twenties and thirties, in his attack on the Versailles settlement, that Brailsford seemed to articulate widely-shared sentiments, but even then he was more committed to appeasement than most socialists before 1936 and more belligerent thereafter. Despite these shifts of viewpoint, particularly in regard to Hitler, there was an underlying consistency in Brailsford's attitude towards Germany. For nearly forty years he preached the importance of concessions as a basis for reconciliation. If he was inclined to overlook German faults while identifying British ones, it was not from sentimental germanophilia, but because his radical conscience responded to the German sense of inferiority, which constituted a stumbling block to peace in Europe. What characterised Brailsford was his independence and integrity, qualities that set him apart from so many other publicists. While he was prepared to shift his position as circumstances changed, he would never violate the dictates of conscience or betray his passion for freedom. Just as he defied received opinion on the left in order to denounce the Soviet trials, so too he remained independent on German questions, refusing to yield to patriotic or popular sentiment. Above all, he was an internationalist who abhorred xenophobia, a socialist whose sympathies could not be confined within national boundaries. If he was credulous at times, he was never vindictive or mean-spirited, and his commitment to peace and understanding among peoples could not be impugned. Whatever his mistakes, the labour and progressive movement in England gained in stature by having in its midst such a man of principle. That his ideas were unlikely to sway statesmen on either side of the Channel does not invalidate them, nor does it alter the fact that had the policies he advocated been pursued consistently, the European stage would have been strewn with fewer corpses. A century that counted its war dead and its genocide victims in the millions could ill afford to ignore the counsels of reason.

Notes

1. F.M. Leventhal, 'H.N. Brailsford and the *New Leader*', *Journal of Contemporary History* IX (January 1974). Also see entry on Brailsford in J.M. Bellamy and J. Saville (eds.), *Dictionary of Labour Biography*, II (1974).
2. A.J.P. Taylor, *The Trouble Makers* (Bloomington, 1958), esp. pp. 122-4, 175-8, 185-7.
3. *Reynolds News*, 26 January 1941. Also see J. Braunthal, *In Search of the Millenium* (1945), p. 323.
4. 'Germany and the Balance of Power', *Contemporary Review*, CII (July 1912); *The War of Steel and Gold* (1914), pp. 37-46. Also see F.M. Leventhal, 'H.N. Brailsford and the Search for a New International Order', *Edwardian Radicalism 1900-1914* (A.J.A. Morris (ed.), 1974).
5. *The War of Steel and Gold*, p. 35.
6. *Nation*, 24 May 1913.
7. *Nation*, 29 August 1914. See *Nation*, 12 December 1914.
8. *War and Peace*, February 1915.
9. *A League of Nations* (1917), p. 241.
10. 'The Shaping of Mid-Europe', *Contemporary Review*, CIX (March 1916).
11. *Nation*, 1 January 1916; *Labour Leader*, 16 December 1915.
12. *A League of Nations*, pp. 243-6.
13. *Nation*, 19 September 1914.
14. *Herald*, 20 October 1917.
15. *Herald*, 8 June 1918. Also see 'The Reichstag and Economic Peace', *Fortnightly Review*, DCIX (September 1917).
16. *Herald*, 7 December 1918.
17. *Montrose Standard*, 6 December 1918.
18. *Herald*, 7 December 1918.
19. Brailsford's reports were collected in a volume entitled *Across the Blockade: A Record of Travels in Enemy Europe* (1919). See esp. pp. 40-7, 106-13, 123-6. Most of the material had appeared originally in *Nation, New Republic, Herald*, and *Manchester Guardian*.
20. Ibid., p. 114.
21. *Daily Herald*, 12 May 1919.
22. *Across the Blockade*, p. 146.
23. Ibid., p. 110. Also see *Daily Herald*, 21 May and 18 June 1919.
24. *Daily Herald*, 20 May 1919.
25. *Manchester Guardian*, 30 May 1919.
26. *Manchester Guardian*, 3 June 1919. See *Across the Blockade*, pp. 148-9.
27. *After the Peace* (1920), pp. 21, 33-4.
28. Ibid., p. 82.
29. Ibid., p. 30.
30. Ibid., pp. 22-3.
31. 'The Survival of German Civilisation', *Manchester Guardian Commercial*, 4 January 1923. Brailsford had interviewed Lukacs, in exile in Vienna, during the summer of 1922. Their initial encounter was in Budapest in 1919. Cf. *Across the Blockade*, pp. 32-3.
32. 'Unemployment, the Peace and the Indemnity', Labour Party Advisory Committee on International Questions Memorandum 188(a), pp. 3-4, 8-9

(Transport House). Also see *New Republic*, 23 March 1921.
33. *Nation*, 15 July 1922.
34. *New Leader*, 5 January 1923. The *Labour Leader* had taken the name *New Leader* when Brailsford became editor in October 1922.
35. *New Leader*, 19 January 1923.
36. *New Leader*, 26 January 1923.
37. *New Leader*, 6 July 1923.
38. *Olives of Endless Age* (New York, 1928), pp. 428-30.
39. *New Leader*, 19 September 1930.
40. *New Leader*, 31 July 1931.
41. *World Tomorrow*, 28 September 1932.
42. *New Republic*, 17 August 1932. Also see *Property or Peace?* (1934), pp. 41-5.
43. *Property or Peace?* p. 290.
44. *World Tomorrow*, 1 March 1933.
45. *Property or Peace?* pp. 47-8; *The Nazi Terror* (1933), 9 pp.
46. *Property or Peace?* p. 291.
47. *Reynolds' Illustrated News*, 26 March 1933.
48. *New Clarion*, 3 June 1933; *Property or Peace?* pp. 291-2.
49. *Reynolds' Illustrated News*, 8 October 1933.
50. Miles [pseud. of Walter Lowenheim], *Socialism's New Start: A Secret German Manifesto* (1934). The pamphlet was published by the National Council of Labour Colleges. Also see *Reynolds News*, 28 December 1941.
51. *Reynolds' Illustrated News*, 21 January 1934.
52. *Reynolds' Illustrated News*, 9 December 1934.
53. *Reynolds' Illustrated News*, 6 January 1935.
54. *Reynolds' Illustrated News*, 24 March 1935.
55. *Reynolds' Illustrated News*, 12 May 1935.
56. *Reynolds News*, 15 March 1936.
57. *New Statesman*, 9 May 1936.
58. *New Fabian Research Bureau Quarterly*, No. 11 (Autumn 1936). Also see *Reynolds News*, 19 July 1936.
59. *Reynolds News*, 18 October 1936.
60. *Reynolds News*, 3 January 1937.
61. *New Statesman*, 19 March 1938.
62. *Reynolds News*, 29 May 1938.
63. *Reynolds News*, 4 September 1938.
64. *Reynolds News*, 18 September 1938.
65. *Reynolds News*, 2 October 1938. 'All the press welcomed the Munich agreement as preferable to war with the solitary exception of *Reynolds News* (and, of course, the Communist *Daily Worker*).' A.J.P Taylor, *English History 1914-1945* (Oxford, 1965), p. 430.
66. *New Statesman*, 5 November 1938.
67. *New Statesman*, 19 August 1939.
68. *Reynolds News*, 8 October 1939. Brailsford had so far forsaken his earlier views that he could write a year later that the leaders of the Western democracies had 'appeased, when they ought to have armed and rallied a whole continent for resistance', whereas 'the progressive Opposition, in England at least, had no illusions about appeasement. It called steadily for resistance.' *America Our Ally* (1940), pp. 43-4.
69. *Daily Worker*, 9 October 1939.
70. *Reynolds News*, 15 October 1939.
71. *Reynolds News*, 26 November 1939.
72. *Germans and Nazis* [? 1941], 16pp. See *Reynolds News*, 26 January 1941; 'Guilt and Tragedy of the German People', *International Socialist Forum* (October 1941); Lord Vansittart, *Black Record: Germans Past and Present*

(1941).

73. 'Peace, the Poles and East Prussia', *Left News* (February 1944).

74. I am grateful to Evelyn Anderson, the late Julius Braunthal and Heinrich Fraenkel for information on this period of Brailsford's life. See *Reynolds News*, 17 November 1940; J. Braunthal, *Auf der Suche nach dem Millenium* (Nürnberg, 1948), pp. 637-46; W. Röder, *Die deutschen sozialistischen Exilgruppen in Grossbritannien 1940-1945* (Hannover, 1968), pp. 88, 218.

75. H.N. Brailsford to Clare Leighton, 6 June 1943 (courtesy of Clare Leighton).

76. H.N. Brailsford to Clare Leighton, 3 September 1944 (courtesy of Clare Leighton). Brailsford first sketched his proposals in a talk to the Fabian International Bureau's group on Germany in March 1943. I am grateful to Evamaria Brailsford for information concerning the publication of *Our Settlement With Germany*.

77. *Our Settlement With Germany* (New York, 1944), pp. 61-3, 81-2, 136-40. Much of this material was also incorporated in a series of articles, entitled 'What to Do with Germany', in *New Republic*, 10-24 July 1944. On the issue of reparations, see *Making Germany Pay?* (1944), 8pp.

78. *Our Settlement With Germany*, pp. 43-53.

79. Ibid., pp. 94-100; 'The Re-education of Germany', *Contemporary Review*, CLXVII (August 1945).

80. *Our Settlement With Germany*, p. 57.

81. Ibid., pp. 57-63.

82. Ibid., pp. 38, 113-16, 135-6.

83. Ibid., p. 154.

84. H.N. Brailsford to Luther Allen and Robert Weaver [?1945] (courtesy of Professor Robert L. Weaver).

85. Author's conversation with Kingsley Martin, 4 July 1968.

86. Ilya Ehrenburg, 'Mr. Brailsford, Devil's Advocate', *Labour Monthly*, XXVII (February 1945).

87. *Labour Monthly*, XXVII (April 1945).

88. *New Statesman*, 11 October 1947. Also see *New Statesman*, 4 October and 25 October 1947.

89. *New Statesman*, 15 November 1947.

90. *New Statesman*, 29 November 1947.

91. 'Germany's Influence on War or Peace', *Contemporary Review*, CLXXV (September 1949). See letters to editor, *New Statesman*, 7 May 1949; *Manchester Guardian*, 25 October 1949; *News Chronicle*, 26 October 1949.

92. Brailsford received replies to his proposals from, among others, Hugh Dalton (3 October 1949) and L.S. Amery (8 November 1949).

7 THE SOCIETY FOR SOCIALIST INQUIRY AND PROPAGANDA

Margaret Cole

The Society for Socialist Inquiry and Propaganda (SSIP) and the New Fabian Research Bureau (whose history is told, in part, in a number of places[1]) between them tell the story of a radical movement which, though it was always small in actual numbers, and was regarded by many as negligible, was nevertheless of historical importance throughout the depressing thirties. It provided a rallying point for constructive socialist thought, which eventually, working through the revived Fabian Society and alongside the much more spectacular Left Book Club, played a considerable role in securing that the Labour Party went into the 1945 election with a simple and definite social programme, and in its return with a majority so large as to startle most observers. But in order to understand what happened it is necessary to go back a few years.

By the winter of 1926, when the miners had all gone back to work on the owners' terms, it was clear that the day of aggressive industrial action, which the radicals of the left had been pursuing, on and off, for something like ten years, ever since the wartime scarcity of labour had put the organised working class in a position of unprecedented strength, was completely over, even if the victorious Establishment had not proceeded to spell out the defeat by passing the 1927 Trade Union Act, whose obvious intention was to put the trade union movement — and the Labour Party — firmly in their proper place. In this they were not entirely successful. The membership of trade unions fell; and so of course did the affiliated membership of the Labour Party, and not only because the public service unions were forbidden to attach themselves to it. But the feelings of those who remained attached to the party were strengthened rather than lessened; the Trade Union Act was regarded as a vindictive measure, which must be repealed as soon as that should become possible. In fact, pro-Labour feeling among the working classes was politically strengthened, as became apparent in the results of the 1929 general election. Some of that feeling, moreover, was distinctly left-wing. The Independent Labour Party, whose finances had been put on a much firmer footing by Clifford Allen[2] in the early twenties and had sponsored 24 MPs in the Parliament of 1924 (with a good many

190

others enrolled as ILP members) was starting to feel its oats. James Maxton, the Member for the Bridgeton division of Glasgow, a man of strong emotions and considerable personal charm though rather lacking in tactical sense, became its leader, and joined with Arthur Cook of the Miners' Federation in drawing up a strong left-wing programme. 'Socialism in Our Time', it was called; and it embodied proposals for 'A Living Wage' all round, and a measure of workers' control. All through 1927 and early 1928 these policies were being pressed; by mid-1928 Maxton was already talking of the ILP as 'a Socialist Party within the Labour Party'; and in 1929 an ILP conference went the length of laying down that ILP candidates should sign a pledge to support in Parliament the policies of the ILP, whether or not these formed part of official Labour policy. Some, even of Maxton's own party, thought this an unwise decision.

The leaders of the official Labour Party, however, had no sympathy whatever with this leftward trend. As early as 1927 — possibly with some recollection of the widespread rumour which credited the Russian Communists with having inspired the General Strike, both the General Council of the TUC and the Labour Party Executive initiated the move against 'quasi-communist organisations' which led to the drawing-up in 1929 of the first Black List of banned organisations. MacDonald described the ILP's proposals as 'flashy futilities'; and the policy pamphlet *Labour and the Nation,* produced for the 1929 election, for all that R.H. Tawney had had a hand in the drafting, was both weaker and woollier than *Labour and the New Social Order.* Many of the suggestions for domestic policy were really due to Maynard Keynes, and were more vigorously stated in Lloyd George's election manifesto, though the deep dissensions among the Liberals made that document useless when the election came.

After the election, fought in the fine warm weather which made it easier for Labour voters, who lacked cars and in a good many cases overcoats, to get to the polls, Labour came back to Westminster as the largest party — though still without a clear majority. Ramsay Mac-Donald was still the obvious choice for Prime Minister, his bungling over the second 1924 election and the Zinoviev Letter being apparently forgotten. He did not, it is true, have the same enthusiastic support from the Clyde as had ensured him his first term of office; but by now the Clyde was not so important a factor. The *proportion* of ILP-sponsored candidates had declined as the number and size of divisional Labour parties rose rapidly; but as a good number of the MPs whom they had sponsored were members of the ILP, MacDonald's name and presence made up an electoral asset which could not be lightly thrown away.

Nevertheless, MacDonald's rightward shift was, in retrospect, clear enough. From the Cabinet were dropped, beside Colonel Wedgwood, the left-wingers John Wheatley and Fred Jowett of Bradford. Wheatley died in the following year. As Housing Minister, he had been one of the unquestioned successes of the 1924 government, and would certainly, had he survived, have given good practical advice to Maxton. Newcomers included Lord Sankey, who was not a Labour man, but believed to have Labour sympathies ever since he had chaired the 1919 Commission on the Coal Mines, Wedgwood Benn the ex-Liberal, Arthur Greenwood, who was not a strong man, William Graham, who as Philip Snowden's junior at the Treasury had little chance of indulging leftist views, and Margaret Bondfield, a trade union officer who turned out to be very much in the hands of the civil servants in the Ministry of Labour. William Jowitt, the Liberal KC, crossed the floor to become Attorney-General. Arthur Henderson, the secretary of the Labour Party, who can scarcely be described as a man of the extreme left, only succeeded in getting the Foreign Office after a hard struggle; and the only real exception to the drift to the right was George Lansbury's accession to the Cabinet as Minister of Works. It would, however, have been impossible to pass over Lansbury again, in view of the widespread popularity which had accrued to him after his successful Poplar battle in support of the poorer boroughs of London against wealthy ones like Westminster; and as Snowden cynically pointed out in his own autobiography, the leaders felt that in the Ministry of Works he would not be able to do much harm or waste much public money — there is something ironical in the fact that Lansbury, in doing the best he could within the limits set to him to improve the prospect for the leisure and enjoyment of Londoners, should have established, in 'Lansbury's Lido' in Hyde Park, the best-known legacy of the second Labour Government.

Some have suggested that the appointment of Oswald Mosley, an ILP member at the time, to the chancellorship of the Duchy of Lancaster, was another exception to the general trend; but this is flatly disproved when it is recalled that Mosley was charged, along with Lansbury, Thomas Johnston of *Forward*, and (of all politicians!) J.H. Thomas, with producing a general remedy for unemployment. This appointment was clearly no more than a meaningless sop thrown to the left to keep it quiet: MacDonald's own object, to sell to other parties the policies of his minority government, was much more clearly shown when he set up, early in the New Year, an enormous Economic Advisory

Council, to meet monthly with himself in the chair. Its membership included the industrialist Arthur Balfour, Sir Andrew Duncan, Sir Josiah Stamp, Ernest Bevin, Walter Citrine, R.H. Tawney, G.D.H. Cole (who had moved some way from the intransigent Guild Socialism of his early writings), Hubert Henderson of the *Nation,* Keynes, Colin Clark, and a number of businessmen; it met a number of times without producing any noticeable results. Snowden, writing his own autobiography a good while later, after he had broken with MacDonald, stated categorically that his late chief had flirted with the Tories; and Beatrice Webb's *Diaries* gave several indications that she and her husband may have thought so too.[3] It has been suggested that MacDonald had the coalition of 1931 in mind as a possibility long before it actually happened; as to which, since there is as yet no detailed biography of MacDonald available, the only possible comment is that the conjecture is not in the least incredible.

At the beginning of the government's term, the omens seemed moderately favourable. The economic climate had improved slightly for the British; and in the external world Stresemann in Germany and Briand in France were sympathetically disposed to a social-democratic Britain, and Henderson as Foreign Secretary was making an impressively good start. On the home front, a programme of reform was announced; and in the course of the brief summer session some of it was put into effect. The most detested regulations affecting the administration of unemployment benefit were cancelled: the three Boards of Guardians which had been sacked for endeavouring to follow Poplar's example were reinstated; the Housing Act was renewed; and plans for assisted development for home industries and for similar developments in the Colonies were formulated, though in the nature of things these could not mature very quickly. Other reforms — though not specially socialist reforms — were also promised, and the autumn session was to show some improvement in the conditions obtaining for women and old age pensioners. But already the skies were beginning to darken. The first Wall Street crashes began late in 1929, with the result that American money invested in Europe took fright and started to go back home again; and the way was thus opened for the spectacular collapse, during the next year and a half, of so many of the institutions of Central Europe and of the whole fabric of 'reparations'. (Though in May of 1930 the Young Plan of reparations replaced the by then unworkable Dawes Plan, the change came too late to be of any use.)

The bulk of the British public took very little serious note of these happenings — were not the Americans traditionally gamblers and Continentals anyway unreliable? The fall and disgrace of Clarence Hatry at the end of September was seen more as an exciting 'horror story' than as a serious indication of danger; and the same was true, a year or so later, of the collapse and suicide of the Swedish match king, Ivar Kreuger. What did influence the ordinary Briton was the rise in the percentage of unemployment — from 9.6 to 15.4 in twelve months, and in totals from 1,163,000 to 1,912,000 (a year later it was 2¾ million) — and the government's complete failure to do anything about it. Mosley, doing what he was certainly not intended to do, worked at his supposed assignment, and early in 1930 produced a series of proposals (most of which have long since been put into effect) which became known as the Mosley Memorandum. These were promptly rejected by his superior, J.H. Thomas; and in May Mosley impatiently resigned from the government, making at the end of the month a speech of angry indictment which caused Beatrice Webb to speculate on whether he was possibly aiming at the leadership of the Labour Party. He did not, at this juncture, resign from the party itself; he waited until after the October party conference had rejected by an enormous majority a frontal attack by Maxton on the Executive Committee while turning down by only a few thousand votes a motion put forward by the Doncaster Labour Party calling for a full enquiry into his proposals. Encouraged by the latter vote Mosley rewrote them into the 'Mosley Manifesto' of December (published as a pamphlet in the following February) and then proceeded to break with his former comrades and set up his New Party. Of the many MPs who had displayed sympathy, only a very few followed his example; but when at a by-election at Ashton-under-Lyne in April 1931 Allen Young, standing as a New Party candidate, took enough former Labour votes to present the seat to the Tory, the Labour Party not surprisingly barred Mosley and his supporters altogether.

The organisation with which this chapter is chiefly concerned began to take shape before the Mosley dispute had fully developed. In the early autumn of 1930, during the course of the annual conference of the Tutors' Association,[4] the author of this chapter was having a drink with H.L. Beales, who two years earlier had come from Sheffield to become Reader in Economic History at the London School of Economics, and with R.S. Lambert, who had been a tutorial class tutor for the University of London and was then editor of the *Listener*. Over our drink we discussed at some length the disappointment which was being so strongly felt by radical intellectuals (many of them members of the Association and attending the conference) with the performance of the government to date, and reached the conclusion that something drastic and public ought to be done to recall to Ministers the programme and the policies on which they had fought the election. *What,* however, we were not quite certain, and felt that the next step was to consult G.D.H. Cole, the Association's chairman, a prominent figure in Oxford and author of a long book recently published which set out in detail the kind of social reforms which a non-revolutionary government of the left ought to be actively promoting.[5] I was deputed to sound him, and did so at the earliest opportunity — having incidentally ascertained that our next-door neighbour C.M. Lloyd, a Fabian of long standing who was presently head of the Ratan Tata foundation at the London School of Economics and assistant editor of the *New Statesman,* was a hundred per cent in agreement with us.

The consultation was successful beyond anticipation. Cole thought the thing over for a very little while — as he was bound to do in view of his relations with Arthur Henderson, his recent acceptance of a parliamentary candidature, and his membership of the National Economic Council; but almost immediately he agreed to the necessity, suggested the holding of a weekend gathering of selected persons, and further promised to consult with Ernest Bevin, with whom he was at that time on very friendly terms, and see if he could be induced to co-operate. Bevin agreed, and so did Arthur Pugh of the Iron and Steel Trades Confederation; and the trade union element was thus firmly secured. (The adhesion of W.R. Blair, who as well as being a socialist was a director of the Co-operative Wholesale Society, was another — and unexpected bonus; Blair proved a tower of strength until, sadly, he died in the following year).

Cole also undertook to ask Lady Warwick, the Red Countess of Easton Lodge near Dunmow in Essex, whether she would allow the suggested meeting to be held at the Lodge.[6] She was delighted with the idea; and the informal and relaxed atmosphere in which the gathering took place gave it a quite exceptional flavour. The inconvenient but impressive house — subsequently pulled down — the Friendship Garden started by Edward VII, the almost stagnant swimming pool fringed with exotic-looking vegetation, the pet black lamb of Lady Mercy Greville's gambolling on the hearth, and the chatelaine herself, with her flowing dresses, her tight white curls and her electric smile, wandering in and out of meals and discussions trailing a group of suspicious and snapping Pekinese behind her — all was very unofficial: and few could remain stiff and controlled while the peacocks strutted up and down the terrace screaming PIGOU! PIGOU! to embarrassed economists, and in the trees beyond a cuckoo continuously interrupted George

Lansbury's address. 'Yes, brother, I *know* I am!' the Minister of Works
at last replied. It was all very friendly, the more so as all the invitations
had been issued by personal letters, and none, so far as I am aware, had
been declined on principle. Of the personnel who attended, I quote
from my own account in *The Story of Fabian Socialism* (p. 223):

> The chief recruits were the young Oxford Socialists, who came
> practically *en bloc*; but from the *Daily Herald* (only on the verge of
> being taken over by Odhams Press) came George Lansbury, his son-
> in-law Raymond Postgate, historian, and later editor of *Tribune* and
> of that remarkable monthly FACT, and Francis Meynell of the
> Nonesuch Press; from the Parliamentary Labour Party, as well as
> Lansbury, C.R. Attlee and Stafford Cripps; from the quondam Guild
> Socialists William Mellor, Ellen Wilkinson MP, W.H. Thompson the
> Labour solicitor who had defended dozens of conscientious objec-
> tors, shop stewards, and others in trouble with the authorities, and
> the cartoonist J.F. Horrabin; from the I.L.P. Dick (afterwards Sir
> Leslie) Plummer and H.N. Brailsford the brilliant journalist and ex-
> pert on central European affairs;[7] and from the Workers' Educa-
> tional Association Tawney, E.S. Cartwright and H.P. Smith of
> Oxford, and many other tutors and organisers.

The highlight (or the prize exhibit!) of the whole conference was Bevin,
who took full part in all discussions, formal or informal, and enjoyed
himself immensely, holding a kind of court in which he told anecdotes
of the past of THE MOVEMENT — he always put it in capitals — to an
admiring ring of questioners, and also displaying a grasp of economic
and financial essentials which some of the younger intellectuals had
scarcely thought to find in a trade union official. The discussions were
unscripted and practically unrecorded; but they were wide-ranging and
keen, and the general consensus of opinion was so strong that a decision
to meet again and again at Easton Lodge was carried without question.
In December, at the third meeting of those whom Francis Meynell nick-
named 'the Loyal Grousers', the decision was taken to form a society
with a nation-wide appeal.

   This was the Society for Socialist Inquiry and Propaganda, its
initials being intended to carry a suggestion about its methods; it was
known as ZIP from the start. Bevin agreed to be Chairman; as vice-
chairmen it had Cole, Blair, Pugh, and D.N. Pritt KC. Its Treasurer was
G.R. (later Lord) Mitchison, and its joint secretaries Beales and myself;
and these officers, together with Postgate, Horrabin, Colin Clark the

young economist, and Honor Scott (later Mrs Croome), granddaughter
of Scott of the *Manchester Guardian,* formed the executive committee.
The organisation, at the start, was rudimentary: recruiting of membership, at five shillings per annum, was done by individual postal appeal
from our house in Hampstead until in the early weeks of 1931 it decided
to provide itself with a tiny office in Abingdon Street opposite the
Houses of Parliament; but that membership was full of enthusiasm.
Lloyd, whom long years of generally unprofitable toiling in the radical
interest had rendered sceptical of new movements, wrote to the Webbs
urging them to look kindly on the new venture, and a simultaneous
letter from Cole to Beatrice ends 'I'm bubbling too much with ideas at
the present time to get them down properly on paper.'

Rudimentary or not, SSIP went ahead fast. A suggestion of Cole's,
made at one of the Easton Lodge gatherings, that potential members
might join the now nearly moribund Fabian Society — he himself
having recently rejoined it — and take it over, had met with little support, as 'take-over' seemed not likely to be as easy as he had envisaged,
and some who in pre-war days had been fierce and vocal opponents of
'Fabian gradualism' were not prepared to swallow their past words quite
so easily. The New Fabian Research Bureau, set up in the early months
of 1931, which did eventually 'take over' the Fabian Society, was supported by the Webbs. So SSIP was organised by itself, and had about
five hundred members when the formal 'foundation conference' was
held on 15 June 1931, in the hall at Transport House — secured, of
course, by the Chairman of the Society. Five hundred does not sound
much of a membership, though it was many times that of the original
Fabian Society at the date of *Fabian Essays in Socialism;* but already
there were embryo branches in being (one, as readers of today will note
with amusement, was at *Selsdon*); duplicated draft reports on a variety
of important subjects were laid before the conference; a duplicated
monthly bulletin was in course of preparation, and pamphlets, in
striking scarlet and white covers, were beginning to appear. A note by
Cole, casually preserved in the files, suggests no fewer than 21 *Study
Guides,* of which only some came out, under the imprint either of
SSIP or of the Socialist League. The Society was also planning public
lectures, like the Fabian Autumn Lectures, started more than forty
years previously and then still kept going by the monies of the many
who bought course tickets in order to hear Bernard Shaw. One course
(including a lecture by Bevin) was held in the winter of 1931-2. Two
pamphlets by Cole, *National Government and Inflation* and *The Need
for a Socialist Programme,* foreshadow the development which was to

come.

For external events were not obliging enough to stay put while the
Loyal Grousers got going. The general economic situation, as already
described, grew worse and worse, and the government's programme for
social reform at home faded steadily. To mention only a few examples:
a Bill for the reorganisation of the mining industry was so mutilated as
to be almost unrecognisable; the Bill for raising the school-leaving age
was so badly knocked about by Tories and Roman Catholics that it had
to be dropped (this resulted in the resignation of C.P. Trevelyan, the
Minister of Education); Bills to set up consumers' councils, to establish
holidays with pay, and to regulate the hours of shop assistants were
postponed, with no indication of any future date. In the early spring
Philip Snowden, as Chancellor, set up the notorious May Committee
(presided over by a former secretary of the Prudential) with the charge
of looking into government expenditure, particularly in relation to unemployment, and suggesting economies. The May Report (with the
two Labour members dissenting) was not published until 31 July, after
Parliament had risen; but in June, the very month of the SSIP's foun-
ding conference, the government pushed through the detested
Anomalies Act, severely revising the conditions under which benefit was
granted — this made Margaret Bondfield, the Minister of Labour, extremely unpopular in the country. During the first weeks of August the
discussions on 'cuts' went on between the Prime Minister, the Chancellor of the Exchequer and the General Council of the TUC, growing
gradually more and more bitter, until on the 24th the Labour Cabinet
met for the last time, and MacDonald told them of his intention to head
a government of National Emergency. So the stage was set for the final
breach of the Labour Party and the trade unions with their once-adored
leader, the tearing down of the large photographs of MacDonald which
had adorned so many local party committee-rooms — and the general
election of October, with its staggering result for Labour.[8]

Neither SSIP's membership nor its leaders were very much surprised
by the events of the summer, though nobody could fail to be somewhat
startled by the size of the anti-Labour majorities in the election, by the
spectacle of MacDonald waving a valueless million-mark note and
Snowden declaring that Post Office savings accounts would be
swallowed up. In September Bevin and Cole jointly wrote a pamphlet
on 'The Crisis', which was published by the *New Statesman*; and the
general feeling was that the Loyal Grousers must press on even harder
and faster with their proposals. But in this course there was a snag; and
its name was ILP.

The ILP, under Maxton's guidance, had steadily kept up its quarrel with the Labour Party Executive, both on policy and on questions of internal discipline. The Labour Party had introduced new standing orders, forbidding MPs, whether sponsored by the ILP or by anyone else, to vote in defiance of Labour Party policy decisions. To this the ILP strongly objected; but at the annual conference of 1931 a motion moved by Fenner (later Lord) Brockway to refer back the Executive's report on this was turned down by 2,117,000 votes to 193,000. This was a pretty heavy defeat, and during the winter it became clearer and clearer that a head-on clash was coming. At the ILP conference of Easter 1932, a positive motion to disaffiliate from the Labour Party was lost in favour of one moved by David Kirkwood[9] calling for 'conditional' affiliation — conditional on the party's amending its Standing Orders. This, in view of the previous vote, was highly unlikely, and it seemed certain that disaffiliation would soon be carried; in July it was. But there was a large element in the ILP membership, headed by Frank Wise and Patrick Dollan,[9] which very much disliked the idea of being forced into the wilderness; and Wise, for example, resigned instantly from the ILP governing body.

These developments (which were not secret) posed a problem for SSIP, since if the dissident ILP'ers formed an organisation of their own there would be an unholy and probably disastrous scramble for membership between two organisations of individuals pledged to support the Labour Party.[10] Cole, realising the difficulty promptly, induced his own Executive to prepare a letter (which in the end was never sent) inviting dissident ILP'ers to join SSIP. The letter was never sent because Wise and Dollan, probably anticipating something of the sort, had formed a National Affiliation Committee, which approached SSIP with the proposal that the two groups should amalgamate into a new Socialist Society, which should then seek affiliation to the Labour Party. Cole, knowing their strong love of politics and parliamentary action, was very doubtful about the suggestion; but many leading members of the SSIP, such as Cripps, Brailsford, Mellor and Horrabin, were also members of the ILP; and the pressure was so strong that he agreed to the opening of negotiations. There was to be an emergency meeting of the SSIP Executive; and so it was essential to find out the attitude of the two trade unionists. In September the TUC was in conference at Newcastle upon Tyne. G.D.H. and I were staying with the Mitchisons at Paxton near Berwick-upon-Tweed, and Dick Mitchison drove us over in order to talk with Bevin and Pugh. Bevin gave leave to go ahead, but just a look at his face showed plainly that he did not like the idea; and this attitude was justified when after negotiations began it became clear that, though they were ready to make some concessions — about not trying to run parliamentary candidates or force particular politics on the party — Wise and Dollan were determined on two points — that the new organisation should apply for affiliation to the Labour Party, and that its Chairman should be not Ernest Bevin — but Frank Wise. These demands the SSIP Executive accepted by a majority, out-voting Cole, who nevertheless acquiesced when it was done, and agreed to serve on the Executive of the new body, which called itself, in rem-iniscence of William Morris, the Socialist League. The first condition might not have mattered very much — it would depend a great deal on what line the Socialist League representatives decided to take. But the second was disastrous. For Bevin was deeply offended, and not only in his personal vanity. He took it as an insult to the trade union movement at large, and his subsequent actions and correspondence[11] show clearly that all the understanding between him and the 'intellectuals' which had been gained by the early meetings at Easton Lodge had been irre-coverably lost. Coming directly on top of the actions of Mosley and the New Party (and, incidentally, of MacDonald) it confirmed, in the mind of one of the best brains produced in the ranks of manual trade unionists, the conviction that intellectuals of the left were people who stabbed honest working-class leaders in the back. This obsession had a noticeable effect on working-class history in the following years: the really ironical reflection is that if the amalgamation had not been so speeded up in the heat of the summer, and if Cole had not been partly disabled by the first onslaught of the diabetes which finally killed him, the disputed clauses might never have been carried in that form, and Bevin's personality and experience might not have been lost to the left. An additional irony is that Wise, whose attitude was the most intransi-gent and who would never have got on with Bevin at all, died unex-pectedly in November 1933: his place as leader of the Socialist League was taken by that most unpractical of socialist politicians, Stafford Cripps.

The amalgamation was hurried on because the promoters of the Socialist League wished to get it recognised by the Labour Party in time for the annual conference at Leicester in October. This they did by the skin of their teeth — and mainly through the efforts of William Mellor carried an amendment (on joint-stock banks) to the Executive's policy resolution, which was an additional annoyance to Bevin. Mean-time the rank-and-file members of SSIP itself, who had certainly not been properly consulted, put up an angry resistance in the press and at the emergency meeting called for ratification. But there was really very little they could do about it. The thing was done, and in November the Society dissolved itself, not without angry recriminations. It is not suggested that the Society could really have carried on by itself; it was too much a creation of amateurs personally recruited, and would . probably have been open to capture by Communists or other possible groupings; the 'self-denying ordinance' of the reconstituted Fabian Society of 1939 was drafted as a check on just that possibility. And the competition with the ILP would not have helped the wider movement. But one cannot but feel that the whole affair might have been better done. In its short life, however, SSIP did a good deal to galvanise up-to-date thinking within the labour movement; and though it died, the New Fabian Research Bureau carried on the spirit and the momentum in the years which followed.

Notes

1. G.D.H. Cole, *A History of the Labour Party from 1914* (1948), pp. 282-4; *idem, A History of Socialist Thought* vol. 3 (1956, repr. 1963), 127; M. Cole, *The Story of Fabian Socialism* (1961), p. 225ff.; L. Woolf, *Downhill all the Way* (1967), p. 220; M. Cole, *The Life of G.D.H. Cole* (1971), pp. 178-80.
2. Reginald Clifford Allen (1889-1939), created Lord Allen of Hurtwood, 1932. Fabian dissentient and chairman of University Socialist Federation, 1912-15. During First World War Conscientious Objector (absolutist) and Chairman of No-Conscription Fellowship. Treasurer and Chairman of ILP, 1922-6; in ILP disputes, and in 1931, sided with MacDonald. See also *Dictionary of Labour Biography*, Vol. 2 J.M. Bellamy and J. Saville (eds.), (1974).
3. See Beatrice Webb's *Diary*, 15 March 1924, 24 April 1924 (quoting Maxton), 14 July 1931 (letter to Lord Passfield), 20 July 1931. MacDonald (but not Henderson) was prepared in 1911 for coalition with Balfour and Lloyd George, *Diary*, 28 October 1931. See also Sidney Webb's article on the 1924 government, printed for the first time in the *Political Quarterly* of January to March 1961.
4. The Tutors' Association, which catered for tutors employed by universities and other bodies to teach extra-mural classes, was founded by G.D.H. Cole while he was, from 1922 to 1925, Director of Tutorial Classes in the University of London; and he was for many years its chairman. It was a lively little association, bringing together class tutors, whole-time and part-time, from many towns, endeavouring with varying success to establish standards of pay, and engaging in much vigorous discussion of policy, programmes, syllabuses, training and methods in non-university adult education.
5. See *The Next Ten Years in British Social and Economic Policy*, published by G.D.H. Cole in the spring of 1929. This book, whose foreword expresses appreciation of Beatrice and Sidney Webb, describes the changes in

his political and social opinions since the days of the National Guilds League, and sets out in detail a full programme of reform for the next Labour government. The author had quietly rejoined the Fabian Society in 1928, and early in 1929 was billed to lecture to it on 'Nationalisation Old and New'; he had also become friendly with the Webbs, and he and his wife had stayed several times with them at Passfield Corner. (See Beatrice Webb's *Diary* for 12 September 1928).

6. Frances Evelyn (1861-1938), Dowager Countess of Warwick on her husband's death in 1924, Victorian society beauty and one of the loves of Edward VII, was converted to a simple faith in socialism by Robert Blatchford. When she was very young he wrote in the *Clarion* a strong denunciation of a party of hers, and expounded the faith to her when she asked him for an explanation. Conversion did not stop her from spending money on the entertainment of her royal lover (and frequently getting into debt); but she was active in the cause. She befriended Joseph Arch, the agricultural workers' organiser — and wrote a rather naive book about him; she consistently supported Conrad Noel, the Red vicar of Thaxted, who displayed the Red Flag and the banner of Sinn Fein alongside the Union Jack in his church; she was a Poor Law Guardian, founded Studley Castle for training girls in horticulture etc., and a scientific and technical school for girls, and was president of many local societies such as the Essex Needlework Guild. She loaned Easton Lodge for conferences of the ILP, and in the spring of 1924 let it to the Labour Party for a year for £300. (Beatrice Webb's *Diary*, 7 April 1924). Her acquaintance with Cole began in 1925, when the now-forgotten project was drawn up of establishing a working men's residential college in Easton Lodge, financed by the trade unions, of which Cole would probably have been the head. The project came to nothing, partly because of the General Strike; but the friendship remained.

7. Henry Noel Brailsford (1873-1958), socialist, journalist and historian, was editor of the *New Leader* — Keir Hardie's *Labour Leader* transformed — from 1922 to 1926. He was a leader-writer on the *Manchester Guardian* and the *Daily News,* and wrote also for the *Nation* and *Tribune.* In 1913 he was a member of the Carnegie International Commission in the Balkans, and out of his experience wrote *The War of Steel and Gold* (1914), the book which first made him famous. He was a strong critic of MacDonald. See also *Dictionary of Labour Biography,* op. cit., and Chapter 6 of this book.

8. The crisis of 1931 has been very often described. The fullest account is in C.L. Mowat, *Britain between the Wars.* See also a very pro-MacDonald book, *1931,* by R. Bassett; and for day-to-day contemporary detail, Beatrice Webb's *Diary* for July 1931 and 2 September 1931.

9. David Kirkwood (1872-1955), was leader of the engineers of Clydeside in the troubles of the First World War. He was deported from Glasgow by the government in 1916, was Labour MP for Clydebank and Dumbarton from 1922 to 1951, when he was raised to the peerage as Lord Kirkwood of Bearsden. Sir Patrick Joseph Dollan (1885-1963), started life as a grocery apprentice and was eight years a miner in Lanarkshire: he became author, journalist and left-wing politician, served on the Corporation of Glasgow where he led the Labour Party from 1913 to 1946, and was Lord Provost from 1938 to 1941. Edward Frank Wise (1885-1933), civil servant, was economic adviser to the Russian Centrosoyus in 1923 and MP for Leicester East from 1929 to 1931. He had attended a conference at Easton Lodge before the ILP broke with the Labour Party.

10. Frank Wise led the ILP dissidents, who included Brailsford, Horrabin, Dollan, Mellor and several other members of the SSIP.

11. Bevin's attitude developed only slowly. In May 1931 he had written to J.R. Bellerby, an economist of Liverpool, a letter about SSIP in which he said 'We have kept clear of dogma and this is an attempt to study and project in order to fill the niche for the next decade, like the Fabians and early Socialists did for us.' (Quoted in Bullock, *Life and Times of Ernest Bevin*, Vol. 1, p. 501). This was also Cole's purpose; but Bevin believed that the formation of the Socialist League had sold the pass. He refused to join the New Fabian Research Bureau, saying that he ought now to stick to his last; and a later letter of his to Cole, dated 31 December 1935, shows pretty clearly his final view; 'one difference', he wrote, 'between the intellectuals and the trade unions is this: You have no responsibility, you can fly off at a tangent as the wind takes you. We, however, must be consistent and we have a great amount of responsibility. We cannot wake up in the morning and get a brain wave, when father says "turn" and half a million people turn automatically' (quoted in Bullock, op. cit., p. 532).

8 FACTIONALISM WITHIN THE LABOUR PARTY: THE SOCIALIST LEAGUE 1932-1937

Patrick Seyd

Factionalism has been a permanent feature of Labour Party politics. Throughout its life party members have coalesced into formal organisations pursuing demands over a range of issues in attempts to influence their party's policies and leadership. The existence of these factions is a function of two factors — the ideology of socialism and the party's democratic value system.

The Labour Party in its formative years encapsulated a wide variety of socialist ideas including Marxist, Fabian, Christian, ethical, sentimental and romantic. To treat these strands as mutually exclusive would be incorrect since the people within the particular bodies which represented these strands of opinion often intermingled and co-operated. Nevertheless a distinctiveness of approach is apparent in the internal debate within the Labour Party as to the nature of socialism. By 1918, however, the balance of debate tilted in favour of Fabian and sentimental socialism. The political agreement between the Labour Party and the trade union movement, based upon a new party constitution and party programme, incorporated a belief in national efficiency combined with the rhetoric of system change. But this political agreement did not provide the Labour Party with a coherent ideology which united the disparate elements within it. Rather, it was 'a rallying point around which the adherents of different ideologies and the representatives of different interests assembled'.[1] Reformist ideas were dominant, however, and the personnel in political control supported this reformist tendency: this has remained the case with only few exceptions since 1918. While the party has been continuously fed large supplies of the rhetoric of system change[2] the practice of Labour governments has been somewhat different. Wariness on the part of many within the party concerning the *actual* relationship between rhetoric and practice has been consistently voiced, while Labour governments' attempts to patch rather than transform capitalist society have produced their critics. Left factions, or those groups demanding a fundamental change in society by means of the elimination of a very large part of privately-owned industry and its substitution by publicly-owned industry, have therefore been a constant part of the Labour Party scenario, challenging the socialism as

interpreted by Webb, Henderson, MacDonald and other leading figures
in 1918 and perpetuated since, and critical of the performance of the
nine Labour governments, whether minority or majority. In contrast
right factions, or those groups pursuing demands for social reform within the prevailing capitalist economy, are a rarity. Informal networks and
contacts between certain trade union and parliamentary leaders have
existed but no open organisation has normally been necessary because
the parliamentary party, the National Executive Committee, the party
bureaucracy and the annual conference have reflected the opinions of
the predominant reformist tendency. The Campaign for Democratic
Socialism (1959-1964) and the Manifesto Group (1974-) are aberra-
tions in the history of the Labour Party; their existence reflects the
changed internal political balance that has taken place within the
Labour Party since the mid-1950s.

The divisive nature of British socialism is reinforced by the fact that
the Labour Party's procedural value system lays great stress on argument and debate. Division of opinion is taken to be a basic part of its
political philosophy and thus should be tolerated. The virtues of such
tolerance are openly advocated in drawing comparisons with the mono-
lithic uniformity adopted by the Labour Party's political opponents.[3]
Such a value system affords the opportunity for individuals within the
party to challenge prevailing orthodoxy and, inevitably, strength in
such conflict comes from the organisation of like-minded persons. In
practice, however, toleration of argument and opposition is tempered
by another ideal, that of political unity. In fighting the political enemy,
a working-class organisation's strength lies in its unity and this can only
be undermined by factional criticism.[4] While left factions have existed,
the tolerance of party leadership towards them has been limited. They
have been categorised as 'splitters', undermining the party's electoral
potential, and the history of left factions has been one of expulsion,
disaffiliation, proscription or a general harassment by the leadership.
The Socialist League was no exception; its five-year existence ended in
its disaffiliation from the Labour Party.

Formation of the Socialist League

During the period from 1918 until the fall of the second Labour government the Independent Labour Party (ILP) acted as the left faction
within the Labour Party. After the defeat of the first Labour government the ILP demanded a more precise and immediate programme of
socialist legislation; policy reports were presented and approved at ILP
conferences under the general title of 'Socialism in Our Time'. By 1927

the ILP had become increasingly critical of the TUC and the Labour
Party, the first for its policy of industrial co-operation with the employers, and the second for the absence of anything more than vague
generalisations and rhetoric in its statements about future programmes.
The ILP's fears that the Labour Party was led by men whose ideas of
socialism were limited to very particular reforms of capitalist society
were confirmed during the two years of the second Labour government. Dismay at the incompetence of the Labour government was not,
of course, confined to members of the ILP. Others in the Labour Party,
concerned at the lack both of socialist ideas and of socialist propaganda, established the Society for Socialist Inquiry and Propaganda
(SSIP) and the New Fabian Research Bureau.

The defection of the ILP from the Labour Party in July 1932 left a
political vacuum on the Labour left. The basic argument between the
two had been concerned with their rival interpretations of socialism,
with the ILP rejecting the Labour Party's gradualist philosophy as
resulting only in the administration of a capitalist economy and the
inevitable compromising of socialist values. The particular argument
concerning the role of the ILP parliamentary group within the Parliamentary Labour Party (PLP) was a second-order, tactical issue which
inevitably became embroiled in the more fundamental argument.[5]
Within the ILP there was disagreement over the course of action to be
taken in this dispute, with one element arguing in favour of remaining
attached to the Labour Party. This element, led by E.F. Wise[6] and H.
N. Brailsford, determined to form a new faction within the Labour
Party and established the ILP Affiliation Committee in 1932. The
SSIP had feared that the formation of a new body would overlap and
rival SSIP activities. G.D.H. Cole, in a memorandum to the SSIP Executive Committee, recommended that SSIP should appeal to ILP members and branches to join the existing organisation.[7] Cole recognised
that this would drastically alter SSIP — it would become a large,
formally organised socialist body which would need to affiliate to the
Labour Party — but he personally was in support of this change so long
as SSIP, contrary to ILP practice, did not sponsor parliamentary candidates either directly under its own name or indirectly under the auspices of the Labour Party. Cole's suggestion was approved by the SSIP
Executive but before the appeal could be launched the ILP Affiliation
Committee had been formed; and in August and September negotiations took place between the two bodies over their amalgamation into
a new organisation, the Socialist League. Many SSIP members were
opposed to this proposal. Bevin, SSIP's Chairman, failed to sign the

letter inviting people to the inaugural conference of the Socialist League[8] and, at an SSIP meeting called in November 1932 a resolution to approve SSIP's incorporation into the Socialist League failed to secure the necessary two-thirds majority.[9] Instead, a resolution was passed dissolving SSIP.[10] Hugh Gaitskell, Evan Durbin, George Dallas and Colin Clark were among those who opposed amalgamation, preferring to remain with the New Fabian Research Bureau rather than join the Socialist League.[11]

Fifty-four people signed the letter sent to constituency Labour parties and trade union branches inviting them to the inaugural conference of the Socialist League to be held in Leicester immediately preceding the Labour Party's annual conference in October 1932. Among the signatories were 13 members of the SSIP executive and 15 members of the ILP Affiliation Committee; others signing included Katherine Glasier, Harold Laski, R.H. Tawney, Charles Trevelyan and Dan Griffiths. Upon approval of the formation of the Socialist League by this specially convened conference, the National Executive Committee (NEC) of the Labour Party immediately considered the situation. At a meeting of the NEC on 5 October, Arthur Henderson moved a resolution that 'Head Office be empowered to affiliate the Socialist League upon its application being received'.[12] Herbert Morrison countered that 'no decision be registered on the subject until an application from the Socialist League had been received'.[13] The NEC was equally divided on the merits of the two motions and the Chairman had to use his casting vote in favour of Henderson's resolution, with the further amendment 'provided the Constitution of the Socialist League is in harmony with the Constitution, Policy, and Programme of the Party'.[14] On 19 October the NEC's Organisation subcommittee approved a report from the party's National Agent that the Socialist League's constitution did not contravene the Labour Party constitution and its decision was approved by the NEC in November.[15]

A faction of the left had been formed to take the place of the ILP. Its initial role was believed to be that of a socialist propagandist organisation for the Labour Party; it soon moved its position, however, to one in which it was challenging the policies of the Labour Party and finally, after numerous defeats in this quest, to one of attempting to win support in the labour movement as a mass organisation rivalling the Labour Party.

Organisation of the Socialist League

Membership of the Socialist League was open to all socialists but they were expected to be individual members of the Labour Party, the Co-operative movement and of a trade union.[16] A highly organised and formal structure was created. A branch organisation was established and by March 1934 it was reported that 74 branches had been formed and that the total membership was in the region of 3,000.[17] During the next twelve months it was claimed that the number of branches had increased by 30 per cent,[18] and later in 1935 it was claimed that the London area alone contained over 40 branches.[19] Branch organisation would appear to have been somewhat exaggerated, however, since only 28 branches are detailed in the annual report of the National Council for 1934. The largest number of these branches was in London and immediate surrounding area (14), with Tyneside (5) and South Yorkshire (3) being the only other areas with any extensive branch organisation.[20] It is difficult to assess branch organisation in any accurate manner for 1935 and 1936 but it would appear to be doubt-ful whether it increased. The final agenda for the 1937 Socialist League conference — a crucial one since it discussed the future of the organisa-tion — contained 12 motions and 19 amendments, only one of which was moved by a branch from outside London;[21] the remainder were in the names of nine branches from London or surrounding area. It would appear, then, that the Socialist League, notwithstanding its national structure, followed a pattern which has since prevailed for most Labour left factions, namely, of being London-based with little organisational strength elsewhere. Whilst the Socialist League's individual membership was dispersed throughout the country, and in particular areas, such as Bristol, did have an impact on local Labour politics, the focus of Labour party activities was Westminster and the Socialist League congregated and organised in its immediate environs.

Superimposed upon the branch organisation was a structure of seven regional committees,[22] an annual conference, and an elected National Council responsible for the day-to-day affairs of the Socialist League.[23] The National Council elected Cripps as its Chairman in June 1933 and he was annually re-elected until in 1936 he was succeeded by William Mellor.[24] The elected leadership of the Socialist League was predomi-nantly a public-school and university-educated group of people. One of the few trade unionists to take a leading part was Harold Clay, the assistant General Secretary of the Transport and General Workers' Union. He was a National Council member, elected by the London and Home Counties region for one year from 1933. By the time of the 1936 Labour Party conference he was speaking out against the Socialist League's call for unity of working-class organisations. Among those who were involved in the affairs of the Socialist League by being regularly elected as members of the National Council were Constance Borrett, Ruth Dodds, H.L. Elvin, J.F. Horrabin, William Mellor and G.R. Mitchison. Others who were involved as elected members for shorter periods of time were Barbara Betts, H.N. Brailsford, G.D.H. Cole, D.N. Pritt and Sir Charles Trevelyan. Cole resigned from the National Council in June 1933, the same month in which he had been elected. Whereas the annual report of the National Council states that he resigned due to pressure of work Cole wrote that he resigned 'feeling that the political line which the League, under Wise's leadership, was taking was certain to bring it into direct and unfruitful collision with the official Labour Party.'[25] In retrospect he argued that the Socialist League was doomed to failure because of its adoption of a collective programme; if it had abjured policy commitments, as did the New Fabian Research Bureau, it would have been saved from ultimate disaffiliation from the Labour Party.[26] Cole's actions at the time, however, suggest that his later writings were an *ex post facto* justification of his resignation. For after his resignation he prepared a pamphlet study-guide to the 16 policy resolutions passed by the first annual conference of the Socialist League as a basis for further discussion amongst members.[27] Further, he wrote a Socialist League pamphlet demanding that the Labour Party adopt a co-ordinated plan of action with more precise and detailed indications of socialist policy.[28] However, he did make it clear that the pamphlet's intention was to stimulate discussion rather than lay down a final scheme of programme. Cole was certainly aware that the Socialist League could become 'a home for straying intellectuals', but he argued in 1934 that there must be an organised body of socialists within the Labour Party since

> keen and active Socialists . . . need an organisation in which they can come together to devise policies for the long as well as the short run, to work out the general strategy of class conflict, to discuss and constantly reinforce their faith by putting it to the test of unflinching analysis in the light of changing facts and situations.[29]

There seems no doubt that Cole held a strong attachment to the discussion of ideas within the Labour Party, but he was also in favour of the Socialist League attempting to persuade the Labour Party to abandon its piecemeal social welfare approach to politics for a comprehensive plan for socialist revolution.

The Socialist League recruited a permanent staff[30] and maintained a permanent office, first at SSIP's old premises in Abingdon Street and, from June 1933, in Victoria Street. In its first year the Socialist League published 13 pamphlets and one leaflet, the sales totalling 21,000.[31] During its five years in existence it published about 27 pamphlets. In 1934 it began publication of a monthly journal, *The Socialist Leaguer*, with a print ranging from 3,000 to 4,500; in September 1935 the paper was retitled *The Socialist* and this continued to be published until superseded by *Tribune* in 1937.

Socialist League/Labour Party Relations

The prevailing ideology of the Labour Party has always generated intense factional argument, and the structure of the party offers factions considerable opportunities to campaign for their particular points of view. The tensions which exist within the Labour Party over the ultimate source of authority provide opportunities for factions to mount campaigns at various levels of the party and, if defeated at one level, to counter by mobilising support at another. Left factions have consistently failed to secure a majority within the PLP, and have thus been forced into mounting their campaigns in the various organisations of the extra-parliamentary party. Here again structural factors aid factional activity, for the indirect structure of the party enables campaigns to be undertaken within the trade unions as well as the constituency parties. The focus of such campaigns is always to mobilise majority support at the party's annual conference. Left factions, although managing to draw upon a good deal of political support amongst the party activists, have generally been defeated by an alliance of the reformist parliamentary leadership with the leadership of certain large trade unions.

The distribution of power and of political opinion within the Labour Party in the 1930s made it inevitable that the Socialist League would concentrate upon the party's annual conference as the major forum for mounting its challenge. The electoral débâcle of 1931 left the PLP as a mere rump with a number of the leading figures missing from its ranks; amongst the 46 members of the PLP, the majority of whom were trade-union-sponsored, there was little support for the Socialist League. Lansbury and Attlee were sympathetic, initially at least, but the majority of the Executive Committee of the PLP were hostile. Cripps was the only member of the Executive Committee known to be a supporter. The case was similar after the 1935 General Election. Both the Executive Committee and the PLP were hostile. It was inevitable that with the reduced number in the PLP the NEC would play a more important role in policy deliberations. Support for the Socialist League among its members was, however, minimal. During the five-year period 1932-7, membership of the NEC remained virtually static, with Henderson and then Morrison and Dalton occupying key positions, and none of them was sympathetic to Socialist League arguments.[32] It was, therefore, at the yearly conference that the Socialist League concentrated its attacks on the party's domestic and foreign policy documents.

The Socialist League's attempt to influence the Labour Party should not be considered as confined solely to particular aspects of policies. Rather it mounted a challenge to the very basis of party policy; it questioned the Labour Party's fundamental assumptions. Samuel Beer has argued that the Labour Party during this period displayed a broad consensus 'on ideology, program and strategy', and that the major party policy statements were accepted since they were all intent on pursuing the agreed objective of the Socialist Commonwealth.[33] The Socialist League was, however, suspicious that the rhetoric employed by the party leadership was far removed from its intended actions, and that the capitalist system would be tampered with rather than transformed. It was also highly sceptical of the party's parliamentary strategy since it believed parliamentary political institutions to be a bulwark against such transformation.

A class analysis of politics

The Socialist League started from the belief that politics needed to be examined in terms of class conflict and that the Labour Party should adopt a distinctively class approach to political issues. It believed that British society was divided into irreconcilable classes and conflict between them was inevitable. J.T. Murphy described the Socialist League's objective as being to transform the Labour Party 'into the Party of the working class revolution'.[34] Cripps argued that the basic task of all socialist policy was to advance the interests of the working class:

> If we remember that all the time, and if we make the touchstone of our propaganda and our decisions the stark but unpleasant fact that within Capitalism there always is and must be class struggle in which the dominant class for ever exploits the servient class, then we shall not go far wrong in assessing the necessities of the political situation, national or international . . .[35]

The 'acid test' of a socialist government's measures, argued J.F.

Horrabin, should not be whether it added to economic efficiency or made the capitalist machine work more smoothly but whether 'it raise[d] the status and conditions of the workers as a class, and correspondingly weaken[ed] the power of the owning class.'[36]

One sees the Socialist League's class approach to political issues especially in its attitude towards foreign policy, the issue which increasingly dominated its deliberations from 1934 onwards. It believed, first, that the consequences of foreign policies pursued by capitalist and imperialist nations were of no benefit to the working classes of these nations and, second, that by international co-operation the working class could determine the foreign policy of these nations. The Socialist League argued that war was a certainty between capitalist nations pursuing economic sovereignty and it further argued that since the working class had no quarrel with the working class of any other nation war should be resisted by organised opposition. If war broke out then the working class should use the general strike as a weapon to stop the war and also bring about the downfall of capitalism.[37] It rejected the idea that there might ever be a 'just' war, as for example in the case of the League of Nations' action to curb Italian aggression in Abyssinia. While the Socialist League supported British membership of the League of Nations, since it could be used as a meeting place and a talking shop, it argued that it was built upon foundations that preserved unequal relationships in Europe and the world, and since the League of Nations could not curb national sovereignty it could not therefore curb war.[38] By 1935 the Socialist League had become increasingly critical of the League of Nations. Cripps opposed the NEC's call for all necessary measures to be taken under the League of Nations to curb Italy's attack upon Abyssinia. He argued that the League of Nations was 'nothing but the tool of satiated imperialist powers'[39] while Mellor contended that to support the League of Nations was to 'support the interests of British imperialism . . .'[40] No capitalist government could be trusted not to misuse its power to the detriment of the workers. 'Had we a workers' Government in this country', said Cripps, 'the whole situation would be completely different . . . [for] there would be no risk of imperialist and capitalist aims being pursued . . .'[41] As late as 1936, Cripps was arguing that in the event of a war between Britain and Germany the British working class would not necessarily suffer if there was a German victory.[42]

The Socialist League not only called for international working-class action to curb imperialism; it also called for united working-class action in Britain to curb the growth of Fascism. Fascism was the major threat facing the working class; it was the product of declining capitalism, with the state seeking, by means of violence and repression, to crush socialist and Communist movements and reverse the process of social evolution.[43] The National Government displayed many of the features of a Fascist régime, and the only means of curbing it was by the united action of the working-class movement.[44] It therefore urged the Labour Party and the Trades Union Congress to take the lead in uniting the working class,[45] supported the Communist Party's application for affiliation to the Labour Party,[46] and ultimately called for united action between the Independent Labour Party, the Communist Party and itself. However, both the Labour Party and the Trades Union Congress were consistently opposed to any united working-class action which involved any co-operation with the Communist Party. While a large number of individual members of the Labour Party were attracted by the demands for unity, the Socialist League was unable to convince many trade unions of such a need.[47]

Critique of reformism

The Socialist League rejected any schemes for capitalist rationalisation and declared that such schemes 'have nothing in common with socialism . . .'[48] It was opposed to any policy of the Labour Party to secure particular economic palliatives. Capitalism could not be made more human; it had to be abolished. It was inefficient and inhuman and was moving inexorably into deeper crises. The competition for world markets had led to the establishment of protective economic barriers and recurrent currency crises. Domestic industries were ailing and required state aid, while the charging of higher prices for goods led to unemployment and poverty. Imperialist war and a Fascist government introducing reactionary policies to crush labour was the inevitable result of the capitalist crisis. A Labour government should immediately acquire the 'vital points of power'[49] through public ownership. Within its first five years in office the government should acquire with only limited compensation the coal, gas, electricity, oil, iron and steel, munitions, chemicals, cotton, woollen and shipbuilding industries, all forms of inland transport and the health services. The government should plan the distributive trades and should fix the hours and wages of all labour. Taxes on large incomes should be raised and the inheritance of wealth should be restricted. Thus during discussion of domestic policies at Labour Party conferences the Socialist League was intent on ensuring that the party was committed to fundamental change rather than to any particular economic palliatives. In 1932 Wise successfully demanded the public ownership of joint-stock banks as well as of the Bank of England.[50] In 1933 the Socialist League submitted 13 amendments to the NEC policy document *Socialism and the Condition of the People*, all intent on ensuring that the Labour Party's general objective should be 'to eliminate all private enterprise as quickly as possible . . .' [51] Only two of the Socialist League's amendments were called for debate.[52] The first instructed the NEC to specify the means to be adopted by a Labour government in securing a 'rapid and complete conversion of the Socialist system . . .',[53] while the second would have deleted the NEC proposal that a National Investment Board should provide long-term credit for small firms. Wise argued that if such capital was injected into small firms there would then be pressure not to nationalise them. Rather the NIB should replace the individual investor and use the provision of capital as a means of securing public ownership and control.[54] In 1934 the Socialist League submitted amendments to the NEC policy document *For Socialism and Peace*, in an attempt to ensure that the Labour Party, both in general statement and in particular detail, should be committed to complete industrial and social reorganisation. Cripps demanded that the policy document should include a specific programme of action in order that rhetoric could be translated into practice and that such a programme should include the acquisition of sufficient economic power to proceed with industrial and social re-organisation. He rejected any idea of a Labour government proceeding by introducing a number of measures of social reform for he believed that 'it is impossible for the capitalist system to give to the workers the rewards that are promised under a policy of social reform.'[55] Mellor attacked the policy document from another angle. Why, he asked, did the Labour Party not reaffirm its working-class basis and purpose rather than establish a government which 'expresses the needs and voices the aspirations of the community as a whole'?[56] In two further amendments debated at the party conference of 1934 the Socialist League first challenged the idea that compensation to owners of private industries should include capital repayment and second, proposed that publicly owned industries should be run not by the Morrisonian public board but by the Minister in direct control who would be less likely to pursue capitalist objectives and more likely to establish socialist priorities.[57]

Scepticism

While individual Socialist League spokesmen advocated that the pursuit of power should be through the ballot box, as a body the Socialist

League appeared ambivalent, if not hostile, to the idea. On some occasions the Socialist League stated that its objective was to secure a socialist, parliamentary majority.[58] The working class made up a majority in British society and thus socialists had everything to gain by a democratic rather than a violent seizure of power. However, the Socialist League had little confidence in the amenability of the political institutions to secure socialist change, especially since it believed that the capitalist ruling class would sabotage the policies of a socialist government. The lesson to be drawn from the fall of the second Labour government was 'the power of capitalism to overthrow a Government by extra-parliamentary means'.[59] On other occasions, therefore, the Socialist League rejected the idea of the parliamentary road to socialism. Two proposals at the first annual conference of the Socialist League, one to reaffirm the belief '. . . that only by the free-will of the people expressed through a democratically elected Government [could] the Socialist idea of a Cooperative Commonwealth be achieved and retained . . .', and another to commit it in its constitution to 'use constitutional means to bring about the Socialist Commonwealth', were both defeated.[60] Others argued that even if a socialist majority was worth pursuing through the ballot box it might then be necessary for socialists to defend their democratically won power by violence since others might choose to adopt unconstitutional methods of opposition.[61] Laski considered it likely that any future Labour government would face the opposition of city, monarchy and the Conservative Party all intent on removing it from office by any means.[62] Attlee believed that a Labour government would face a crisis and the atmosphere would be akin to that of wartime.[63] Delay in implementing socialist policies would be disastrous since it would enable the economic interests to organise and destroy the elected government. Thus the Socialist League advocated the introduction of an Emergency Powers Act to enable Ministers to act by decree.[64] It called for the abolition of the House of Lords in order that legislation could be speedily implemented without the usual parliamentary delays and, in the intervening period, any opposition by the House of Lords should either be avoided by the creation of new peers or, along with the judiciary, it should be ignored. Such a policy would lead to political conflict and confusion and 'would almost certainly result in an uprising of the capitalists which would have to be quelled by force . . .'[65] In any constitutional impasse the monarch might look to a person with support from the armed forces to take office and in such a situation the socialist government should 'make itself temporarily into a dictatorship until the matter could . . .

be put to the test at the polls.'[66] The use of such terms as uprising, force and dictatorship was a challenge to the niceties of the language of parliamentary politics. The Socialist League went further by arguing that socialists should act as agitators stimulating the political unrest which existed in society.[67] Such language was regarded as intemperate by many within the Labour Party and as electorally damaging.[68] Members of the Socialist League were, themselves, aware of the controversy that such argument stimulated in parts of the labour movement and made efforts to modify the language. G.D.H. Cole wrote in March 1933 that it was impossible to 'put limits to the degree of dictatorial power which, under stress of the emergency, our Socialist Government may have to assume',[69] but later in the same year he had modified this by substituting 'administrative power' for dictatorial power.[70] Similarly, his statement that a socialist government would 'at the outset . . . establish a system that can be relied upon to work quickly and dictatorially . . .'[71] was later omitted, while his suggestion that Parliament must meet 'as seldom as possible' became 'as often as is needed for some clearly practical purposes.'[72] But the NEC felt it necessary to issue a statement in which it asserted that the Labour Party:

> stands for parliamentary democracy. It is firmly opposed to individual or group dictatorship whether from the Right or the Left. It holds that the best and, indeed, the only tolerable form of government for this country is democratic government with a free electoral system and an active and efficient Parliamentary machine for reaching effective decisions after reasonable opportunities for discussion and criticism. In so far as any statements which are at variance with the declared policy of the party on this question have been, or may be, made by individuals, these are hereby definitely repudiated by the national executive.[73]

It is worth noting, however, that the NEC statement *Parliamentary Problems and Procedure*, presented to the party conference in 1934, did state that parliamentary procedure was antiquated and in need of reform, that the House of Lords should be abolished and, in the event of an emergency situation for which the normal powers of government were inadequate, a Labour government would seek the necessary emergency powers from Parliament.[74]

It was clear that the Labour Party was very firmly committed to the institutions and procedures of parliamentary government. The Socialist League, by contrast, while expressing the hope that the transition to socialism could be achieved without civil war, gave the impression that it believed the power of vested capitalist interests and the bias of political institutions to be such that it was unlikely that a peaceful transition could succeed without the use of emergency powers.

Impact upon the Labour Party?

This challenge to Labour Party policies was very limited in its success. In 1932 the opportunity for the Socialist League to exert its influence was relatively great since a political vacuum temporarily existed within the party. This was the result of the defection of some of the leading parliamentary figures, a disillusionment within the party over the policies pursued by the second Labour government, and tension between the trade unions and the party. It was an opportune moment for a left faction to argue its case.

At the 1932 and 1933 party conferences the NEC was subjected to defeat or forced into making concessions to its critics. In 1932 NEC opposition to the demands for the public ownership of joint-stock banks and for a future Labour government to introduce socialist measures was overriden.[75] In 1933 the NEC declared, as a result of Socialist League pressure, its willingness to think again about particular aspects of its economic policy and it accepted a resolution pledging the party to resist war by means which included a general strike.[76] It was only on such issues as the application of the Communist Party for affiliation to the Labour Party and the demand for a united front of working-class organisations that the NEC at this time was able to secure comfortable victories in ballots.

It was significant, however, that Ernest Bevin spoke out against the Socialist League, and against Stafford Cripps in particular. At the 1933 party conference he accused them both of being out of touch with reality. Bevin's intervention in the debate and his opposition to the arguments of the Socialist League reflected the increasing importance of the trade union movement in the internal affairs of the Labour Party. After the 1931 débâcle Henderson and Bevin co-operated in the revival of the National Joint Council, renamed the National Council of Labour in 1933, as a means of improving the relations between the trade unions and the Labour Party.[77] It met monthly to discuss matters common to the labour movement and soon became the dominant centre of power in Labour's intra-party politics. All Labour Party policy documents emanated from its discussions as well as statements on day-to-day issues.[78] It was composed of seven representatives from the TUC and three from the NEC and PLP respectively. Policy matters discussed at this body then

went to the annual Trades Union Congress and subsequently to the
annual party conference for approval. It was unlikely, once the National
Council of Labour had agreed a policy, that it would be defeated at
either the TUC or party conference for the natural response of many
trade union delegations was to support the policies drawn up by their
own leaders. During this period the votes of the trade unions at the
Labour Party conferences totalled approximately two million whilst
constituency parties, socialist and co-operative societies ranged from
approximately four to five hundred thousand. While neither trade
unions nor constituency parties have ever cast their votes as a unified
bloc it was the case that, however much the Socialist League could
attract support for its arguments in constituency parties, the combined votes of any of the leading unions were large enough to dominate
conference proceedings.[79] During this period the alliance of the largest
trade unions in providing support for the policies being presented to the
party conference by the party leadership, these having been discussed
and approved in the National Council of Labour, guaranteed that there
would be approximately one to one and a quarter million affirmative
votes prior to the debates taking place.

By 1934, the Socialist League was thus faced with a situation in
which the NEC was no longer responding to policy initiatives at the
party conference but was itself taking the initiative. These initiatives
were in part trade-union-inspired, thus drawing upon the support of
the trade union delegations at the party conference and often leaving
the Socialist League isolated. Thus the Socialist League's 'euphoric'
phase of 1932-3 was transformed into a second phase in which it was
consistently voted down at party conferences. There was some NEC
accommodation in 1934 in that the party policy document *For Socialism and Peace* contained a section stating the need for reform of the
parliamentary procedures but the Socialist League had little success in
the major debates on economic and foreign policy issues. Morrison
recommended that the Socialist League's amendment to the section in
For Socialism and Peace on 'Labour's Aims' should be rejected as
woolly and full of platitudes, and in a card vote the amendment secured
only 206,000 votes as compared with the 2,146,000 in favour of the
NEC's line.[80] The two Socialist League amendments on economic
policy were heavily defeated and so were the amendments to the
foreign affairs section of *For Socialism and Peace*, and the NEC policy
document *War and Peace* was accepted.[81] This pattern of voting was
repeated at ensuing conferences. Socialist League challenges to the
NEC's policies of support for the League of Nations in any action over

Abyssinia, of support for a policy of non-intervention in Spain, of
support for a policy of rearmament at home, and of rejection of a
united front campaign, were all defeated in 1935 and 1936.[82] The
Socialist League had been steadily defeated in its confrontations with
the NEC. As a consequence of such defeats, a special Socialist League
conference was held in November 1934, which decided that the time
had come for it to act as 'a disciplined organisation founded on a
common policy and working as part of the Labour movement' which
had 'passed out of the realm of programme making into the realm of
action'.[83] No longer was it to be a case of the Socialist League preparing plans for effecting the transition to a socialist society but, instead, of rousing the will to power amongst the working class by agi-
tating on such issues as war, Fascism, unemployment and the operation
of the means test. The Socialist League had veered away from its
original position as a research and propaganda faction within the
Labour Party to become a faction campaigning within the *labour movement* for socialists, and competing with the Labour Party for their
allegiance.

In 1935 the Socialist League arranged 16 conferences in England and
Wales on the theme of mass resistance to war.[84] During the latter part
of 1935 and early part of 1936 the Socialist League held mass meetings
in 40 towns in pursuit of its objective of making and recruiting
socialists. In this type of recruiting campaign it was inevitable that it
would come into frequent contact with the ILP and the Communist
Party and that suggestions would be made for the three organisations
to co-operate. Yet such co-operation, in particular with the Communist
Party, was destined to split the Socialist League and provide a ready
reason for its expulsion from the Labour Party.

Moves for an alliance of the ILP and the Socialist League had commenced early in 1935. Fenner Brockway noted that discussions had
taken place between ILP leaders and Mellor, Elvin and Mitchison on
drawing up a common policy and uniting to campaign on specific
issues.[85] The Socialist League was a good deal more wary of any
formal alliance with the Communist Party. Moves to forge such an
alliance had been defeated at the Socialist League's annual conference
of 1934 and 1935. The prevailing view was that it did not wish to be
'diverted into activities definitely condemned by the Labour Party which
will jeopardise our affiliation to and influence within the [Labour]
party.'[86] But in February 1936 the National Council adopted a resolution supporting the Communist Party's request to affiliate to the
Labour Party. Unknown to the majority of Socialist League members,

Mellor, Cripps and Bevan entered into negotiations with the ILP and
Communist Party over the possibilities of the Socialist League com-
bining with the two other bodies in a united front campaign. There is
no doubt that some of its members were opposed to any formal collaboration with the Communist Party.[87] However, a special meeting of the
Executive Committee approved the idea and agreed that if the ILP did
not enter into the unity agreement then the Socialist League would proceed in alliance with the Communist Party alone.[88] The division among
Socialist League members was reflected at a specially convened conference, held in January 1937, when approval for a unity manifesto was
only given by 56 votes to 38 votes with 23 abstentions.[89] Two days
after the conference the Unity Manifesto was published, signed by
Mellor, Cripps and Mitchison on behalf of the Socialist League,
Maxton, Jowett and Brockway on behalf of the ILP, and Pollitt,
Gallacher and Dutt on behalf of the Communist Party. It called for a
united campaign of the working class against 'Fascism, Reaction and
War', for the 'adoption of a fighting programme of mass struggle' and
'the return of a Labour Government, as the next stage in the advance
to Working-Class Power'. Instructions were sent to Socialist League
branches and members that they 'should immediately establish contact
with the Communist Party and the ILP and set up a Unity Campaign
Committee composed of three representatives from each organisation.'[90]
Demonstrations were to be held in January, February and March in 21
cities and towns in England, Scotland and Wales. The fact that the
Unity Manifesto was signed and instructions sent out to Socialist
League branches with such speed, when only a minority of those
present at the special conference approved of such action, reveals the
essential nature of the organisation. Notwithstanding the formal structure of the Socialist League, policy and strategy were in fact determined
by a very small group of people.

The response of the NEC to the Socialist League's action was swift.
It had issued an appeal to party members, entitled 'Party Loyalty',
four days before the Socialist League special conference in which it
reminded them that decisions had been taken at the 1934 and 1936
annual conferences rejecting either Communist Party affiliation to the
Labour Party or any joint action with the Communist Party in a united
front. When this warning failed to deter members of the Socialist League
the NEC, at its January meeting, decided that the Socialist League should
be disaffiliated from the Labour Party.[91] Two months later it decided
that, because the Socialist League was still involved in the united front
campaign, membership of the Socialist League and the Labour Party

should be incompatible and that this should operate from 1 June.[92] The annual conference of the Socialist League held in May, perhaps appropriately in its original meeting place, Leicester, then decided that it should disband rather than enable the NEC to expel individuals from the Labour Party and, in the meantime, a campaign was to be mounted to reverse the NEC's decision at the annual party conference. The NEC's clamp-down on any campaign in favour of the united front went further than proscription of the Socialist League. It refused to endorse as parliamentary candidates any persons known to be in favour of a united front.[93] At its July meeting it warned that it would not tolerate any organised campaign within the Labour Party by party members to persuade other party members of the merits of united action with the ILP and Communist Party.[94] Further, it announced that none of the resolutions submitted on the issue of the united front for discussion at the forthcoming annual party conference would be called under the 'three year rule';[95] instead delegates wishing to raise the matter would have to discuss it during the presentation of the NEC report. Inevitably the NEC's decision was overwhelmingly approved at the party conference.[96] The Socialist League was officially dead.

Conclusion

The Socialist League was a small organisation by contrast with the ILP.[97] In some ways, however, the comparison is unfair since prior to 1918 the ILP had been the major recruiting agency for individual members of the Labour Party. Many people felt a loyalty to the ILP, irrespective of political stance, and thus remained members throughout the 1920s. In contrast the Socialist League could not call upon such traditional loyalty; its membership was small, as has been the case since with all the left factions within the Labour Party. What the Socialist League lacked was not necessarily numbers but leadership of a particular type. What it needed was a working-class, trade union leadership, instead of which it found itself with a body of middle-class leaders who could be pejoratively classified as intellectuals by their opponents. Intellectuals were regarded suspiciously by many within the labour movement and it was possible for trade union leaders to play on this suspicion by suggesting that such men were likely to abandon the working class when it suited them, as had Ramsay MacDonald and Oswald Mosley.[98] Stafford Cripps certainly generated such suspicion; this was the man who had displayed little commitment to transform society as a member of the second Labour government,[99] but had then rapidly adopted a very critical attitude to gradualism after the fall of the Labour government and had assumed the leadership of the Labour left. Trade union leaders claimed that such a man knew nothing about the working class or the trade union movement.[100] Among some he generated a good deal of loyalty and support but in general his personal aloofness considerably limited his ability as a mass leader.[101] Cripps further suffered from being a poor tactician and politically naïve.[102] It was inevitable that the leader-writers of Fleet Street would present a grotesque parody of the man, but he did offer them rather easy opportunities by making forthright speeches which he would then modify or clarify in consequence of press misreporting and exaggeration. His modifications often gave the impression of a man unaware of the implications of some of his thoughts and unsure of them when controversy arose.[103] It is also likely that the Socialist League suffered as a consequence of Cripps' wealth; however generous he was in offering his professional services to the labour movement,[104] critics would accuse the Socialist League of being a 'rich man's toy',[105] and it being a means of his buying influence and power within the Labour Party. While there is no doubt that Cripps in particular, and the Socialist League in general, attracted criticism on account of their respective social origins and social composition, there is also no doubt that among others they attracted support and loyalty. They played an important role in rallying the flagging spirits of the party members disappointed and disillusioned by the insensitivity of the party leadership to their demands for greater action in meeting the serious threats to social democracy in Britain and abroad. To these people, and there were many activists among them, the Socialist League was a haven in a distinctly hostile political environment.

Throughout the life of the Labour Party a core of party activists has existed, operating within both the trade union branches and constituency parties, who have always been committed to the radical transformation of society, both national and international. They believe that the Labour Party will achieve this only by eliminating private enterprise in Britain and by abandoning the traditional features of British foreign policy. The existence, and permanence, of this core is revealed by an examination of the resolutions submitted to the party's annual conference by affiliated organisations. Every year resolutions are submitted which would commit the Labour Party to the introduction of considerable social, economic and political change — a great deal more than that envisaged by those dominant within the Labour Party. This activist group has always been in a minority when votes are taken at party conferences, except on certain rare occasions such as 1932 and 1933. But in general the 1930s was a disquieting and dispiriting period for such activists. In the face of the very serious threats posed by the growth of Fascism the party leadership seemed to present the appearance of indifference through its desire to have nothing to do with the Communist Party. Its hostility to the Communist Party was perfectly understandable but its willingness to allow the Communist Party to take the lead in organising protests against domestic and foreign injustices was inexcusable. In this frustrating period the Socialist League offered solace to party activists demanding action. The frustration of the party members reached its climax in October 1936 when the Labour leadership seemed to be ignoring the opinions within the constituency parties on Spain and rearmament. As a consequence party activists organised a campaign to secure the election of constituency party representatives to the NEC solely by delegates from the constituency parties, in order that such representatives would be more sensitive to constituency opinions. The NEC was forced to recognise the strength of feeling within the constituencies on this issue.[106] The NEC must also have been worried about the possible drop in individual party membership which had been taking place in 1937.[107] The reform demanded was therefore accepted by the NEC and introduced at the 1937 party conference. The elections for the constituency party representatives to the NEC resulted in Cripps, Laski and Pritt being amongst the seven elected. It is dangerous to interpret the election of particular individuals to the constituency parties' section of the NEC as reflecting a particularly dominant set of ideas amongst party activists, since the impact of personality also plays a large part in determining voting patterns. But in the very first election to be determined solely by constituency party delegates, it is reasonable to draw the conclusion that the support for a more radical and vigorous party leadership was not so small within the party as might be assumed from a glance at the voting figures on particular policy issues upon which the Socialist League had challenged the party leadership at successive party conferences.

Every opportunity has been taken by the party leadership to harry the Labour left. Harold Shepherd, the National Agent, outlined the attitude taken by the party leadership:

> We always allow latitude for differences on particular points, but we do not believe that the doors of our party should be open to persons who want to come in merely for the purpose of changing its policy.[108]

Left factions *do* want to change policy, to inject the socialist element into policies which they feel is lacking. Life can always be made extremely difficult for such factions but they continue to exist, because they feel that the Labour Party, with its links with the trade union movement, remains the most effective vehicle for working-class action.

The alliance between the leading personalities in the trade union movement and the dominant right wing of the Parliamentary Labour Party was sufficient to defeat the left in the British movement during the 1930s. In the confrontations between the Socialist League and the Labour leadership at party conferences the latter always won, once they had learnt the lessons of the immediate aftermath of the 1931 débâcle. But qualitative changes in ideas and attitudes are not to be measured only by votes and in particular by votes at Labour Party conferences. The Socialist League, with all its mistakes and short-comings, did provide a centre of opposition and of political activity for a significant number of activists who might otherwise have stayed in the wilderness. The League included among its members some of the most attractive socialists of the decade, and it undoubtedly made its own contribution to the radicalisation of sections of the movement that was a noticeable characteristic of the closing years of the thirties. In the evaluation of the contribution the Socialist League made to the history of the British labour movement, the war years must be included as an extension as well as an enlargement of the preceding decade. For those on the left of the movement, the 1930s was a decade of political frustration and of lost opportunities; but the Labour victory of 1945 cannot be understood simply as a response to wartime radicalisation. It is this which in part at least accounts for the importance of the Socialist League as of the other movements of the left in the years which pre-ceded the outbreak of war.

Notes

1. R. Harrison, 'The War Emergency Workers' National Committee 1914-1920', in A. Briggs and J. Saville, *Essays in Labour History 1886-1923*, p. 259.
2. A good example from the period under examination is the following: 'The choice before the Nation is either a vain attempt to patch up the super-structure of a capitalist society in decay at its very foundations, or a rapid advance to a Socialist reconstruction of the national life. There is no half-way house between a society based on private ownership in the means of production, with the profit of the few as the measure of success and a society where public ownership of those means enables the resources of the

nation to be deliberately planned for attaining the maximum of general well-being.' *For Socialism and Peace.* (The Labour Party, 1934), p. 12.

3. A classic statement of the democratic value system was made by Harold Laski in the debate on the disaffiliation of the Socialist League at the 1937 Labour Party conference. *LPCR* (1937), p. 158.

4. The tension between these two ideals was revealed during the intra-party disputes of the 1950s. Michael Foot, writing in *Tribune*, argued that 'people with heretical, unorthodox or minority views must have the means of discussing politics and political attitudes with like-minded people. Otherwise they will never have the chance of making converts to their outlook . . . Groups of one form or another within national parties are as essential to democracy as the right of free speech itself.'

   To which came an immediate response in the correspondence columns that some 'would rather discuss differences of opinion within the party confines than ostentate their views by sensational public declarations of opposition. And they would hotly deny that discussion of policy is not possible within the confines of the party. There are numerous ways of opposing or trying to change the policy of the Labour Party other than by organising factions. The machinery of organisation within the Labour Party, Trade Unions and Co-operative Party and in the various Socialist societies is immensely flexible . . . Many people are opposed to the present 'defence' policy of the Front Bench of the Labour Party. They are appalled at the seeming inadequacy of the leadership. And, quite rightly, they are determined to work within the party to change this state of things. What they will not do is to parade their discontent — like political skifflers — so that copy hungry capitalist newspapers may be provided with ammunition with which to damage the Labour Party. They think it is folly to imperil the party by this kind of rowdy display of petulance. *Tribune*, 7 and 14 March 1958.

5. Both McKenzie and Beer regard the breakdown between the two bodies as basically concerned with the tactical issue. See R. McKenzie, *British Political Parties* (1963, 2nd. ed.) pp. 433-46 and S. Beer, *Modern British Politics* (1965, pp. 158-9). But see Brockway's speech to the 1931 Labour Party conference on the difference of policy. *LPCR* (1931), p. 174.

6. Frank Wise, an ex-Civil Servant, was Labour MP for East Leicester from 1929 to 1931. He was very active within the ILP.

7. July 1932. Cole Papers, Nuffield College, Oxford.

8. Alan Bullock writes that SSIP representatives were out-manoeuvred in their negotiations with the ILP group and had to accept Wise's terms or risk losing half their members. One of those terms was that Wise rather than Bevin should be Chairman of the new organisation. A. Bullock, *The Life and Times of Ernest Bevin: 1881-1940* (1960), p. 515.

9. The meeting was held on 6 November 1932. The resolution to amalgamate was passed by 67 votes to 42. Cole Papers, Nuffield College, Oxford.

10. The resolution was passed by 70 votes to 27.

11. Margaret Cole writes that her husband was 'vehemently opposed' to the amalgamation of the two bodies. But G.D.H. Cole did sign the letter inviting socialists to the inaugural conference of the Socialist League and he also became, for a short period, a member of the Socialist League's National Council. See M. Cole, *The Story of Fabian Socialism* (1961), p. 231.

12. *Minutes of the NEC*, 5 October 1932, The Labour Party Library.

13. Ibid.

14. Ibid.

15. The Socialist League's affiliated membership was 2,000. This was raised to

3,000 in 1933.

16. *Rules of the Socialist League* (1932), Section 1.

17. *Annual Report of the National Council*. Presented to Socialist League annual conference, May 1934.

18. J.T. Murphy, *Socialist Leaguer*, 11 May 1935.

19. *The Socialist*, 2 November 1935.

20. The Socialist League did not organise in Scotland, leaving the field to the Scottish Socialist Party which had been formed following ILP disaffiliation from the Labour Party. The Scottish Socialist Party affiliated to the Labour Party in 1932. Consultations between the Socialist League and the SSP took place in 1936 with a view to amalgamation of the two bodies. A successful completion to these negotiations was only halted when the Socialist League joined the United Front campaign which the SSP had decided not to join.

21. Norwich.

22. The seven regions were: North-West England, North-East England, North and South Wales, Yorkshire and North Midlands, East Midlands, South-West England, London and Home Counties. It is clear from a reading of Socialist League material that London, South Wales and Tyneside were the only areas which sustained Socialist League activity throughout the lifetime of the organisation.

23. In addition to the Treasurer and General Secretary, ten members were elected annually to the National Council and seven represented the regions.

24. Wise acted as Chairman of the Socialist League until its first annual conference in June 1933. He then became Vice-Chairman until his death in November 1933.

25. G.D.H. Cole, *A History of Socialist Thought*, Vol. 5 (1960), p. 69.

26. G.D.H. Cole, *A History of the Labour Party from 1914*, (1948), p. 284.

27. G.D.H. Cole, *A Study Guide on Socialist Policy* (Socialist League pamphlet, 1933).

28. G.D.H. Cole and G.R. Mitchison, *The Need for A Socialist Programme* (Socialist League pamphlet, 1933).

29. G.D.H. Cole, 'The Working Class Movement and the Transition to Socialism', in S. Cripps et al., *Problems of the Socialist Transition* (1934), pp. 65-7.

30. F.C. Henry was the first General Secretary. He was succeeded by J.T. Murphy in January 1935. Murphy resigned in September 1936 due to a disagreement over policy; he supported the idea of a Popular Front whereas the Socialist League's policy was that of support for a United Workers' Front. Murphy was succeeded by Margaret McCarthy who remained in the post until the Socialist League's disbandment.

31. *Annual Report of the National Council*, presented to Socialist League annual conference, May 1934.

32. Between 1932 and 1937 16 of the 23 elected members served continuously.

33. S. Beer, op. cit., pp. 154, 162 and 127.

34. *New Clarion*, 15 April 1933.

35. *The Socialist*, 1 September 1935, p. 4.

36. 'The Class Struggle', in S. Cripps et al., op. cit., pp. 183-4.

37. Trevelyan successfully moved a resolution at the 1933 Labour Party conference along these lines, *LPCR* (1933), p. 186. At the 1934 Labour Party conference the NEC issued a policy document, *War and Peace*, in which it rejected many of the demands contained in the Trevelyan resolution. A Socialist League amendment to the policy document *For Socialism and Peace* called upon the workers in capitalist countries 'to make every effort to prepare resistance to War declared by their own Governments, and undertakes to resist a War entered into by this Government by every means in its

power, including a General Strike.' *LPCR* (1934), pp. 176-7.

38. H.N. Brailsford, *The Socialist Leaguer*, 11 May 1935, p. 169.

39. *LPCR* (1935), p. 157.

40. Ibid., p. 171.

41. Ibid., p. 157. It is interesting to note the division of opinion within the Socialist League on this issue for, in the same debate, Trevelyan argued that the League of Nations should stop Italy and that Britain as a member was bound to support the policy of sanctions.

42. Cripps' statement reported in the *Manchester Guardian* (20 November 1936), naturally caused considerable publicity and excitement in the national press.

43. J.T. Murphy, *Fascism: the Socialist Answer* (Socialist League, 1934), p. 1.

44. Cripps described the National Government as a form of 'country gentleman Fascism'. Speech to the Fourth Annual Conference of the Socialist League, *The Times*, 1 June 1936.

45. *Annual Conference Report*, Socialist League, 1933, p.1.

46. Letter from J.T. Murphy to Secretary of the Labour Party, 5 February 1936, Socialist League file, The Labour Party library.

47. Among the six largest trade unions the MFGB and the NUDAW supported proposals for working-class unity.

48. Resolution approved by the annual conference of the Socialist League in 1934, *The Socialist Leaguer*, 1 June/July 1934, p. 13.

49. *Forward to Socialism*, Socialist League, 1934, p.9.

50. The NEC recommended that the demand should be rejected but was defeated. The voting was 1,141,000 to 984,000, *LPCR* (1932), pp. 182-94. A significant measure of the *decline* of the left's influence within the Labour Party during this period is that by 1937 Morrison could reject the idea of public ownership of joint-stock banks and claim that they could be regulated through a publicly owned Bank of England, *LPCR* (1937), p. 186.

51. *Amendments to Socialism and the Condition of the People*, The Labour Party, 1933, p.6.

52. One of the means by which left factions have been constantly outmanoeuvred at party conferences is through, first, the compositing of motions and, second, the selection of motions for debate. The Conference Arrangements Committee plays a crucial role in both these procedures. This committee is elected by all the delegates to the annual party conference and thus it is dominated by trade union votes. Left factions have rarely been in a position where any of the five members of this committee are sympathetic to their arguments.

53. *Amendments . . .*, op. cit., p. 2.

54. *LPCR* (1933), pp. 174-5.

55. *LPCR* (1934), p. 159.

56. Ibid., p. 161.

57. Ibid., p. 191 and 201.

58. *Forward to Socialism*, Socialist League, p. 8; S. Cripps, Preface to C. Addison *et al.*, *Problems of a Socialist Government*, 1933, p. 12.

59. S. Cripps, 'Can Socialism Come by Constitutional Means?', in C. Addison *et al.*, op. cit., p. 38.

60. *Annual Conference Report*, Socialist League, 1933, pp. 2 and 6.

61. S. Cripps, 'Democracy: Real or Sham?', in S. Cripps *et al.*, op. cit., p. 31.

62. H. Laski, *The Labour Party and the Constitution*, Socialist League, 1933.

63. C. Attlee, 'Local Government and the Socialist Plan', in C. Addison *et al.*, op. cit., p. 189.

64. *LPCR* (1933), p. 159.

65. S. Cripps, 'Can Socialism Come By Constitutional Methods?', in C. Addison

et al., op. cit., p. 45.

66. S. Cripps, ibid., p. 46.

67. *The Socialist Leaguer*, 9 February 1935, p. 131, and *The Socialist Leaguer*, 10 March/April 1935, p. 146.

68. 'Every time this self-appointed spokesman of the Labour Party (Cripps) opened his lips in public he lost the Labour Party 20,000 votes and at least two seats.' Rev. H. Dunnico, a former Labour MP, *The Times*, 18 January 1934.

69. *Socialist Control of Industry*, Socialist League pamphlet, 1933, p. 15.

70. Reprinted in C. Addison, *et al.*, op. cit., p. 173.

71. *Socialist Control of Industry*, p. 14.

72. C. Addison, *et al.*, op. cit., p. 173.

73. *The Times*, 26 January 1934.

74. *LPCR* (1934), pp. 261-3.

75. The Socialist League was only formed immediately prior to this conference and therefore its impact as an organised body was minimal. But the two individuals prominent in moving these items (Wise and Trevelyan) were both leading members of the Socialist League.

76. Hugh Dalton states that the NEC accepted the resolution on war and peace in order to preserve the 'façade of unity'. Arthur Henderson was due to speak immediately after the debate and the NEC '. . . did not want a wrangle and an excited vote immediately before this speech by the President of the Disarmament Conference.' *The Fateful Years: Memoirs, 1931-1945*, (1957), p. 45. Dalton notes that the NEC determined that in future 'on such important questions, not to leave the initiative to the floor'; instead the major policy questions should be covered by NEC resolutions to which alternative policies would have to be presented as amendments, thus giving the NEC the initiative in the debates.

77. Bevin referred to its revival in a speech at the 1935 party conference, *LPCR* (1935), p. 180. For its official powers see *LPCR* (1932), p. 67.

78. By 1938 one constituency party, at least, was worried at its power: 'This Conference declares that there is a growing tendency for the National Council of Labour to exceed the advisory functions allotted to it at the time of its re-formation and increasingly to usurp the authority of the NEC. It regards this as a highly unconstitutional and dangerous situation and demands that the National Council of Labour should confine itself to the functions for which it was formed.' Eastbourne DLP, *Agenda for Labour Party Conference*, 1938, p. 12. [See the discussion below on this matter in John Saville, 'May Day 1937', pp. 241 ff.]

79. The voting strength of the six largest trade unions during the period was:

	1932	1937
Miners' Federation of Great Britain	400,000	442,875
Transport and General Workers' Union	254,500	337,000
General and Municipal Workers' Union	250,000	242,000
National Union of Railwaymen	234,729	224,809
United Association of Textile Factory Workers	181,556	129,890
National Union of Distributive and Allied Workers	93,339	150,000

80. *LPCR* (1934), p. 165.

81. An amendment to the section in *For Socialism and Peace* on 'Key industries and services' challenged the notion of fair compensation to owners at time of public ownership, suggesting an income allowance for previous owners but not provision for capital repayment. It was defeated by 2,118,000 votes to 149,000 votes. Another amendment, rejecting the traditional public corporation as the means to control the iron and steel industry was defeated on

show of hands. The foreign policy amendments were lost on a show of hands, and *War and Peace* was adopted by 1,519,000 to 673,000 votes. *LPCR* (1934), pp. 199,202, 175-7, 178.

82. The NEC's motion calling on the Government to 'use all the necessary measures provided by the Covenant to prevent Italy's unjust and rapacious attack . . .' was adopted by 2,168,000 to 102,000 votes. *LPCR* (1935), pp. 153 and 193. The NEC motion reaffirming its policy of non-intervention in Spain was carried by 1,836,000 to 519,000 votes. *LPCR* (1936), p. 181. Cripps' reference back of a resolution containing a commitment to maintain a defence force consistent with membership of the League of Nations was defeated by 1,438,000 to 652,000 votes: ibid., p. 207. The motion calling for a united front was defeated by 1,805,000 to 435,000 votes: ibid., p. 257.

83. *Socialist Leaguer*, December 1934.

84. The conferences in Birmingham, Brighton, Bristol, Cardiff, Durham, Eastleigh, Hull, Leeds, London, Luton, Manchester, Newcastle, Norwich, Reading, Sheffield and Swansea were addressed by Socialist Leaguers including Cripps, Bevan, Pritt, Elvin, Mellor, Trevelyan and Murphy. A resolution was to be introduced at each conference pledging all members of the conference to take immediate action to mobilise every available force for the mass resistance to war. *The Socialist*, 1 September 1935. The London conference, held in September, 1935, attracted approximately 1,500 delegates from the trade union branches, constituency Labour parties and co-operative Guilds. In Cardiff, Newcastle, Leeds, Manchester and Hull the number of delegates ranged from two to three hundred.

85. Letter to members of the ILP National Administrative Council, Socialist League file, The Labour Party Library. The Labour Party's response to these discussions reveals its autocratic mentality. The NEC instructed its Secretary to write to Mellor asking for his comments on this 'highly questionable activity'. Letter from J.S. Middleton to Mellor, 23 May 1935, Socialist League file, The Labour Party Library. Mellor replied that such discussions were informal, and Murphy, the Secretary of the Socialist League, when asked for his comments by Middleton, confirmed that the discussions were personal and informal, in no way committing the Socialist League as a body.

86. *New Leader*, 14 June 1935.

87. Reg Groves, a member of the National Council, campaigned against uniting with the Communist Party. He was an ex-member of the Communist Party who had shifted his support to Trotsky. R. Groves, *The Balham Group*, 1974.

88. *Minutes of the Executive Committee*, 20 November 1936. Reg Groves was absent from this meeting.

89. The resolution passed was: 'This conference of the Socialist League endorses the action of the National Council in concluding the agreement between the Socialist League, the ILP and the Communist Party, approves of the Agreement's terms and policy, and calls upon all branches and members to support wholeheartedly the Unity Campaign. This Conference authorises William Mellor, Stafford Cripps and G.R. Mitchison to sign the Unity Manifesto on behalf of the Socialist League'. *Circular to all Socialist League branches and members*, 19 January 1937, Socialist League file, The Labour Party Library.

90. Ibid.

91. A move to defer the decision for one week in order to allow consultation between the NEC and the Socialist League was lost by 14 votes to 9. A resolution to disaffiliate the Socialist League was then carried by 23 votes to 1, Mrs Agnes Dollan being the sole dissentient. *Minutes of the NEC*, 27 January 1937.

92. The NEC decision was carried *nem. con.*, as Mrs Dollan was not present at

the meeting. *Minutes of the NEC*, 24 March 1937.

93. William Mellor as candidate for Coventry and A. Campbell as candidate for Hendon. Mellor's further candidature at Stockport and Ben Green's at South-West Hull were approved later in 1937 but only after months of consideration by the NEC.

94. Margaret McCarthy, the Secretary of the Socialist League, with others who opposed its disbandment, had formed the Socialist Left Federation in June 1937 with the purpose of organising '. . . all those Socialists who seek to win the Movement to a militant Socialist policy of class struggle, for the achievement of working class power and the establishment of Socialism.' *A Call To the Socialist Left*, Socialist League file, The Labour Party Library.

95. Standing Order 2(iv), *The Constitution and Standing Orders of The Labour Party*.

96. 1,730,000 to 373,000 votes, *LPCR* (1937), p. 164.

97. The ILP's affiliated membership to the Labour Party was 21,000 in 1931.

98. 'Sir Stafford Cripps is a rich man with rich pals around him, and they are the biggest danger to the Labour Party in this country. You will find those chaps where Mosley is before much longer.' J. McGurk of the Miners' Federation speaking at a Labour Party conference, *LPCR* (1937), p. 160.

99. Cripps was offered a place in the National Government by Ramsay MacDonald and it took him some time to reject the offer. In his letter of rejection he writes of his admiration for Ramsay MacDonald's courage and conviction. C.A. Cooke, *The Life of Richard Stafford Cripps* (1957), p. 127.

100. Charles Dukes, of the National Union of General and Municipal Workers, criticised the Socialist League's policy of mass resistance to war on the grounds: 'What does Sir Stafford Cripps know about "mass action"? I do not mind a Bevin or a Marchbank, or anybody else, who really can say to this Movement: "I tomorrow will lead my men"; but I resent people who have no ideas as to what those people think – people who have no authority, no responsibility, no influence – talking in this Conference as though it were possible to organise mass action against political action.' *LPCR* (1935), p. 173. In similar vein, Ernest Bevin: 'The middle classes are not doing too badly as a whole under capitalism and Fascism. Lawyers and members of other professions have not done too badly. The thing that is being wiped out is the Trade Union Movement.' Ibid., p. 179.

101. '. . . Stafford was a lone wolf, too conscious of his superiority to those around him and completely incapable of making intimate contacts with the rank and file.' K. Martin, *Editor* (1968), p. 51.

102. '. . . oddly immature in intellect and unbalanced in judgement . . . ignorant and reckless in his statement and proposals.' M. Cole (ed.), *Beatrice Webb's Diaries 1924-32* (1956), p. 304.

103. Cripps' response to his 'Buckingham Palace speech' is a good example. In a speech made in January 1934 he had stated that when the Labour Party came to power it would have to 'overcome opposition from Buckingham Palace and other places as well.' After the predictable press uproar he stated that he was 'most certainly not referring to the Crown'. See C.A. Cooke, op. cit., p. 159.

104. For example, his services to the North Wales and Border Counties Mineworkers' Association in the enquiry following the Gresford Colliery disaster in 1934.

105 Hugh Dalton speaking in the Rhondda in April 1937. H. Dalton, op. cit., p. 130.

106. The Committee of Constituency Labour Parties had been formed after the 1936 party conference with Stafford Cripps as its Chairman. The organisation

claimed that 'the platform was riding to victory over the constituency delegates . . . [and] it became clear that the opinions and views of the divisional party delegates carried no weight even on matters which were of more importance to the divisional Parties than to any other section of the conference. *Circular issued by the Provisional Committee of Constituency Labour Parties*, 1936. This organisation attracted wider political support than the Socialist League on this particular issue, but there is no doubt that many of its members, who believed that the NEC should more accurately reflect the views of party activists, were also critical of the party leadership's gradualist approach to political issues. The NEC disapproved of the formation of this organisation and attempted to undermine its existence by calling regional conferences to discuss party organisation. But at these conferences there was a strong demand for the reform of the election procedure for the NEC. The agenda for the 1937 annual party conference contained over eighty resolutions demanding reform of the election procedure.

107. At their meeting on 23 June 1937 NEC members had before them a report from the Organisation Subcommittee that party membership cards issued to the constituency Labour parties in the first six months of the year had dropped by 17,500, whilst in the first three months of 1936 they had increased by 50,000. NEC members could either interpret this as meaning that constituency parties were not carrying large stocks of party membership cards or as a significant decline in party membership.

108. *LPCR* (1934), p. 140.

9 MAY DAY 1937

John Saville

On Monday the third of May, 1937, the author of this article was standing on the steps of the London School of Economics in Houghton Street. With him was an American research student, Hap Poulson. Their talk was about the exciting May Day demonstrations of the previous Saturday and Sunday, the unprecedented London busmen's strike, and Spain: the issues everyone would be discussing that Monday. Harold Laski crossed the road to enter the School and as he came up the steps Hap Poulson said to him: 'Things are really beginning to move, aren't they?' 'You bet they are,' said Laski; but in the optimistic context in which the question was asked, and answered, he was wrong.

I

There were two May Day processions in 1937, as indeed had been customary for many years in London. The Labour Party always celebrated May Day on the first Sunday of the month, and they did so in 1937, despite the fact that May the first happened to fall on a Saturday. But May the first was always appropriated by the left — that is, the Communist Party and groups of militant trade unionists — and any change might be misinterpreted as a gesture towards the 'united front'. Since that was unthinkable, Transport House rejected a request from the May First committee for a united demonstration; and the official May Day march remained on Sunday.

The May First Committee held its initial conference on Saturday 16 January. Among the intellectuals sponsoring the Committee were J.B. Priestley, Jacob Epstein, Hamilton Fyfe, Ivor Montagu, Professor H. Levy, Stephen Spender and John Strachey. The last named gave the opening address at the Saturday conference, which was attended by 300 delegates representing 150 organisations, most of them trade unions. The main issues listed by Strachey were Spain, trade union recruitment in London, and working-class unity. A small ILP group argued that the central slogan 'For the Defence of Democracy and for Social Advance' was a betrayal of working-class aspirations; but their amendment, 'United Working-Class Action for Working-Class Power', received only 16 votes. The officers of the May First Committee, elected unanimously at this Conference, were Joe Scott, a well-known

232

Communist engineer, as chairman, and John A. Mahon, a full-time
Communist functionary, as secretary.[1]

Between January and the first of May, new issues intruded themselves. The two most important domestic matters were the Harworth
miners and the strike of the London busmen.

The Harworth story had its origins in the aftermath of the General
Strike of 1926 when company unionism established itself in the
Nottinghamshire coalfield. Its last phase started in the middle of August
1936 when two boys employed at the Harworth Pit were assaulted by a
colliery official, and this began a long chain reaction of events. The
majority of Harworth colliers belonged to the Nottinghamshire Miners'
Association, which was not recognised by the owners. The national
Miners' Federation became involved, and so did the National Council
for Civil Liberties which, through its Secretary, investigated allegations
'of high-handed action by the police'. During March and April 1937 the
situation in Harworth village became more and more tense. A miners'
national ballot voted seven to one for a national strike to achieve recognition of the MFGB in Nottinghamshire and for a guarantee of no
victimisations at Harworth. A special miners' national conference on 30
April rejected their Executive's recommendations, and voted for a
national strike on 22 May. A contingent of Harworth miners marched
on May Day: the symbol that the Union makes us strong.[2]

On the same Friday evening that the miners' delegates went home,
there began in London a stoppage of 26,000 metropolitan busmen. This
London strike was official; it was matched in a dozen counties by
unofficial strikes of provincial busmen. The strike in London
threatened the Coronation celebrations on 12 May, and it was felt by
many on the May Day processions that it was a fitting counter to the
environment of bunting and tinsel that was celebrating the abdication
of Edward VIII and the accession of George VI and his intelligent wife.

The London busmen were led by the Central London Bus Commit-
tee, an official part of the structure of the Transport and General
Workers' Union. From the early 1930s a Rank and File committee had
worked successfully to achieve a hundred per cent unionism in
London's garages. The Committee published a lively monthly journal,
Busmen's Punch. Its leaders were a group of remarkably vigorous trade
unionists: Bill Ware (Enfield); Frank Snelling (Merton); Bernard
Sharkey (Willesden); Bill Payne (Dalston) and Bert Papworth
(Chelverton Road). By no means all the leaders of the rank and file
movement were members of the Communist Party but the driving force
behind the success of the movement was undoubtedly Communist. The

leaders of the rank and file had controlled the Central Bus Committee
for several years before 1937, and Bert Papworth was also on the
national executive.[3] It was a situation Ernest Bevin found exceedingly
irksome since he was pushed into negotiations in support of demands
which he often considered too advanced. After negotiations in 1937
had dragged on for at least two months past the time appointed for a
new agreement, the Union officially gave a month's notice to strike,
and every bus in London came off the streets at midnight on 30 April.[4]

Four days earlier, on 26 April 1937, the Basque town of Guernica
had been partly obliterated by bombing. It was a new phenomenon in
the list of horrors of war and Guernica became a symbol: of the power
that the new technology could inflict on urban populations, and above
all of Fascist bestiality.[5] The cause of the Spanish Republic was
arousing more positive commitment among the politically progressive
in Britain than any other external set of events in the twentieth century.
No foreign struggle, save perhaps the American Civil War, had so divided the classes in Britain.[6] The cause of Spain greatly increased the
hatred and loathing of the left for the ruling groups in British society;
and the retribution exacted by the Fascists upon the people of
Guernica emphasised the argument of the left that the war against international Fascism was also a war of the classes in their own country.

But very few, in the May Day marches of 1937, believed anything
but that the cause of the ordinary people in Spain would triumph; and
despite the horrors of the Spanish war, and the evidence of Nazi bru-
tality and subversion throughout Europe, those who marched in the two
days' demonstrations in London — or in the many Sunday processions
of the big towns outside the capital — were optimistic about their
movement and its future. The year that had just gone by had witnessed
what a Chartist journal once described as the 'stirring of the old bones'.
The marchers in London had some great days to look back upon: the
many thousands who greeted the last national Hunger March on its
arrival in Hyde Park on Sunday 8 November 1936;[7] the equally enthusiastic welcome given to the Jarrow marchers; the unforgettable day of
4 October 1936, when the people of London blocked Gardners Corner,
Commercial Road and Cable Street in the East End to prevent the long-
advertised march of Oswald Mosley and his Fascists. And now, on this
lovely May weekend, the hundreds of London busmen in their white
coats and blue uniforms, and the miners of Harworth, were further
proof of the stirrings in the movement, and the hopes that could be
expected of the future. There was reasonable optimism and there was
certainly enthusiasm on these May Day demonstrations, and by general

agreement they were the largest and liveliest for many years.[8] It was felt to be a good time to be marching, even though *The Times* thought differently, since while it reported May Day demonstrations in Moscow, Paris, Warsaw and New York, there was nothing at all in their columns about either of the two demonstrations in London, or anywhere else in the country.

II

The greater political vigour of the second half of the thirties had its numerical reflection in the increased number of individual members of the Labour Party, in the rapid growth of the Communist Party, especially in London, and in the improvement in trade union recruitment.[9] The total number of trade unionists affiliated to the TUC had markedly fallen after the débâcle of the General Strike, and the pre-1926 level was only reached again in 1937. While these developments on the political and industrial fronts were modest but encouraging, they had not yet been reflected in electoral terms at the national level. In this important area, there was a notable difference between the two decades of the inter-war years. During the 1920s, Labour was steadily enlarging its electoral base in the country. By 1922, with 142 seats it had clearly emerged as the alternative party, and by 1929, its peak year in electoral voting, it obtained 289 seats. What had happened since the end of the war was that the Labour Party was winning votes in working-class areas where previously it had had no support; and it was not only the pre-1914 Lib-Labs who were being converted to Labour Party supporters. There were now also the beginnings of change in social and political consciousness in towns like Birmingham and in regions such as Lancashire, where the classical Lib-Lab tradition was never very strong. The total Labour poll in 1929 was 8,365,000 against 4,237,000 in 1922 and 2,225,000 in 1918. The upward secular trend in the 1920s was unmistakable, and it was broken only when the political crisis of August 1931 compounded the industrial collapse of 1926. In the hysterical general election of October 1931 which followed the cobbling together of a National Government by Ramsay MacDonald, the Labour Party suffered a catastrophic decline in the number of MPs elected — 46 (excluding 5 ILP members) against 289 in 1929 — while its total electoral vote fell by only two million. It was, however, the shrinking of its geographical base in British society that mattered. The West Midlands, which include Birmingham, returned no Labour members in 1931, against 25 in 1929; Lancashire and Cheshire showed a decline from 44 to 5, Scotland from 37 to 3 (excluding the ILP). It was the coalfields, together with those parts of the larger urban areas whose socialist traditions went back before 1914, which provided the core of the parliamentary remnant. Twenty-three of the 46 elected members were miners, with South Wales and Monmouth accounting for 15 of this total.[10]

The general election of 1935 came almost exactly four years after 1931; years of massive unemployment, although the economy had been moving upward from the low point of 1932, the result mainly of growth in the building sector and the development of the 'new' industries in the Midlands and the London region. Labour added just over 100 seats to its 1931 figure. As Dalton noted, 'The results were very disappointing.'[11] The total number of votes cast nearly reached the previous peak of 1929, but the electorate had increased by two and a half million, and the turnout on election day was 8 per cent lower. The main Labour gains in 1935 were in London, Scotland and Yorkshire. The main centres of strength — which in terms of seats in 1935 all continued to fall short of 1929 — were still the coalfields and selected urban areas. Trade union MPs numbered 79 out of a total of 154, the miners remaining the largest group with 34. As in 1931 there was not a single Labour MP for any of the twelve Birmingham constituencies, and it was the county boroughs in England outside the coalfields, most of the industrial north and London that remained the main source of electoral weakness. The rural areas, almost everywhere in Britain, were well beyond the chances of a Labour victory. There was a fairly steady improvement in Labour's local election results over the whole decade; but again the geographical spread was uneven. The labour victory of 1934 in the LCC elections was, of course, the most notable.[12]

What Labour was failing to do in the 1930s was to continue to win over the very large numbers of manual workers, and even more their wives and daughters, who either voted for one of the other two major parties or were politically uncommitted. At the time, Harold Laski noted that the unemployed, outside the coalfields, voted in 1935 for the Tories.[13] He might have added, 'or did not vote at all'. It was the working-class vote that was in question, and it was this failure to shift the social consciousness of large numbers of working people to the point of voting Labour that provides the major domestic question of the decade. It is a large question, to the solution of which the answers that have been traditionally offered — the long-term consequences of the General Strike, the collapse of Labour morale after 1931 and the ineffectiveness of Labour leadership throughout the decade — are relevant without being comprehensive. The problems of minority parties of the left always relate to the effectiveness and efficiency of their agitation and propaganda in terms of the economic and social interests, as well as aspirations, of their constituents (or their potential constituents). A minority Labour Party must clearly address itself in the first and main instance to the working people. In the 1930s the British Labour Party was still, in the social composition of its leadership as well as in its rank and file, a working-class party. There was a middle-class element in the Parliamentary Labour Party, and it was growing; but apart from Hugh Dalton and a few lesser personalities who were strongly identified with the right wing of the party, most of the middle class in the PLP were not obviously aligned one way or the other, and the tendency was more towards the left or left-centre. Since the national constituency for the Labour Party was the working class, the answer to the question posed must above all be concerned with the definition of working-class aims and aspirations.

III

There were two main strands in the 1930s to working-class 'interest'. The first, and obvious, was unemployment, wages and working conditions, and the second was international affairs in general and in particular the emergence of Fascism and the growing threat of war. The two did not necessarily meet, or relate to each other, except in the theoretical formulations of the left; in the consciousness of ordinary working people, jobs, wages and homes were the paramount considerations.

The political problem confronting the labour movement has already been stated: how to encourage the upward trend in Labour voting that had been so clearly expressed during the 1920s. It is worth remarking that the shift to Labour after the failure of the General Strike was exactly what could be expected to happen; the phenomenon had occurred many times in the past at the local or regional level.[14] But the collapse of the Labour government of 1931 was an unprecedented event, as was the desertion of the Labour Party by its leading personalities. There was no obvious resurrection available to the labour movement after the disastrous collapse in the General Election of 1931, except the patient acknowledgement of the theory and practice of the long haul. What made the disaster worse was the combination of trade union weakness and caution characteristic of the years following the General Strike, and the sharply deteriorating economic situation with its very rapid increases in unemployment. The choice before the Labour Party in the 1930s was never between moderation and caution, on the one hand, and a revolutionary programme on the other, although it was often presented by contemporaries in these ways. On no meaningful analysis could the British situation be described as revolutionary, or potentially revolutionary, and those on the left who did take this view were seriously at fault in their analysis. Their mistake is, of course, easily understood. Capitalism as a world system was in deep and serious crisis between 1929 and 1933, and the fact of crisis had penetrated social consciousness on a wide scale, in both the industrial and the underdeveloped worlds. But it was an elementary error of vulgar Marxism to infer from economic crisis an automatic revolutionary response from those who were its victims.[15] The contrary would seem to have been true in most periods in the history of British labour. Naturally, what the actual response will be in a given historical situation depends upon a variety of factors, but a common reaction to economic depression, and its accompanying unemployment, has often been an overwhelming sense of being at the mercy of forces beyond one's control, as well as a desperate fear of not being able to provide adequately for one's family. Those manual workers whose social psychology has been conditioned by the practice of solidarity over many years through trade union activity will be able, with the help of the union itself, to withstand the retreat into passivity and despair; and those with a degree of political understanding will be able to go further. But for the mass of working people in the thirties what Labour had to do was to rehabilitate itself in terms of its collective capacity to govern; the Labour Party could only do this if it was able to sustain a vigorous and continuous critique of government policy and practice and at the same time offer what could be presented as a viable alternative. It is, however, unlikely that even had these conditions been fulfilled — which they were not — the shift towards Labour would still have been of the magnitude necessary to obtain a parliamentary majority.[16] In the long history of the evolution and development of a working-class party in Britain, there has always been a subtle and complicated inter-play between unionisation and political attitudes. In very broad terms in the twentieth century, the greater the unionisation of a given industry, town or region, the more likely has been the shift towards the Labour Party in voting terms. Psephological studies in the post-1945 period have established that the chances of a trade unionist voting Labour are certainly greater than for a non-trade unionist.[17] Moreover, the political working-class militant has almost always been a trade unionist, and the trade union has normally been the school through which the young militant has first learnt his political ideas. There are exceptions, of course, not least with the emergence of youth movements attached to militant groups of the left; but to find a working-class militant not also

active in his union is very unusual. There are some wider implications
of this matter. There is nothing in England (until fairly recently one
could have written Britain) comparable with the appeal to the masses
of anarchism in Catalonia, or republicanism in Ireland, or revolutionary
ideas for sections of the Parisian workers. Certainly for the ordinary
British worker in the twentieth century, untouched by political radicalism, the changing attitudes pushing him towards the labour movement
have mostly come as a result of the trade union connection. Politics
cannot, of course, be ignored, and there are, therefore, two questions
to be asked of the thirties in order to disentangle the reasons for the
slow, and only partial, recovery of the labour movement from the
catastrophe of 1931. The first relates to the quality of the political
leadership being offered and the second to the trade union history of
the decade.

Labour's political history of the thirties is for the most part unin-
spiring and certainly ineffective. The Parliamentary Labour Party was
wedded to the constitutional struggle inside Westminster, and while the
Labour Party in certain parts of the country, notably London, was at
times more lively, the general tone of the movement was largely
dictated by the national leadership.[18] The immediate problem after
1931 was to re-build the confidence of the Labour rank and file. A
great deal of the energy of the first half of the decade went into the
preparation and discussion of programmes and policies for a future
Labour administration; and these were presented successively at annual
conferences from 1932. But coherent ideas about the future, though
welcome and necessary, were no substitute for action on contemporary
problems. It was above all the working-class electorate which Labour
had to convince as to its ability to govern. The Labour victory in the
London elections of 1934 was an important advance; recognised as such
abroad as well as in Britain. But there was no comparable achievement
at the national level, and the most striking political characteristic of the
1930s was the way in which successive Conservative governments were
able to ignore, on all fundamental matters, the Labour Party inside
Westminster and the political and industrial movements outside. There
were occasions when the government had to submit to outraged public
opinion — the retreat on the new UAB regulations in January-February
1935[19] or the resignation of Samuel Hoare after the disclosure of the
negotiations with Laval in late 1936[20] — but the exceptions were few,
and government submission was never simply the result of Labour
Party pressure alone. Conservative governments in the 1930s went their
own way, and the feebleness of the Labour opposition was a constant

theme of political journalists and the leader writers.[21] The crux of the
matter was not only or even mainly to be found in Westminster; George
Lansbury's leadership, between the two general elections of 1931 and
1935, was within limits quite skilful and energetic, given the poor
quality of much of the PLP and the small size of the Parliamentary
group. The problem was much more the general approach to politics
in the country at large. The most serious social question of the 1930s
was unemployment. The extent of unemployment was never fully
revealed in official statistics[22] and long-term or short-term unemployment affected all sections of manual workers, with only obvious exceptions, such as railwaymen, printing workers, and most municipal
workers. Apart from these favoured groups, there was never full
employment in the post-1945 sense, and even in the relatively active
years of the mid-1930s, seasonal fluctuations in employment were to
be found in most trades and industries.[23] The TUC always insisted that
the unemployed worker was the responsibility of his appropriate union,
but most unemployed had not been union members; and for the rest the
TUC advocated provision of social facilities. It was all half-hearted and
certainly ineffectual. What was not lacking in vigour was the denunciation by the Labour leadership of bodies outside the Labour Party who
were engaged in agitation on behalf of the unemployed. The most
important group was the National Unemployed Workers' Movement,
who organised national hunger marches to London on four occasions:
1930, 1932, 1934 and 1936. Not one of these marches was officially
supported, and in the first two the local Labour parties and trades
councils were specifically instructed to offer no help. The reason was
that the NUWM was led by Communists. Only in 1936 – and to a
lesser extent in 1934 – were the bans imposed widely disregarded. In
the 1936 reception in Hyde Park Attlee was among a number of leading
Labour personalities who spoke from one of the platforms.[24] The most
extraordinary episode, which illuminates more clearly than any other
the stupid, reactionary and politically self-destructive attitudes of the
Labour establishment, was the negative approach adopted towards the
Jarrow march of October-November 1936. The march was organised
by Ellen Wilkinson, the sitting MP, and the Town Council; and the
Conservative agent for the Division, Councillor Suddick, was among the
advance guard of the march. The continuous publicity the Jarrow March
achieved was enormous: far greater than any of the NUWM marches.
The TUC, the Labour Party National Executive and the National Council
of Labour all adopted a policy of non-co-operation. The 1936 Edinburgh
Labour Conference, which met just before the Jarrow March began, gave

it no specific approval.[25]

Everyone in the Labour movement was concerned with unemploy-ment; the bitterness of these years has not been exaggerated. But it was not until the annual conference of the autumn of 1936 that the Labour Party set up a special Commission of Inquiry into the Depressed Areas,[26] and the general failure to maintain a national campaign against the major social evil of the decade was typical of Labour's general political attitudes and approaches. Despite, for example, the extra-ordinary passion evoked by the Spanish Civil War, the Labour Party never conducted a major campaign throughout the country on any of the issues involved, except for a desultory attempt after the 1937 annual conference. All the major political initiatives and campaigns for which the 1930s are remembered were conducted either against the expressed wishes of the Labour leadership or without their approval. The decade is connected above all with the hunger marches, the street battles against Mosley and his Fascists, and Spain. The energies un-loosed around these issues, and the political commitment entered into, can at no point be credited to the Labour leaders. Only against appease-ment is the record acceptable, but even here the fatal weakness was the restriction of the struggle to the parliamentary scene, and, many would argue, because of the confusions about rearmament. Be that as it may, to characterise the Labour leadership as incompetent and ineffectual is not only a judgement of hindsight; it was precisely and exactly what was pronounced at the time, by increasing numbers of Labour activists as well as by non-Labour commentators.[27]

The crucial influence in the political decisions of the 1930s made in the name of the official Labour movement belonged to the leading trade unionists of the period, and in particular to Ernie Bevin and Walter Citrine. They had important allies among Labour politicians, notably Hugh Dalton, but real power remained with the trade union leaders. There was no major issue of the decade that went against the wishes of Bevin and his colleagues in the TUC. Through their 'ownership' of the block vote they controlled the annual conferences of both the TUC and the Labour Party; above all they dominated the National Council of Labour. Henry Pelling, in his *Short History of the Labour Party*, very properly heads the chapter dealing with the 1930s as 'The General Council's Party'.

It was the product of exceptional circumstances that the National Council of Labour emerged during the 1930s as a policy-making body. In 1921 the newly formed General Council of the TUC joined in equal numbers with the National Executive of the Labour Party and the

Parliamentary Labour Party to form the National Joint Council of the
Labour Party and the TUC. After the massive Labour defeat of 1931,
the TUC circulated a memorandum during the winter of 1931-2 propo-
sing changes in the structure and functions of the National Joint
Council of Labour, so renamed in 1934. The unions were allocated
seven seats on the National Council as against three each for the executive of the Labour Party, and the PLP, and they had always in reserve
the block vote of their unions to bludgeon opposition at both the TUC
and the Labour Party conferences.[28] They left, however, nothing to
chance. The National Council of Labour, according to Citrine, always
met the day before the national executive committee of the Labour
Party; and it would have been very difficult for the latter to proffer
a political line different from that already stated by the Council of
Labour.[29] As an American observer wrote in 1938:

> Although the acceptance of National Council's decisions theoreti-
> cally is voluntary on the part of the participating organisations, the
> structure of the Trade Union and Labour movements and the pub-
> licity given to Council action makes rejection by the Labour Party
> or the Parliamentary Labour Party virtually impossible. If, on a
> specific issue, the Labour parliamentary group declined to accept
> the National Council's stand, Labour's opponents would gain
> support for the frequent charge that the forces of labour are divided.
> Similarly, considerable embarrassment would result if the Party
> conference or Executive refused to accept as final a Council decision.
> To maintain the front of internal harmony, declarations of the
> National Council of Labour must be followed. (D.E. McHenry,
> *The Labour Party in Transition, 1931-8,* p. 43.)

There was, in fact, no change of any serious divergence from the policies of the National Council of Labour. Under the 1918 constitution,
the National Executive Committee of the Labour Party was elected by
the annual conference as a whole. Thirteen of the executive total of 23
were to represent affiliated organisations (mainly trade unions); five
were to represent local Labour parties; and there were four seats
reserved for women. The Treasurer was to be elected separately. Out of
the 23 members in 1936-7, the unions had 12 members and the Royal
Arsenal Co-operative Society one. The 1937 Conference made a minor
constitutional change which at the time was exaggeratedly regarded as
an important victory for democracy. The membership of local constituency parties had been increasing throughout the thirties and there was

growing discontent with the system of election of the Labour parties'
representatives (which were subject to the unions' block votes). Debate
on a revised Constitution had been deferred for two years running, but
after a long debate in 1937 the proposal to increase the representatives
of the local Labour parties by five to seven was carried by 1,408,000
to 1,134,000. It was not often the margin was so narrow, or that some
of the big battalions were defeated. A second resolution, easily passed,
restricted voting for the Labour Party representatives to the constituency parties themselves. These changes, hailed with naïve enthusiasm,
made no difference to Labour policy in any fundamental way. Their
main result was to 'imprison' certain of the left who, having been
elected to the Party Executive, now had to accept collective responsibility for many decisions with which they did not agree. The unions
still controlled a majority on the national executive and on the National
Council of Labour and there was always the block vote in reserve at
annual conferences.[30]

There was, undoubtedly, a heightening of political understanding,
and a radicalisation of attitudes in the last few years before the outbreak of war, but very little can be attributed in any direct way to the
official leadership of the Labour movement. The rank and file certainly
found many outlets for their energies and numerous opportunities by
which to demonstrate their commitment. Many of the initiatives for
which the thirties are remembered, such as the extraordinary success
of the Left Book Club, or the notable radicalisation of the university
students and of groups of intellectuals, were developed quite outside
the Labour establishment. The heightened political consciousness
was to expand further under the conditions of World War Two, and its
origin is therefore, important. But before the war began in the late
summer of 1939 our estimate must be different, and in the analysis of
the general working-class electorate, very different. It is, in other words,
doubtful how far the undoubted radicalisation of certain groups among
the manual working class and the lower middle class really penetrated
the mass of the working people. The impact of unemployment and job
insecurity must have had some effect, just as the improvement in real
incomes for those who remained in work is another factor to be
evaluated; and their political consequences may be opposed. But
it is by no means certain that the Labour Party was making significant
inroads into the voting patterns of the 1935 general election. The
psephological evidence of 1936-9 suggests that it is an open question, if
war had not come, whether Labour would have won the general
election of 1940.[31] What was missing, apart from a credible political

leadership at the national level, was unionisation of any size or significance.

IV

The peak affiliation of trade unionists to the TUC was in the years 1919 and 1920, when around six and a half million workers were represented. By the year of the General Strike this total had fallen to about four and a quarter million, and following the defeat of the General Strike, the number affiliated to the TUC remained under four million from 1927 until 1935. Trade union numbers were moving slowly upwards after 1932, the trough year of the depression, but while the total was just over four million in 1936, the five million mark was not passed until 1940, the first full year of the war.

The failure of the trade union movement to initiate a forward development was widely commented on at the time, most notably by G.D.H. Cole. There had taken place, during the whole of the inter-war years, certain basic shifts in occupational structure which inevitably had direct consequences for the unions. Mining and textiles were sectors of severe contraction; engineering (especially in the 'new industries'), building and distribution were among the growth points in numbers employed. Trade unionism was still strong in the older industries: those in which unionisation had already been well established before 1914. It was in the newer, post-World War One industries that unionisation was weak or practically non-existent. The distributive trades, the largest insured occupational group, with some 10 per cent only in unions, were exceptionally difficult to organise; and by the middle 1930s the rapidly growing automobile industry was still largely unorganised, except for the fully skilled workers, and unionisation was weak among other branches of the metal trades located in the Midlands and the London metropolitan area. Road transport workers, including busmen, were mostly unorganised, with London as an outstanding exception for the passenger services; and building, despite the boom of the 1930s, had low proportions of organised workers, even among some groups of craftsmen. 'In all', wrote G.D.H. Cole,

> out of about twelve million employed males over 16, the Trade Unions at the end of 1936 had enrolled about four and a half million. Out of about five million employed women, they had enrolled only 800,000 of whom 350,000 were non-manual workers.[32]

The fastest-growing manual unions were the two general unions – the Transport and General Workers and the General and Municipal Workers.

Both had high turnovers of membership, a relatively high proportion of Irish Catholic labour — often industrially militant but always anti-Communist — and a hierarchical structure which kept power firmly in the hands of the full-time officials. These two general unions exercised the leading influence within the TUC during the 1930s.[33] They could be, and on occasions were, defeated by the combined vote of other big unions, but in Bevin they had the outstanding union personality of the decade, and behind Bevin was Citrine, General Secretary of the TUC, whose efficiency and competence worked for the same policies and programmes as those of Bevin. Their personal relationship, according to Citrine, was not close,[34] but this did not affect their close agreement on most issues of policy.

The TUC, and the individual unions affiliated to it, had a distinctly unsuccessful record during the 1930s. The geographical shift in employ-ment opportunities towards the Midlands and London and the South-East was not matched by a new vigour in union activity. There was nothing in Britain to set against the achievements of the CIO in the United States, or the French unions during the Popular Front period. The mass of the working people were not stirred into new forms of action and activity at their places of work. The union leaders lacked imagination, inspiration and energy. Their minds were closed to the new possibilities that had opened up before them; and in the case of Bevin and those in the majority on the General Council of the TUC, anti-Communism was a stronger sentiment than anti-employer. The opportunities open to them were never exploited and this rejection aggravated several times over the failures on the political front.

Unionisation was the key to the revitalisation of the labour move-ment after the traumatic defeats of the early 1930s. Only a direct appeal to the economic self-interest of the unorganised masses would have begun that transformation of consciousness without which the shift to a new politics could not be expected to take place. The 1935 general election showed clearly that, except in Lancashire, there was a close connection between trade unionism and the Labour vote. G.D.H. Cole, writing in 1939, said this in the closing paragraph of his study of contemporary trade unionism:

At the present moment British trade unionism is in serious danger of missing its chance. As I write, a boom has been in full swing; but very little attempt has been made to take advantage of it. Now, assuredly, is the time both for the organised workers to win advances by militant action and for the movement to bring effectively within its ranks the mass of unorganised workers in the rapidly-developing new industries and services. But the old leaders only found, in the recent boom, a new excuse for inaction. Every sign of trade union militancy can now be attributed to the machinations of a handful of Communists, who have somehow found the art of being in a hundred places at once, and in whom it is regarded as a crime to induce non-Unionists to join a Trade Union, or to suggest to the workers that they had better act promptly, while profits are high, instead of staying quiet until the precarious chance passes away. In 1934 the Trades Union Congress made a great affair of celebrating the centenary of the Tolpuddle Martyrs. If George Loveless and his friends got into trouble with the police today, they would probably be told that they were a pack of Communist agitators, who deserved all they got.[35]

There were groups to the left of the Labour Party which might have offered alternative leadership, although as the thirties went along, the Communist Party became the only serious possibility. The Independent Labour Party was already a declining force by the late 1920s, and after 1931 it was dominated by the internal discussions concerning continued affiliation or disaffiliation from the Labour Party, a not untypical example of the extraordinary importance of doctrinal issues within a sectarian group of the left. The background to these intense and interminable discussions was, after all, the greatest crisis in the history of world capitalism. When the matter was finally resolved by the Bradford Conference at the end of July 1932, those who remained within the ILP quickly found themselves in a political isolation from which the party never recovered; and apart from the traditional loyalties of Glasgow voters, the ILP, in theory and in practice, was largely irrelevant to the problems of the decade.[36] The Socialist League had a somewhat different history. It was founded in 1932 at Leicester immediately before the Labour Party conference by the amalgamation of the Society for Socialist Inquiry and Propaganda (SSIP) with that part of the ILP, led by Frank Wise, which refused to accept the disaffiliation policy. The Socialist League was dominated by intellectuals, although J.T. Murphy did later become its secretary. The League was not in any serious way concerned with developing a base within the manual workers, but its presence certainly kept alive the debate about principles and policies which was important for the health of the movement. A statement of this kind does not offer blanket approval for the arguments put forward by the Socialist League at any one particular time; it is as a general point of substance that it is made.[37]

The weakness of the Socialist League lay in its lack of contact with the industrial working class; and it was this which was the main difference between the ILP and the Socialist League on the one side, and the Communist Party on the other. At the beginning of the 1930s the CP was still enmeshed within the sectarian stupidities of the social-Fascist period; a policy well summed up by Miliband as 'grotesque in Britain', and 'catastrophic in Germany'.[38] With the economic depression steadily worsening through 1930 and 1931, the Communist Party both increased its sectarianism and eroded its influence. The very promising grouping of disaffiliated Labour parties which went under the name of the National Left Wing movement had been disbanded on CP instructions, and the National Minority movement was allowed to run down into ineffectiveness.[39] The basic assumption upon which the British Communist Party operated — derived from the decisions of the Sixth World Congress of the Communist International and refracted through policy-making bodies such as the Red International of Labour Unions — was the belief that the crisis of world capitalism was irreversible and would inevitably encourage a revolutionary upsurge on a world scale. Whatever happened, or was likely to happen elsewhere, this was never a possibility in Britain; and what Keynes said of a volume by von Hayek — that it was an example 'of how, starting with a mistake, a remorseless logician can end up in Bedlam'[40] could equally be applied to some at least of the theoretical writings at this time of R. Palme Dutt, the Communist Party's outstanding theoretician. It is a very common error of vulgar Marxism which assumes a simple and direct relationship between material conditions and social consciousness; and the blind faith with which the British CP followed the Moscow line produced a situation in which they were at their lowest point, in numbers and influence, during the years of the worst-ever crisis of capitalism. By the beginning of the decade their total membership was between three and four thousand; according to the report of the 1932 Battersea Congress they had 5,400 members, of whom 60 per cent were unemployed. The party's influence in the trade union movement had shrunk to quite negligible proportions, and it engaged in such puerile exercises as the expulsion of Maxton from the League against Imperialism, and of J.T. Murphy from the Communist Party itself for his advocacy of increased Anglo-Soviet trade.[41]

The Communist Party did not, however, remain in this situation of political impotence. It had never wholly lost touch with social reality, and it contained within its membership a number of outstanding per-

sonalities. Some, like Arthur Horner, had been disciplined for refusing
to accept completely the sectarian approach to trade union work;[42]
others, like Wal Hannington, continued their independent activity on
behalf of the unemployed. The party, moreover, had always retained
a foothold in industrial affairs, and it was, unquestionably, a party of
working people, almost all of whom, and this was true of the leadership as well as the rank and file, had come to politics through the trade
union movement. Their own native political sense began to reassert itself, and the changing line of the Comintern, much accelerated after the
victory of the Nazis in Germany in 1933, permitted a fresh turn
towards the mass organisations of the British working class. The
Communist Party never overcame the consequences of these disastrous
years between 1928 and 1932, and the mistrust and bad faith engendered were never forgotten.[43] Despite the inspiration which it provided
in the second half of the decade, and the energy it imparted to the
whole movement, the Communist Party was a prisoner of its past as
well as of its continuing acceptance of Moscow directives. But without
the Communist Party, the history of the 1930s, from about 1933-4
onwards, would have been very different. They provided the dynamic
behind the organisation of the hunger marches, much of the opposition
on the streets to Mosley, and a great deal of the extraordinary efforts
that went to support Republican Spain in the Civil War, including the
recruitment of a high proportion of the British section of the International Brigade from among party members.[44] The party was also
central to the radicalisation of the student movement, and its influence
over intellectuals was not inconsiderable.[45] Whether the Communist
Party ought to have concentrated more of its efforts on industrial
work, in particular on the establishment of rank and file movements, is
an interesting question upon which further research is required. There
was, in fact, a good deal more Communist shop-floor activity than has
so far been recorded: in aircraft factories, for example. It could be
argued, as Hinton and Hyman have done for the years before the
General Strike, that a different strategy might have achieved qualita-
tively different results. Against the background of international Fascism
and the menace of war, the argument is highly debatable; but it is one
that certainly demands debate.[46]

V

The second strand to working-class 'interest' in the 1930s was the
emergence of Fascism, its political and social implications, and the slide
towards war. The central international issue of the decade for the labour

movement, after the accession to power of Hitler in 1933, became rearmament in the context of British foreign policy; and as we shall see in the discussion which follows, this was a matter which could not be divorced from the more general problems of leadership and policies within the labour movement as a whole.

The labour movement entered the 1930s with foreign policy attitudes that had remained broadly unchanged since the end of the First World War. Throughout the 1920s there was relatively little dissension on foreign policy issues within the labour movement — except for the extreme left — and there was never anything comparable with the bitter controversies of the second half of the 1930s. The majority of the movement were against the Versailles Treaty, which they regarded as predatory and unjust, and they were firmly wedded to the ideals of the League of Nations, especially to policies of disarmament; and running right through the positions adopted was a strand of political pacificism inherited from the ILP during the war years, and increasingly intertwined, in the 1920s, with the view that all wars were imperialist wars. The left of the movement — the more militant groups within the ILP, and the Communist Party — took more extreme positions. They regarded the League of Nations as a thieves' kitchen of the victorious imperialist powers; and they were much more vehement on issues such as Indian independence.[47] The 1930s were different: above all in the bitter divisions over the issues of the war and defence. The decade divided roughly into two main phases, with no very clear chronological division between them. The first phase saw a marked growth in pacifist and anti-war attitudes, in many ways stronger and more deeply felt than in the 1920s. The second, overlapping in time, was the varying reaction to the coming to power of Fascism in Germany in the early months of 1933.

The spread and deepening of pacifist attitudes was an interesting phenomenon. In his book on the British Labour Party published in 1929, Egon Wertheimer, the German social democrat, had already underlined the pacifist and anti-war tendency which he regarded as deeper than anywhere else in Europe. After noting that many people in Europe still affirmed the heroism of war as a positive virtue, he continued:

> In Great Britain the nation, both individually and as a whole, was inwardly less prepared for the War [i.e. 1914] . The mentality of the people underwent a more direct change than on the Continent, where every able-bodied young man was trained for war by having

to serve from one to three years as a soldier, and throughout his life took for granted the possibility of being called upon for active war service. To the average Englishman the War was incomparably more upsetting and more incomprehensible. And in England, therefore, the reactions of the War were far more profound than in any other country. In spite of victory, Great Britain is at heart much more anxious to do anything possible to ensure that such a thing shall never happen again. The romance of war, for Great Britain, is dead. Although she signed the Pact of Paris only subject to reservations, in her heart she has outlawed war without reservations. Great Britain is, as a nation, more instinctively pacifist than any other nation in Europe.[48]

What happened in the thirties was that the various strands of pacifism and anti-war sentiment received much encouragement and support from a number of different sources which together provided a very powerful backing to the trend of ideas and values revealed by the quotation from Wertheimer. One was the quite extraordinary spate of war novels, plays, memoirs and autobiographies published in the late 1920s and early 1930s, all of which revealed a deep and profound disillusionment with, and revulsion from, the events of 1914-18.[49] They were, of course, almost all by middle-class authors. The roll-call — not a comprehensive one — is impressive:

1928	Edmund Blunden: *Undertones of War*
	Siegfried Sassoon: *Memoirs of a Fox-Hunting Man*
	R.C. Sheriff: *Journey's End*
	Richard Aldington: *Death of a Hero*
1929	Robert Graves: *Goodbye to All That*
	Erich Maria Remarque: *All Quiet on the Western Front*
1930	Frederic Manning: *Her Privates We*
	Siegfried Sassoon: *Memoirs of an Infantry Officer*
1931	Wilfred Owen: *Poems*, in an edition by Edmund Blunden

In 1933 Beverley Nichols capitalised on this anti-war sentiment with a widely circulated *Cry Havoc*.[50]

In September 1931 came the first large-scale violation of peace with the occupation of Manchuria by the Japanese. General opinion in Britain towards Japan at this time was equivocal, although the labour movement, and the left in particular, analysed the Japanese forward move into Asia as a direct expression of deepening capitalist crisis.[51]

Pacifist and anti-war attitudes continued to burgeon, and the arrival of
Hitler in Germany made little or no immediate difference. The Oxford
Union resolution — 'That this House will in no circumstances fight for
its King and Country' — passed on 9 February 1933 was largely pacifist
in origin; more significant was the successful resolution at the Hastings
Labour Party conference in the autumn of 1933 — six months after
Hitler had come to power — which underlined 'the deepening of
imperialist and capitalist rivalries'. The resolution went on to make the
point that the working class of any country had no quarrel with the
working class of any other county, and the Conference pledged itself to
take no part in war. Hugh Dalton, who accepted the resolution on
behalf of the National Executive, explained in his memoirs that there
was no immediate alternative to what he described as a 'wildly unreal'
incident, and that all the Executive could do was to avoid being put in
a similar situation in the future.[52] The majority leadership of the
Labour Party and especially that of the TUC never accepted the argument that 'all wars are imperialist wars', but it was held by a powerful
current of opinion within the rank and file. The London Labour
Leagues of Youth, for example, submitted a resolution to the party
conference in October 1934; and while it was not accepted, it was
endorsed prior to the conference at an unofficial meeting of some 70
delegates. It read, in part:

> We do not propose to be betrayed as was the youth of this country
> in 1914. In no circumstances would it be in the interests of the
> youth of this country for the Labour Movement to support a war in
> defence of any capitalist state. 'Defence of Democracy and the
> League of Nations' might well be made the excuse for another world
> war . . . If there is an immediate danger of war involving this country
> while the Labour Party is in opposition, a General Strike should be
> immediately declared, and the opportunity seized to expel the
> existing Government and institute a Socialist Government.[53]

There was a more specific version of this general argument in an article
published by R.F. Andrews[54] in the November 1934 issue of *Labour
Monthly*. The quotation given below is a rather sharper statement of
the original article, re-printed in a pamphlet entitled *The Labour Party
and the Menace of War*'.

> But supposing Fascist Germany attacks the USSR: are you not in
> favour of the workers supporting the British or French governments

in an attack on Fascist Germany? [After putting the question, Andrews went on:] *Under no circumstances*. Such action would help the German capitalists to represent the war as one of self-defence: it would immensely strengthen the British capitalists, and weaken the British workers: it would put British Imperialism, in the event of victory, in a favourable position for going on to attack the USSR: it would mean suppressing the inevitable and natural revolts of the peoples of India and the British Empire.

This interesting statement, which represented the official line of the Communist Party, was made nearly two years after Hitler came to power, and after the Soviet Union, with French support, had become a member of the League of Nations in September 1934. It was only to be a few months — in early May 1935 — before there was signed the treaty of mutual assistance between France and the Soviet Union.[55]

The growth of 'straight' pacifist sentiments, based upon absolutist attitudes and often derived from religious beliefs, found organisational expression in the Peace Pledge Union, which by mid-1936, less than two years from its foundation, had 100,000 members.[56] More central to the politics of the labour movement was the considerable literature on the private manufacture of armaments and of the war-encouraging activities of the arms manufacturers. These were not new themes in the 1930s,[57] but much of the evidence came together in this decade. In the United States the Nye Committee investigations gave a major impetus to the debate; in 1934 Engelbrecht and Hanighen published their famous *Merchants of Death*; and in the same year the British Labour Party issued Noel-Baker's *Hawkers of Death*. Such was the groundswell of public opinion that the National Government in 1935 set up the Royal Commission on the Private Manufacture of Arms. Its recommendations did not include public ownership, but only stricter control, and the rapidly worsening international situation quickly buried its Report; but during the period of its existence, the Commission was indirectly responsible for a considerable pamphlet literature which much encouraged anti-war attitudes in general.[58] The sale of arms by governments in the post-1945 period, partly to influence regional power conflicts, partly to assist balance-of-payments problems, would have been inconceivable to the labour movement of the 1930s. Political obscenity, they would have argued, could go no further.

The Labour Party leadership at the 1934 Conference had remedied the previous year's resolution by a statement which brought the party into support of collective security within the League of Nations. The

following year's conference at Brighton was quite unequivocal. A
month earlier, in September 1935, Walter Citrine at the TUC had spelt
out the argument that collective security could mean war. At the
Brighton Labour Party Conference Bevin savaged Lansbury in a speech
of great power, and with the aid of the trade union block vote the
pacifist position was overwhelmed.[59] The conference went on record
for collective security under the League of Nations. The background
to the discussions included the collective security vote in the national
Peace Ballot in June, the condemnation of Italian aggression against
Abyssinia by the Council of the League of Nations in October, and the
apparent support of the Baldwin government for the policy of the
League in the matter of sanctions against Italy — 'we have no intention
of wavering in giving effect, as a member of the collective system, to
our obligations under the Government,' Sir John Simon, Foreign
Secretary, later said, shortly before the dissolution of Parliament.
Baldwin was provided with a splendid opportunity to go to the country.
Although the election issues were more concerned with home than
foreign affairs — very noticeably so from the speeches of the leading
Conservatives — the general election of 1935 was a piece of brilliant
timing and opportunism by Baldwin, and while there were many
reasons why Labour had such a poor result, one was that they were
completely out-manoeuvred on foreign policy issues.[60] The abortive
Hoare-Laval agreement showed how politically innocent the Labour
leadership had been.[61]

The next two years saw the resolution of the rearmament question.
Defence expenditure, in absolute terms, increased slightly in 1934-5
and then by a larger figure in 1935-6. In the latter year it was 3 per
cent of GNP;[62] and during 1936 and 1937 the issue of support or not
for British rearmament was at the centre of Labour Party politics. Hugh
Dalton was chairman of the Labour Party between the two annual conferences of 1936 and 1937, and Bevin was chairman of the TUC over
most of the same period. They took it in turn to preside over the
National Council of Labour, and these two men were the main archi-
tects of the change. The arguments which Dalton, Bevin and others of
the right wing and centre of the Labour Party used to win support for
rearmament were simple, and for many, compelling: that with or without collective security organised through the League, the presence of
international Fascism demanded a more effective level of armaments.
The issue was often presented as separate from that of foreign policy. In
the middle of 1937, Dalton included in his diary part of the speech which
helped to convince a majority of his parliamentary colleagues to abstain

on the defence estimates:

> I personally could not and would not face my constituents, inclu-
> ding those who lived in mining villages which had been bombed in
> the Great War, and answer, with what would seem to them a Parlia-
> mentary quibble, the question: 'Did you vote against all means of
> defending us from bombers next time? Did you vote against our
> having even a single anti-aircraft gun?' Others had spoken of the
> difficulty of convincing 'our own people' that we should not go on
> voting against defence. . . . But, in addition to holding the support
> of 'our own people' who were not yet numerous enough to give us
> victory, lay the problem of turning over at least two million others
> who must become 'our own people', unless we were to waste all
> our political lines in opposition. I was absolutely convinced that
> there was no chance whatever of doing this if we continued to vote
> against arms. We were putting a gun into the hands of the National
> Government, with which they would shoot down our candidates
> like rabbits all over the country.[63]

The Parliamentary Labour Party first abstained on the defence estimates in July 1937, and at the annual conference later in the year, the
Dalton line, as set out in a policy document, *International Policy and
Defence*, was overwhelmingly accepted. What was meant was spelled
out before the Conference by the *Daily Herald* — still Bevin's paper in
general approach. The new policy, wrote the *Herald*, would remove
'all misunderstandings and check all misrepresentations of Labour's
decisions to withdraw opposition to the re-armament programme.'
Henceforth, the majority position was clear: support for rearmament
while continuing opposition to the Government's foreign policy.[64]
    The response of the left was vigorous, vociferous and muddled:
muddled in that the arguments for opposing rearmament were sometimes incoherently structured and insufficiently thought through,
sometimes wrong in relation to the problems being confronted. The
issue was a much more difficult question to be coherent and logical
about than most of the left appreciated and the case against support
for rearmament had to be argued not just in terms of foreign policy
but widened to include the tactics and strategy of the labour movement as a whole. The left had a strong case to argue, but it was seldom
presented in its entirety, and too often the partial arguments advanced
sounded, and indeed were, flawed.
    Aneurin Bevan offered the most coherent statement for the opposi-

tion to rearmament in a speech to the October 1937 Labour Party
conference. This was the conference which endorsed, with a large
majority, the decision of the PLP not to vote against the defence estimates of the National Government. The debate was on the Executive
Committee's Report on 'International Policy and Defence'. J.R. Clynes
opened on behalf of the EC, and Sydney Silverman countered with a
speech that was an all-too-common mix of good sense and woolly
sentiment. On the one hand there was a clear statement of the main
argument of the left, that armaments were integrally related to foreign
policy; but it was accompanied with traditional guilt feelings towards
the German people and their treatment by the Versailles settlement,
and rhetorical statements about an international police force, collective
security, and the like.[65] Just before the lunch break Ernie Bevin came
to the rostrum in support of the EC: his speech included the statement
which follows:

> I am bound to confess that the more determined attitude taken by
> Great Britain has revived hopes that Britain may yet stand beside
> the liberty-loving nations of the world, and it has put new heart into
> many of those International Movements.

It was a not untypical Bevin speech at his lowest level of competence;
bombastic, windy, and in political terms, semi-literate. It was delivered
just about a year before the Munich agreement.

Aneurin Bevan was the first speaker after lunch, and he delivered
one of the great orations of his career. He began by ridiculing Bevin for
the statement quoted:

> Mr Ernest Bevin said this morning that the present re-armament has
> given reassurance to the peace-loving and democratic nations of
> Central Europe. Does he really mean that the Government's rearma-
> ment policy has re-assured Czechoslovakia in the light of the Govern-
> ment's betrayal of Abyssinia, of China, of Spain? I am very sorry
> that Mr Bevin used that argument, because those words will be re-
> produced all over the country in Conservative leaflets at the next
> General Election — that the National Government by its re-arma-
> ment, has re-assured democratic and peace-loving nations. I am
> very sorry indeed that Mr Bevin used those words, and I hope that
> Czechoslovakia will not take them at their face value.

There is, Bevan went on, only one justification for supporting the rearmament programme of the government, and that can only be the acceptance of the foreign policy the Labour Party was advocating. He noted that, in any case, a government with the size of the present majority in the House of Commons could not be denied arms; and he went on to develop an argument that ought to have remained at the centre of the whole debate: that the left would without hesitation recommend and support a rearmament programme to carry through a socialist internationalist policy. This was an argument which ought to have been both expanded and constantly reiterated. The rapidly growing menace of war − the call for arms for Spain − the extension of the world conflict by the Japanese action in China − all demanded a tough realism on international issues which would accept the necessity for arms provided that the policies of appeasement and collaboration with the Fascist powers were ended. But this part of the thesis, crucial though it was to the intellectual and political credibility of the left, was more often than not muffled or ignored. The mixture of old ideas was very powerful, with many strands of anti-war sentiment closely inter-woven with the general texture of political attitudes on the left, and the reaction to the political behaviour of the men of Munich − before and after the actual event − was so bitter that a straight opposition to re-armament on the single ground of policy seemed overwhelmingly ob-vious. The willingness to support an armament programme in the interests of an anti-Fascist foreign policy was either not accepted, or, where accepted, was usually never defined.

Bevan made a further point, however, that has been overlooked by most commentators on the period. He argued that the question of support, or not, for rearmament was inextricably involved with the more general problems of labour tactics and strategy. People like him-self had been engaged for many years in an endeavour to instil more militant attitudes into the leadership of the movement, inside the House of Commons and outside. As noted above, on all the central issues of the 1930s − unemployment, the hunger marchers, the oppo-sition to Mosley, the campaign for Spain − the actions and activity of the Labour and trade union leaders could hardly be described as vigorous or inspiring. Rather the contrary. Their caution, concern for respectability, and apparent lack of awareness at the grim prospects of a world in which international Fascism seemed to move from one triumph to another with the support of the British ruling class, were the despair and desolation of many in Britain well beyond the groups of the traditional left. Bevan was highly conscious of these problems, and he saw the acceptance of the rearmament policy as further evidence of the

Labour and trade union leadership refusing to commit themselves to outright opposition to this hated gcvernment. In the same speech to the 1937 Conference, Bevan enunciated his theme:

> You cannot collaborate, you cannot accept the logic of collaboration on a first class issue like rearmament, and at the same time evade the implication of collaboration all along the line when the occasion demands it. Therefore, the Conference is not merely discussing foreign policy; it is discussing the spiritual and the physical independence of the working-class movement of this country. It has faced us in the House of Commons, and will face us in the months to come.[66]

This speech by Aneurin Bevan in the early autumn of 1937 provided, or could have provided, the left with a series of coherent and viable propositions with which to oppose their own leadership and to argue the case against support for rearmament in the country at large. But the case was, in fact, rarely debated in these terms. For most, the relationship between arms and foreign policy was sufficient, and as appeasement of the Fascist powers appeared more and more blatant, there seemed to be less to define and more to emphasise. Two aspects of the argument tended to be either completely ignored, or played down. One, and the most important, was that the opposition to rearmament was not based on pacifist grounds, and the left would be prepared to support an arms programme provided the foreign policy was one of total opposition to the Fascist powers. This was what Bevan said, although even he, in this particular speech, did not unravel the argument with the precision required; and it was rarely stated by anyone else with sufficient clarity. And yet without these implications being clearly comprehended, on both sides, the opposition to rearmament appeared obtuse and unrealistic. Some later commentators, despite their general sympathy with the left, have understood the politics of opposition in these terms.[67] Certainly, the failure to develop the argument fully, to take it forward from Bevan's 1937 speech, and make clear all its implications undoubtedly encouraged illusions and a distinctly muffled understanding of the left's position.

The Communist Party had a particular twist to its general line of opposition to the National Government's foreign policy that further confused the issue. With most of what Aneurin Bevan had said in his 1937 Conference speech the Communists were in full agreement. But they also had a very special involvement with the foreign policy of the

Soviet Union; and right up to the beginning of the war in September 1939 they were arguing that a united front of France, the UK and the Soviet Union could ensure the maintenance of world peace, and that talk of an 'inevitable' war was defeatist. Almost all opponents of appeasement were, of course, in favour of the first of these propositions: that an international 'peace-front' was central to any policy concerned to halt Fascist aggression. But the Communist Party logic encouraged euphoric and unrealistic statements about the positive chances of overcoming the appeasers. While the general argument was often ingeniously formulated — as in Palme Dutt's speech at the September 1938 Congress of the British Communist Party — the effect was undoubtedly to encourage illusions about the possibilities of maintaining European peace, and thereby to narrow and limit the debate on the rearmament question.[68]

The second part of the argument, more often than not taken for granted than actually spoken or written about, was the relationship between the Labour leaders, their general feebleness in opposition and their support for the rearmament programme of the Conservative government. No one was in doubt about the weakness of the Labour opposition, but Bevan's insistence upon 'the spiritual and physical independence of the working-class movement' was rarely explicitly formulated; although always understood and appreciated. The official inactivity of the Labour leadership outside Parliament on the Spanish Civil War was indeed scandalous, from the early days when the non-intervention policy was accepted by both the Labour Party and the TUC[69] to the half-hearted and short-lived campaign following the 1937 Labour Party Conference.[70] On the central question of foreign policy which inevitably dominated British politics in the years immediately preceeding the beginnings of the World War Two, the desperation which seized many beyond the identifiable political left is a fact of major significance in any appreciation of the political arguments and tactics of this period. R.H. Tawney, a middle-of-the-road socialist and not one identified with the left of the labour movement at any time in his career, wrote a remarkable letter to the *Manchester Guardian* in March 1938 which illuminated the anxiety and despondency which overtook those confronted with a government believed to be actively abetting the policies of international Fascism. Tawney's letter, spread over two columns, ended with the paragraph given below. It is unlikely he can have believed his advice would be accepted by the ultra-constitutionalists of the Parliamentary Labour Party:

If the Government can be compelled to change its policy by action in the House of Commons, well and good. If not, would not the Labour Party do better — together with such Liberals and Conservatives as may on these issues agree with it — to withdraw temporarily from Parliament and devote its whole energy to arousing in the country a movement of which the Cabinet must take notice? If a Government can behave as this Government is behaving, democracy is a farce. Why should we make and pay for armaments to carry out a policy precisely the opposite from that which our rulers put forward when they asked to be returned to power?[71]

There were always confusions on the left of the labour movement, some of which were shared by many others well beyond the Liberal and Labour parties. There was, for example, the almost universal exaggeration of the size and scale of the Nazi rearmament programme, and the mistaken belief that the differences between the arms power of Britain, or of Britain and France combined, were always overwhelmingly in favour of Germany.[72] There was, too, the equally common exaggeration about the physical effects of aerial bombardment on cities.[73] As discussed already, the left's ideas were nearly always a mixture of guilt feelings about Versailles, hatred of Fascism, the imperialist causes of wars, the unshaken belief that the British ruling class was in general sympathy with the Nazis as the bulwark against Communism, with the result that the case for opposing the rearmament programme was often inadequately and incompletely presented. Nevertheless, it was a more powerful argument than later generations have usually accepted, and it certainly cannot be understood without a close appreciation of the ways in which contemporary opponents of rearmament appreciated, rightly or wrongly, the political realities of their time. Hindsight can sometimes simplify and distort; contemporaries are not always wrong.

IV

The labour movement in Britain in 1937 published a large number of local papers, usually monthly. Most were printed centrally by the Ripley Printing Society of Nottingham, and each issue was of a standard format and size of eight pages. The papers were published by the sponsoring body — most frequently the Divisional Labour Party — and theirs was the financial responsibility. They offered an outlet for local news and views, with sometimes a column from the local MP, if Labour, or the prospective Labour candidate; but there were also syndicated articles, including a review section, available to local editors, and these were quite widely used. These papers offer, at a rather elementary level of analysis, a guide to what local editors thought would be interesting to their readers. There was, it is clear from the items printed, some choice available.

In the May 1937 issues, from a sample of some thirty local papers, Spain, Russia and the reviews column were the most common choices of the syndicated articles. 'A Woman in Spain' was an account of a recent visit by Maude Rogerson on behalf of the Youth Foodship Committee; the reviews column had a number of book reviews to choose from, including Orwell's *Road to Wigan Pier* and Huberman's *Man's Wordly Goods;* and the Russian article was 'May Day in the Soviet Union' by C.H. Parmenter, who had been a member of the British trade union delegation in 1936. Most of the papers which carried the book reviews section — a minority of the total — included a short review of a symposium *What is Ahead of Us* by G.D.H. Cole, Wickham Steed and others; and usually there was excerpted one quotation only, from Sidney Webb:

> At the close of the year 1936, when nearly all the world seems staggering towards economic and social catastrophe, the USSR stands out from every other country as supremely the Land of Hope.

The growing political sympathy towards the Soviet Union is one of the most striking characteristics of the British Labour movement in the 1930s. After the ending of the wars of intervention the greater part of the labour movement in Britain was not noticeably concerned with internal Russian affairs during the 1920s.[74] There was quite a widespread sympathy, but in no way was its intensity or range comparable with the decade which followed. It was the coincidence in time between the beginnings of the world economic crisis at the end of the twenties and the launching of the First Five Year Plan that brought about a much deeper interest in contemporary Russia. Russia's industrialisation apparently offered the sharpest contrast to the collapse of output and the rapid rise in unemployment levels in the capitalist world. As dole queues lengthened, and families became grimly familiar with the problems of subsistence without work, it was not in any way extraordinary that large numbers of working people and intellectuals should begin to look upon Soviet Russia with a new understanding and appreciation. The Webbs mirrored these changes. As Beatrice wrote on 14 May 1932:

Now this new structure and function in Soviet Russia would not be exciting attention among intellectuals and social reformers of all countries — notably by the way, USA and Great Britain, if it were not for the material and moral collapse of capitalism. If prosperity were to return . . . the manifest defects and breakdowns — the lack of luxuries, if not necessities in the USSR — and more important than all the restriction on the personal freedom of the brain-worker — would enable a hostile world to write it off as a failure. But today there is the fact that this new social order is not only promising work and wages to all its subjects, but alone among states is increasing the material resources and improving the health and education of its people. Instead of the despairing apathy, or cynical listlessness of capitalist countries there is enthusiasm and devoted service on the part of millions of workers in Soviet Russia. The one big drawback lies in the activities of the G.P.U. and even here the USA runs Russia very close.[75]

The emphasis Beatrice Webb gave to conditions in the capitalist world as of crucial importance in encouraging sympathetic attitudes towards the Soviet Union must always be appreciated in any political analysis of the 1930s. It is a serious defect of much commentary upon this period that it fails to understand the point of view from which Russia was judged at the time by working people and intellectuals in the West. For the mass of the people in Britain, unemployment and insecurity of jobs were the biggest social facts of their lives. Economic historians have rightly emphasised the improvement in real incomes during the thirties, but what mattered for most working people was the regularity of a job. Historical hindsight commends the labour mobility which helped to encourage the growth of the new industries in the Midlands and the London area, but at the time, even with a job, life was not altogether sweet for the Welshman, separated from his family, and living an alienated existence in Oxford or Slough. Unemployment, it must be recalled, was always above the million mark, even in 1937, the most prosperous year of the decade;[76] and the widely accepted claim that the Soviet Union was growing so rapidly that there was a labour shortage, especially of skilled workers, had an enormous appeal; as did the general contrast between the unused resources of the West and the planned economy of Russia. The literature favourable to the Soviet Union was quite remarkable in its volume, and much of it emanated from non-Communist sources.

During the two years before the May Day marches of 1937 there was available to the Anglo-Saxon reader a selection of material on Russia which covered almost every aspect of social life. Most important of all was the Webbs' *Soviet Communism. A New Civilisation?* published in 1935, with the question-mark removed for the edition of 1937. Among other works may be noted the autobiography of Anna Louise Strong, *I Change Worlds,* which included an account of her fifteen years in the Soviet Union; J.G. Crowther's *Soviet Science;* Dr L. Segal's *USSR Handbook;* Joshua Kunitz' *Dawn over Samarkand. The Rebirth of Central Asia;* Beatrice King's *Changing Man: The Soviet Education System. Moscow Admits a Critic* which Sir Bernard Pares published in 1936, was especially notable as the views of an eminent Russian scholar who had altered his position from hostility to one of general sympathy with the Soviet regime.[77]

A complete list of books and pamphlets favourable to the Soviet Union published in the 1930s would be a very long one: the evidence to the contrary, on the other hand, was not particularly impressive. The most important work was undoubtedly W.H. Chamberlin's *Russia's Iron Age,* published in 1934, the same year that he left the Soviet Union after a stay of twelve years as correspondent of the *Christian Science Monitor.* His first book, published in 1930, had been a balanced, not unfavourable, account; it was the experience of collectivisation and the famines of 1932-3 that finally disillusioned him.[78] No other critical volume in the 1930s — in the English language — was as effective as *Russia's Iron Age,* but it is doubtful if it was to be found on the shelves of many militant workers. For the rest, there were two books that the May Day marchers might have read. One was Walter Citrine's *I Search for Truth in Russia* published in 1936, and the second was the American Andrew Smith's *I Was a Soviet Worker* which in the month of May 1937 was put out in a special cheap edition by the Right Book Club: an imprint that inevitably severely restricted both its circulation and influence. Citrine's book was much more widely commented on. It was the published version of a diary he kept, and it is in fact a more honest and fair account than was accepted by many at the time of its publication. It was naturally damned by the left, but even a man as moderate as Arthur Woodburn, reviewing the book in *Plebs,* thought Citrine was overdoing his criticisms.[79] The main reason for the failure to impress was Citrine's own political position. He was the super-bureaucrat who stood for right-wing policies in the movement; he had accepted a knighthood in 1935, a much more damning gesture than it was to be forty years later,[80] and it was taken for granted that his political prejudices would cloud his assessment of a Communist regime.

Moreover, he was not by any means unsympathetically reviewed in the bourgeois press, and that, too, implied that his judgement belonged to the wrong side of the argument.

One of the more important aspects of the pro-Soviet attitudes of the 1930s was the image that became accepted of Joseph Stalin. Citrine, for example, while highly sceptical about the processes of democracy in the Soviet Union, gave a not unflattering account of the man himself. Western countries' politicians and diplomats had little personal contact upon which to build an appraisal, and Stalin gave few interviews, but the general impression he seems to have made upon the West was of a highly controlled, intelligent leader. His conversation with Howard, the American publisher, and with H.G. Wells, were widely reported.[81] Typical of the liberal attitude was the assessment of Stalin in John Gunther's *Inside Europe,* a book which had a phenomenal sale in Britain and America. It was first published in January 1936 and by October the British edition had gone through fourteen impressions, and a second revised edition came out in the same month. Gunther gave a blistering account of Hitler and Mussolini and their regimes, but while he did not slur over the harsh facts of the 'Iron Age', his approach to the Soviet Union was immeasurably more understanding and sympathetic. The commentary on Stalin which follows is taken from the first edition:

> Let no one think that Stalin is a thug. It would be idle to pretend that he could take a chair in fine arts at Harvard; nevertheless his learning is both broad and deep, especially in philosophy and history. One is instinctively tempted to consider this reticent Georgian as a roughneck, a man of instincts and muscle, not of brains. But his speeches quote Plato, Don Quixote, Daudet; he knew all about the monkey trial at Dayton and the composition of Lloyd George's shadow cabinet and the unionisation of workers in America; in his talk with Wells he showed as much knowledge of Cromwell and the Chartists as Wells himself . . .
>
> Nor are his manners bad. He sees visitors only very rarely, but one and all they report his soberness, his respectful attention to their questions, his attempt to put them at their ease . . . He is the only dictator who is *serene.*[82]

And so on. The new Soviet Constitution of 1936, often referred to as the Stalin Constitution, underlined for much of the outside world the move away from the 'Iron Age' towards a more democratic way of life.

But by 1937 the overriding factor in the general assessment of the Soviet Union was her foreign policy in relation to the growing threat of war from the Fascist countries. The public statements of Litvinov and other Soviet diplomats and leaders — including Stalin — were in striking contrast to the speeches and actions of the National Government in Britain. The deal with Italy over Abyssinia, and above all, the attitude taken towards the Spanish Republic, convinced the greater part of the British labour movement that the leading Conservatives were not to be trusted. Whatever qualifications historians in recent years have placed upon the motivations of Chamberlain and Halifax,[83] contemporaries well outside the left were as convinced as the left was that what became known as 'appeasement' was to be equated with pro-Fascist attitudes, whether pro-Italian or pro-German, or both. What Harold Nicolson was writing in his diary for the 6 June 1938:

> People of the governing classes think only of their own fortunes, which means hatred of the Reds. This creates a perfectly artificial but at present most effective secret bond between ourselves and Hitler. Our class interests, on both sides, cut across our national interests.[84]

— was what informed contemporaries of a liberal or socialist disposition were saying publicly at the time. The issues were grimly defined. Unlike most previous periods of crisis, there was nothing to come between the ordinary people and their 'betters' — no jingoism to arouse the masses to the twentieth-century version of the King and Church mobs; no Labour government to confuse loyalties. What was starkly revealed to the rank and file activists of the labour movement was the inability of the ruling groups to provide employment at home, and their pursuit of a foreign policy that was a craven betrayal of the interests of peace under the threat of international Fascism. The Soviet Union stood in sharply defined contrast; and it was clearly and specifically understood that without the Soviet Union there could be no solid front of opposition to Fascism.

It was the years of the Purge Trials — 1936 to 1938 — that might have begun the first serious debate of the thirties among the left about the nature of Soviet society, although the rapidly worsening international situation in fact considerably restricted — indeed often inhibited — the range and depth of the discussion. The trials were without question a gigantic confidence trick; a frame-up of extraordinary ingenuity and invention. The problem for the historian in trying to explain the reactions of contemporaries is to avoid apologetics on the one hand, and on the other the now more commonly accepted simplistic argument that the left and their allies were the naive dupes of their own dogmas.[85]

There had been a number of Trials in Russia in the late twenties and early thirties, most of them concerned with so-called 'wrecking' activities. The only one that made any impact on British public opinion was the engineers' trial of 1933.[86] But the political trials of the later years were of quite a different order, in that they involved leading Bolsheviks, and purported to show connections between the Fascist governments of Germany and Japan, and the opposition inside Russia.[87]

The first of these major trials, which began on 19 August 1936, was of Kamenev and Zinoviev and fourteen other defendants. The charges included the formation of a 'Trotskyite-Zinovievite Terrorist Centre', the murder of Kirov, and plots to assassinate the Stalinist leadership. Several defendants in their 'confessions' implicated Bukharin, Rykov, Tomsky and a number of former Trotskyists. All sixteen defendants were found guilty on 24 August, and executed a few days later. Tomsky committed suicide on 25 August. Proceedings were begun against Bukharin and Rykov, but terminated in the second week of September, mainly, it is believed, because of opposition within the Central Committee. Bukharin had already been relieved of his editorship of *Isvestia* in August, although his name remained on the mast-head until mid-January 1937.

The second major trial commenced on 23 January 1937. The defendants were Piatakov, Sokolnikov, Radek and fourteen others. Again the 'confessions' implicated Bukharin and Rykov. All seventeen were found guilty, and only Radek, Sokolnikov and two others were not awarded the death penalty. Bukharin was arrested shortly after the end of the trial, and thirteen months later was one of nineteen defendants at the last of the great public trials. Along with him were Rykov, Krestinsky and Rakovsky. The confessions included acknowledgement of the murder of Kuibyshev and Maxim Gorky, wrecking and sabotage, contact with the Fascist powers, and so on. Bukharin was shot on 15 March 1938.

As is now fully accepted, the 'confessions' in these trials were manufactured and rehearsed, and the defendants played their roles as actors. The last speeches in court of Radek and especially of Bukharin were meant by them to be read in code by the outside world, and this is how, many years later, they are now understood.[88] But at the time relatively few observers on the left in Britain outside the Trotskyist or Russian emigre groups appreciated even in part what was happening, although

the range and degree of scepticism was greater than is often believed.
The most remarkable analysis by a contemporary British writer was
published in *Unto Caesar* (1938) by F.A. Voigt, the *Manchester
Guardian*'s diplomatic correspondent and, despite his conservatism,
one of the outstanding journalists of the decade. His main commentary
on the trials, rather oddly, was tucked away in a six-page footnote at
the end of the volume.[89] The *Manchester Guardian* itself, of all the
liberal and radical newspapers, was the most cogent and compelling in
its scepticism. The weekly *New Statesman,* much nearer to the labour
movement than the *Manchester Guardian,* was equally sceptical and, as
always, it articulated clearly the problems and dilemmas of the situation. The biggest question mark over all the trials was the 'confessions'
freely given. The trials were open, dozens of Western journalists and
diplomats were present, and the defendants were mostly old Bolsheviks,
including outstanding leaders with long records of revolutionary
activity. There were no signs of physical torture; Radek joked with the
Court, and Bukharin argued with, and rejected, a number of the accusations put to him by Vishinsky, the Prosecutor. But no one — except
Krestinsky in the last trial and he retracted the following day — spoke a
word which suggested the evidence was faked.[90] A careful analysis of
the verbatim record was a different matter, as Voigt and others argued.
It was the confessions, freely given, that made Koestler's hypothesis in
Darkness at Noon seem plausible, although his reconstruction has now
been specifically rejected by recent biographers of both Radek and
Bukharin.[91] At the time, the question: 'Why did no one stand up as
Georgi Dimitrov.had done in the Reichstag Trial, and denounce the
Court?' was the most telling argument from those who were defending
Soviet justice; and it was a question and an argument which went far
beyond Communist Party circles. Kingsley Martin put it to Trotsky in
their interview in April 1937, and the author of the famous *New
Statesman* article at the time of the Radek trial had made the same
point.[92] Isaac Deutscher put exactly the same question into the mind
of Trotsky's son, Leon Sedov, who was living in Paris during the
period of the trials. It is a remarkable passage:

> Overworked, penniless, and anxious about his father Lyova (Sedov)
> lived permanently in this labyrinth. He went on echoing his father's
> arguments, denunciations, and hopes. But with each of the trials
> something snapped in him. His brightest memories of childhood and
> adolescence have been bound up with the men in the dock:
> Kamenev was his uncle; Bukharin almost an affectionate playmate;

Rakovsky, Smirnov, Muralov, and so many others — elder friends & comrades, all ardently admired for their revolutionary virtues and courage. He brooded over their degradation and could not reconcile himself to it. How had it been possible to break every one of them and make them crawl through so much mud and blood? Would at least one of them not stand up in the dock, abjure his confession, and tear in shreds all the false and terrible accusations? In vain Lyova waited for this to happen . . . [93]

The second aspect of the trials which greatly confused contemporaries was the volume of testimony which insisted upon the correctness of the judicial procedures, the good health of the defendants, and the openness of their testimony. The newspapers reporting the trials were world-wide, the pamphlet and book literature considerable; and the weight of the testimony was overwhelming in favour of the genuineness of the trials. D.N. Pritt, a much-respected left-wing lawyer, published an account of the first trial; Dudley Collard one of the second. The Anglo-Russian Parliamentary Committee's account of this second trial was introduced by Neil Maclean, Labour MP for Glasgow Govan, with a preface by R.T. Miller, the Moscow correspondent of the *Daily Herald*.[94] When Joseph E. Davies — American Ambassador to the Soviet Union from 1936 to 1938 — published his *Mission to Moscow* in 1942, it was revealed that Davies had been convinced of the guilt of the accused and that he had been sending cables back to Washington to that effect. Davies, it should be added, was a lawyer and businessman of good sense and judgement, and his book made a considerable impression when it first appeared. His views in 1937-8 were not, of course, known by the general public; he is quoted here only as an example of a common reaction towards the trials.[95]

The most important factor affecting the attitude taken towards the Soviet trials was the international situation. The events of the years leading up to 1939 underlined the arguments of the Soviet Foreign Minister, Litvinov, that only the firm and steadfast opposition of the Western bourgeois democracies and the Soviet Union would withstand Fascist aggression. As noted above, the activists of the labour movement in Britain were motivated by their hatred of the Conservative government for its domestic policies and increasingly distrustful of its line of appeasement. Spain was the touchstone. The British government backed non-intervention, which to the labour rank and file meant a free hand for Italy and Germany; the Soviet Union gave tangible aid to the Republican government. The issues were understood in simple,

compelling terms, and while there was disquiet among many about the
trials, matters of peace and war were of overriding importance. The
bombing of Guernica evoked a passionately emotional response among
the British left while at the time — because, it must be remembered, the
main facts were hidden — the reaction to the trials was, at best, cerebral.
Bukharin was shot on 15 March 1938, three days after the Germans
marched into Austria. His appeal to the world, made in his last speech
to the court, was drowned by the increasing noise of war machines preparing for action.

It must not, however, be thought that there was no critical response
in Britain to the trials. The right wing of the labour movement was, not
unnaturally, sceptical and questioning. Walter Citrine joined with
Friedrich Adler (the secretary of the Socialist International) in sending
a telegram at the time of the Zinoviev-Kanenev trial, asking for clem-
ency; and Adler's pamphlet on the trial was published in English by the
Labour Party.[96] It was given publicity, among other places, by Leonard
Woolf in the *New Statesman.* Brailsford, the outstanding socialist
journalist of the inter-war years, consistently regretted and sharply
criticised the trials.[97] The most persistent sceptic was Emrys Hughes,
editor of the Scottish *Forward,* who flatly refused to believe that the
confessions were genuine, and who throughout the period of the three
trials was constantly attacking court procedures and asking his readers
to disbelieve the 'fantastic' stories that were being told by the defendants.[98] *Plebs,* organ of the National Council of Labour Colleges, was
also hostile, although since it was a monthly it had less of a consistent
editorial policy than *Forward.* The *New Statesman* was probing in its
appraisal, and no one who read its columns carefully could remain
without doubts and anxieties.[99] All these journals, including the
Manchester Guardian, opened their columns to arguments on both
sides, with the most wide-ranging and interesting selection in the
columns of the *Manchester Guardian.*[100] Communist Party apologists
used all these outlets to argue their case, although the *Daily Worker*
itself never published critical letters. The only journal in which, for a
time, Communists and other members of the left debated their opposing views was in the Trotskyist-supported monthly *Controversy.*[101]
Left News, the widely circulated monthly journal of the Left Book
Club, was almost completely dominated in its writings on the Moscow
trials by Ivor Montagu, a highly persuasive and sophisticated apologist,
John Strachey and Pat Sloan, the last being among the most assiduous
of all pro-Soviet letter-writers to the national press.

The problem for the historian is to explain why the response within

the British left was different from that in France or the United States.
In both these countries there was a vocal and vociferous minority who
either questioned seriously the trials or denied absolutely their valid-
ity.[102] We have seen that there was a sizeable area of scepticism on the
left, too, in Britain, but it was not of the same order of magnitude as in
either France or America. In part, the British situation reflected the
domination of the labourist ethos and the absence of any serious current
of Marxism before the mid-1930s. The practical common sense of the
majority of Labour Party members could hold two discordant themes
in their minds, without apparent contradiction and without any obvious
intellectual tension. One was a broad scepticism in general about democracy in the Soviet Union — a scepticism often barely articulated at
this time — and the other was a vision of the absence of unemployment,
rising living standards and the fierce opposition in international affairs
to Fascism. In the long run, largely because the facts became authen-
ticated without qualification, the 'broad scepticism' about the failure
of internal democracy became confirmed. But the question concerning
national differences can also be posed in another way: why was it that
in Britain in the 1930s there was no Trotskyist movement of any significance, either before 1936 or encouraged by the evidence of the
Trials themselves?

The answer, naturally, is complicated, and it is not within the context of this present essay that it can be fully answered. Certainly the
point already made, the absence of any significant Marxist studies in
Britain before the thirties, is also relevant here. (The Marxism of *Plebs*
and the NCLC was an essentially practical and practice-orientated set of
ideas.) The controversies inside the Russian Communist Party in the
1920s found little echo in Britain, and the *Bulletin Oppozitisii* does not
seem to have been available, except occasionally in obscure bookshops,
or from America. One of the notable aspects of the history of the
British CP is how few leading personalities who resigned or were expelled during the first thirty years or so of its existence went on to
engage in pelemic or argument. There were, therefore, very few people
who had the ability to begin to develop an intellectual base of anti-
Stalinism. Reg Groves was one of the exceptions,[103] but there was
much disagreement on tactics among the very small groups of Trotskyists in the 1930s, and throughout the period they were a mere shadow
of marginal significance within the labour movement. The situation
began to change after the arrival of the South African Trotskyists at the
end of the decade, and the emergence of Jock Haston as an indigenous
leader of political authority; but here one is already moving into the

years of war.[104]

All these things help to explain, without by any means providing the complete answer, the absence of any British name on John Dewey's Commission of Inquiry into the allegations made against Trotsky in the Soviet trials.[105] There was in being a rather shadowy British Committee in Defence of Trotsky, but its adherents outside the very limited number of British Trotskyists were few.[106] When the Trotsky Closed Archives at Harvard are finally open to scholars, there will be more to report. In the meantime, it must be emphasised again that the weak reaction at the time to the Soviet trials among the British left, while owing something to the intellectual and political traditions of the movement, must be analysed mainly in terms of the growing alienation of labour activists from the National Government in general against the increasingly darkening background of international Fascism and the threat of war.

Louis Fischer, one of the great journalists of the inter-war years, who had no illusions during the period of the trials, explained his attitude in 1941. His position can be taken as an exemplar for many of his generation:

> Why, instead of holding my tongue, did I not come out in 1937 or 1938 as a critic of Soviet regime? It is not so easy to throw away the vision to which one has been attached for fifteen years. Moreover, in 1938, the Soviet government's foreign policy was still effectively anti-appeasement and anti-fascist, much more so than England's or France's or America's. It helped China with arms to fight Japanese aggression. It helped Spain with arms to fight the Nazis and Mussolini. It encouraged Czechoslovakia to stand firm against Hitler. I did not know how long it would last. But while it lasted, I hesitated to throw stones in public. Even now I think I was right.[107]

VI

By the time May Day 1938 came round the hopes and expectations of a year earlier had sharply diminished; indeed, had been shown to be illusory. The London bus strike failed, and the powerful Rank and File movement was broken by Ernest Bevin. Mick Kane of the Harworth miners was sentenced to two years' imprisonment and eleven others, including a miner's wife, got sentences of fifteen months to four months. The sentences were among the most severe on trade unionists for many a year, and alarm and protest spread through the whole labour movement.[108] It was part of the price paid for the ending of company

unionism in the Nottinghamshire coalfield, although Spencer drove a
very hard bargain and did not retire from union affairs until 1945. But
above all else, the internatonal situation had worsened steadily. During
the first weeks of March 1938 the Nazis marched into Vienna and
Austria was annexed to Germany; Franco launched a successful offen-
sive on the Aragon front which was to divide Barcelona from Madrid,
and no informed observer could now expect anything but the final
victory of the Fascists. Six months later the betrayal of Czechoslovakia
by the Munich agreement removed the equivalent of over thirty divisions from the anti-Nazi opposition.

The response of the British labour leadership was, predictably,
myopic and parochial. It was also wholly ineffectual against a Government that, in Mowat's words, appeared 'impregnable and imperturb-
able'.[109] Inside the House of Commons the Parliamentary Labour
Party could still exert itself competently, as during the spring and
summer of 1938 when it assailed the Government over the Italian
attacks on British shipping in the Mediterranean. But as always the
protests remained inside the walls of Westminster, and very much more
was needed if the country as a whole, and the full strength of the labour
movement in particular, was to be roused into vigorous action. It would
be straining a counter-factual argument too far to argue that the Labour
politicians or the trade union leaders could have been expected to act
very differently from their actual behaviour in these years. They were in
general consistent and predictable within their own traditions. Their
socialism was of the gradualist kind absorbed, directly or indirectly,
from the Fabians, and it was integrally related to the Labourist theory
and practice of the nineteenth century. Above all, they had no understanding of the nature of power in society; their theory of the state was
of the most simplistic and constitutional variety. Parliament was omni-
competent, the supreme legislative authority; and a majority in the
House of Commons was a mandate to implement the programme on
which the party had been elected. Clement Attlee wrote *The Labour
Party in Perspective* for the Left Book Club in 1937; and his arguments
defined the political understanding within which all the senior members of the party moved and had their being. Attlee emphasised the
way in which British parliamentary institutions had adapted themselves
in the past to changes in the class structure of society, and he took it
wholly for granted that this would continue in the future when an
anti-capitalist body — the Labour Party — achieved an overall majority
in the Commons. It is, therefore, understandable that for the Labour
leaders in Parliament their political lives were devoted to winning the

next election; an objective which dominated and shaped all their thinking. Hence the extraordinary concentration upon what a future Labour government would do that is such a striking feature of Labour Party discussion throughout the 1930s.[110]

It was Harold Laski's major contribution to the debates of the thirties that above all others he insisted upon the need for a new theoretical understanding of capitalist society. We must, he wrote in November 1936,

> re-shape the Labour Party into a fighting instrument of the working-class movement. If we fail to do so, the defeat of the movement is certain. But to re-shape the movement into a fighting movement means the conscious adoption by it of a social philosophy which recognises the nature of the battle in which we are engaged. Until the movement has such a philosophy it can adapt neither the strategy nor the tactics required by the situation. Its present drift arises precisely because such a social philosophy is absent. The leaders of the Labour Party think of themselves as an Opposition which can inherit the mantle of office from the government in precisely the same way as the Conservatives used to inherit it from the Liberals. They forget that the classic form of representative government only worked in this country because Conservatives and Liberals alike accepted the private ownership of the means of production as the postulate upon which all their fundamental policies were built. The Labour Party rejects that postulate. Its accession to power would, therefore, raise problems for those who believe in capitalism different in kind from those to which we have been so far accustomed in the years since 1689. Either the Labour Party must adapt its technique to the faith it is supposed to hold, or it must reveal itself for what it otherwise is — a revised form of the Liberal Party which wants larger social reforms in the periods of upward trends in the trade-cycle. If it decides to be the latter, it is then clear that socialists have no place in its membership. For socialism is a method of action as well as an ultimate goal; and its method of action is built upon the recognition that it is the historic mission of the working-class to capture the state and so end the private ownership of the means of production. The whole technique of socialism as a living philosophy flows from that pivotal insight.[111]

Constitutionalism does not, however, necessarily confer upon its advocates the degree of caution and constraint accepted by Attlee and his colleagues. Even on their own terms they pursued a disastrously narrow approach to the central political problem with which they were concerned: how to convince a much larger proportion of the electorate to switch to voting Labour at the next General Election. As they saw the problem, political struggle was confined to Parliament; and political education outside Westminster was therefore largely a matter of producing blueprints for the future which would convert more people than ever before of Labour's suitability to govern. The pioneering days of the labour movement were long past; the national equivalent of the street-corner meeting was acceptable only on very special occasions but not as a customary part of the processes of political education. Their emotional, as well as their political, responses were by now deeply flawed. No one would guess, reading Attlee's book in 1937, that liberal democracy, of which the Labour Party was a central institution, was in grave and serious crisis; nor would it have been possible to deduce from the political and industrial behaviour of the leaders of the movement that only two years or so remained before a world war would again occur. They had, by this time, fixed reference points from which, regardless of any change in the external situation, they never deviated. One was their dedication to the parliamentary system and what they understood to be the rules of the game, which, *inter alia,* excluded totally the use of industrial action for political ends;[112] a second was the inviolability of the hierarchical power structure of which they themselves were the dominant figures and the main beneficiaries; and the third was anti-Communism, a concept elastic enough to cover most of the opposition from positions to the left of themselves.

These last two assumptions were demonstrated explicitly in the history of the London bus strike. It began, it will be recalled, on the first of May 1937, and it ended after four weeks when the EC of the Transport Union, on Bevin's insistence, revoked the plenary powers of the Central Bus Committee and ordered a return to work.[113] Throughout the strike the trams, trolley buses and Underground had continued to operate normally. Bevin refused to call them out, and although there was a rank and file movement among the tramwaymen, it was too weak to win a majority decision. It is possible to argue that the Central Bus Committee — led by the leaders of the Rank and File movement — ought to have called off the strike when the EC earlier suggested it, since some of the demands had been granted, and others were negotiable. This is certainly, by hindsight, an arguable thesis, given that it was not going to be possible to persuade the other London passenger transport workers to defy Bevin, and that the latter was determined to

smash the Rank and File movement. There is certainly no room for
conjecture on this last point. The busmen went back to work on 28
May 1937; on 4 June the EC suspended the constitution of the Central
Bus Committee and ordered an enquiry into the conduct of its members. Arthur Deakin acted as secretary to the Committee of Enquiry,
and he presented its report and recommendations to the July 1937
Biennial Delegate Conference. Papworth, Payne and Jones were expelled from the union; four others were debarred from holding office
for varying periods; membership of the Rank and File movement was
declared incompatible with membership of the union. Bevin never could
brook opposition; he was always ungenerous to his critics; and as he got
older he became paranoid about those who opposed him. In Deakin,
Bevin had a lieutenant who, in his trade union career, was meaner in
spirit than he was himself. The shattering of the busmen's movement
was vindictive in spirit and vicious in its operation, and the repercussions went far beyond London Transport. Here was one of the few
successful trade union initiatives of the thirties. The London buses were
far from completely organised when the Rank and File movement
showed what could be done; and a victory in the summer of 1937
would have given heart to the whole world of trade unionism. As it was,
another failure, once again imposed from the top of the union machine,
further undermined confidence and encouraged the widespread feelings
of helplessness against the conservatism of the Labour establishment.

As far as it is possible to judge from the evidence at present available,
the trade union leaders, and Bevin in particular, played a rather less
prominent role in the politics of the Labour Party in the period immediately before the outbreak of war than they had done up to the annual
conference of 1937.[114] The political side of the movement continued to
be riven by dissensions over strategy and tactics. The Unity campaign,
launched in January 1937, was an attempt to encourage more vigorous
political activity in the country by the movement as a whole. Despite
well-attended and enthusiastic meetings, proscription by the executive
of the Labour Party brought the campaign to an end within less than
six months.[115] It was soon followed by demands for a Popular Front of
all progressive political forces, under the leadership of the Labour
Party, in order to develop the maximum weight of political opinion
against the government.[116] There was no Labour Party conference in
1938 — Munich was not thought sufficiently critical to warrant the
convening of an emergency conference — and the first phase of the
Popular Front agitation died away. The second began in January 1939
when Stafford Cripps, supported by Nye Bevan and G.R. Strauss among

others, circulated a document, without executive permission, arguing for 'a positive policy of peace by collective action' and a Popular Front campaign in the country.[117] The Labour Party executive took immediate action, and when Cripps refused to be disciplined, he was expelled; to be followed soon after by Nye Bevan, Sir Charles Trevelyan and G.R. Strauss. Some recalcitrant local Labour parties were disaffiliated. An appeal by Cripps against his expulsion was turned down by the Whitsuntide Conference at Southport.

This is not the place to evaluate the tactics of the United Front or the Popular Front; but what needs to be emphasised is that the Labour Party leadership had nothing to offer as an alternative save the injunctions to take note of the parliamentary battles at Westminster and to prepare for the next General Election. Neither the trade union leaders nor the Labour Party politicians took any serious measure of the grim and menacing situation they found themselves in. They gave no hope or inspiration to their own supporters, and were tough, uncompromising and energetic only when their own positions of power were threatened: hence the political and industrial expulsions and excommunications. They placated those who were their enemies, and discouraged their friends. Attlee's leadership of the Labour Party was never secure between the date of his election in late 1935 and the acceptance of office in the Churchill coalition in the spring of 1940;[118] and the divisions and controversies about the leadership confirmed their political weightlessness in the country at large.

It was, therefore, in keeping with the declining morale of the ordinary party worker that the annual conference at Whitsuntide 1939 was the quietest, and the most listless, of any in the decade that had just passed. The Conference had changed the date of its convening from the traditional October to Whitsun in order to avoid coming only a month after the TUC and thereby being unduly influenced by Congress decisions. But 'to judge by this year's proceedings', the *Annual Register* for 1939 commented, 'the change made little difference'.[119]

By the time this last peacetime Labour conference convened, the Spanish Civil War was over and Franco had been recognised by the British government; Hitler had entered Prague; Italy had seized Albania; and Chamberlain had given his extraordinary guarantee to Poland while conducting desultory negotiations with the Soviet Union. This was the background to the conference. Having refused every initiative to build a firmer base of opposition to the government, and having expelled their main critics, the platform at Southport had nothing to propose to their delegates, except to make certain of their own domination over them.

As Dalton wrote in his memoirs: 'Following Cripps' expulsion [in January 1939] we were in a fight to a finish.'[120] Stirring words, which Dalton never used about the Conservative government in these years. But he was right; they fought, and they won. The conference, thanks especially to the block vote of the unions, acquiesced; and the demoralisation among the delegates which observers commented upon was a fair and proper tribute to the narrow and ungenerous vision of those who were to lead the British labour movement into World War Two.

Notes

1. John A. Mahon, 'For the First of May in London', *International Press Correspondence* (Inprecorr), 16 January 1937: see also *Daily Worker,* 18 January 1937, for a brief report on the ILP amendment to the main resolution.

2. For the history of company unionism in Nottinghamshire see R. Page Arnot, *The Miners in Crisis and War* (1961), Ch.V; A.R. Griffin, *The Miners of Nottinghamshire 1914-1944* (1962), Chs. X and XV; 'Spencer, George Alfred', *Dictionary of Labour Biography,* Vol. I (J.M. Bellamy and J. Saville (eds.), 1972). The article by A.R. and C.P. Griffin in this present volume denies the accuracy of the term 'company unionism'. See above, pp. 144ff. The National Council for Civil Liberties published a Report in March 1937 by its Secretary, Ronald Kidd: *The Harworth Colliery Strike: A Report to the Executive Committee of the National Council for Civil Liberties,* 16p.

3. There is a detailed account in H.A. Clegg, *Labour Relations in London Transport* (Oxford, 1950), pp.103-33 and see also Tony Corfield, *TGWU Record* (March 1962), pp. 42-5. The origins of the movement were described in a penny pamphlet, published probably in late 1932: *The Story of the London Busmen's Rank and File Movement; why it was formed; what it has done; its future.* 16p. The present author interviewed Bert Papworth on two occasions in 1972-3. See also W.J. Brown, *So Far* (1943), pp. 199ff. Brown became Honorary President of the breakaway unions, the National Passenger Workers Union.

4. H.A. Clegg, op. cit., pp. 120ff; Alan Bullock, *The Life and Times of Ernest Bevin,* Vol. I (1960), pp. 606ff.

5. Hugh Thomas, *The Spanish Civil War* (1961), gives the background. The report that Guernica was destroyed by the Germans was made by the four foreign correspondents who alone were in Bilbao at the time of the raid. The best known was probably George Steer of the London *Times.* Apologists for General Franco immediately began putting around the story that Guernica was destroyed by the Basques themselves. The most comprehensive account, which documents in immense detail the responsibility of the Germans, is Herbert R. Southworth, *La destruction de Guernica* (Paris, 1975). It was reviewed in *TLS,* 11 April 1975, by Hugh Thomas. See also the later correspondence from Southworth *et al., Times Literary Supplement,* 23 May, 6 and 20 June, 11 July 1975.

6. A.J.P. Taylor, *English History 1914-1945* (Oxford, 1965), pp. 393ff, is notably perverse about the domestic effects of the Spanish Civil War. His

main argument is that the 'emotional experience of their lifetime' – an unpleasantly patronising phrase – was mostly limited to intellectuals, although he contradicts this by his own acknowledgement (p. 396) that the great majorityof the British who fought in Spain were working-class. Mr Taylor is apparently unaware of the existence of sizeable groups of politically conscious manual workers in the British labour movement. The engineers, for example, were especially active in the Spanish cause; and it may be noted here that the history of the working-class contribution to Aid for Spain is as yet far from being fully documented.

7. A recent essay by John Stevenson, 'Myth and Reality: Britain in the 1930s', *Crisis and Controversy. Essays in Honour of A.J.P. Taylor* (A. Sked and C. Cook (eds.) 1976), pp. 90-109, quotes the police estimate of 12,000 for the 1936 demonstration (p. 100). Criticism of Mr Stevenson's inadequate article – a version of 'pop' history – must be left for another occasion, but it may be pointed out that estimates of demonstrations have always – from the early nineteenth century to the present day – differed widely, according to the source. One of the most important features of the 1936 Hunger March is that while it still did not receive any endorsement from the Labour Establishment, the Reception Committee in London was organised for the first time under the auspices of the London Trades Council, an influential body whose secretary was A.M. Wall; and further, that the response to the marchers from local labour and trade union movements along the various routes was more sympathetic and welcoming than on any previous occasion (although the 1934 March was already notable in this respect). Apart from Wal Hannington's own writings – still a most useful source, especially *Unemployed Struggles* (1936), there is a Ph.D. thesis by Ralph Hayburn, 'The Responses to Unemployment in the 1930s, with particular reference to South-East Lancashire' (University of Hull, 1970).

8. For the Jarrow march, see below, p. 226. For the general background to Oswald Mosley and his Fascist movement, see R. Benewick, *Political Violence and Public Order* (1969).

9. Individual LP membership in 1929 was nearly 230,000. Thereafter, numbers increased steadily each year and by the peak year of 1937 the total was 447,000, of whom 258,000 were men and 189,000 were women: G.D.H. Cole, *A History of the Labour Party from 1914* (1948), App. III. In 1935 membership of the Communist Party was reported as being nearly 8,000; by 1939 it was nearly 20,000. The total number of unionists affiliated to the TUC was 4,164,000 in 1926 and it did not again reach just over 4 million until 1936. In 1937 the total was 4,461,000 and numbers continued to increase by about 200,000 for the next two years: H. Pelling, *A History of British Trade Unionism* (1963), pp. 268-70.

10. Figures from Cole, *History of the Labour Party from 1914, passim.*

11. H. Dalton, *The Fateful Years. Memoirs 1931-1945* (1957), p. 75.

12. There is a useful psephological analysis of Labour in the 1930s in an unpublished thesis by J. Jupp, 'The Left in Britain, 1931-1941' (M.Sc.Econ., London, 1956), p. 567ff.

13. H.J. Laski, 'Some Notes on the General Election', *New Statesman,* 30 November 1935.

14. In municipal politics in Britain after about 1890, the failure of a local strike often led to an enhanced political consciousness which showed itself in an increased vote for independent labour candidates and a decline in support of the Liberal Party. Two early examples were the Bradford Manningham Mills strike of 1891: C. Pearce, *The Manningham Mills*

Strike ... (University of Hull Occasional Papers in Economic and Social History No. 7, 1975); and the political aftermath of the Hull Docks strike of 1893; R. Brown, *Waterfront Organisation in Hull, 1870-1900* (University of Hull Occasional Papers No. 5, 1972).

15. As, of course, did the theoreticians of the Communist International; see *The Programme of the Communist International* adopted in its final form by the Sixth Congress of the CI in 1928.

16. It is reasonable to believe that Labour would have been unlikely to win the General Election, which, if war had not intervened, would have occurred sometime in 1940: D.E. Butler, *The Electoral System in Britain* (1963), p. 184.

17. The literature is voluminous: see R.R. Alford, *Party and Society* (1964); D.E. Butler and D. Stokes, *Political Change in Britain* (1969).

18. The standard history of the Labour Party during the inter-war years is the volume by G.D.H. Cole already cited. An excellent liberal account is in C.L. Mowat, *Britain Between the Wars* (1955), with the most interesting Marxist analysis in R. Miliband, *Parliamentary Socialism* (1963). Miliband is especially informative on the 'constitutionalism' of the Labour leadership.

19. A. Hutt, *The Post-War History of the British Working Class* (1937), pp. 262ff; C.L. Mowat, op.cit., pp. 470-3; N. Branson and M. Heinemann, *Britain in the Nineteen Thirties* (1971), Ch. 3, esp. pp. 32ff.

20. C.L. Mowat, op. cit., pp. 556-63; for a recent account, R.A.C. Parker, 'Great Britain, France and the Ethiopian Crisis, 1935-1936', *English Historical Review*, LXXXIX (1974). Contemporary views which indicated the vigorous opposition to the Hoare-Laval plan were well set out in the review in the *Annual Register* for 1935, pp. 105-6.

21. Cf. the comment of F.A. Voigt to W.P. Crozier, 17 November 1937. *Manchester Guardian* Archives: 'I wish the Labour Party were more on the alert in the House. But it never seems to have any inkling of what goes on anywhere'; quoted in F.R. Gannon, *The British Press and Germany, 1936-1939* (1971), p. 135.

22. Among other reasons because many unemployed who were disallowed benefit would disappear from the Register in subsequent months. A larger problem was the difficulties of calculating the numbers of uninsured persons out of work: *Britain in Recovery* (1938), pp. 91-5.

23. A detailed contemporary study was G.T. Saunders, *Seasonal Variations in Employment* (1936).

24. Ralph Hayburn, 'The Responses to Unemployment in the 1930s, with particular reference to South-East Lancashire' (Hull Ph.D. *passim*, 1970).

25. Ellen Wilkinson, MP for Jarrow, gave an account of the march to London, and the lack of response by the Labour and trade union leadership, in Ch. 12 of *The Town That Was Murdered* (1939). The TUC actually circularised Trades Councils advising them against giving help. In Chesterfield, where the Trades and Labour Council obeyed the circular, the local Conservative Party provided a hot meal and accommodation (ibid., pp. 205-6). See also D.A. Reid, 'Response to Misery: the Circumstances Surrounding the Jarrow Crusade 1936' (B.A. thesis, University of Birmingham, 1970).

26. See Ellen Wilkinson, op. cit., pp. 204-5 for a bitter comment on this Inquiry into the Depressed Areas; and Hugh Dalton's complacent-as-ever remarks in *The Fateful Years*, pp. 118ff. Dalton made no reference in his memoirs to the appeal for support for the Jarrow march made at the Edinburgh Conference in 1936.

27. The correspondence columns of all the Labour and pro-Labour journals,

including the *New Statesman,* were full of complaints about the passivity and lethargy of the Labour and trade union leadership; for a brilliant example of left-wing polemic, see H.N. Brailsford, 'What Next After Edinburgh' *Labour Monthly* (December 1936), pp. 726-30.

28. The 1918 Constitution of the Labour Party is printed in Cole, *History of the Labour Party from 1914,* pp. 71-81; and for the National Council of Labour, ibid., p. 123. See also A. Bullock, *The Life and Times of Ernest Bevin,* Vol. I.(1960), pp. 511-12.

29. A point made by many later observers, but not always understood at the time.

30. There is a short account in Cole, *History of the Labour Party from 1914,* pp. 351-2. Nye Bevan was among those who saw the Bournemouth Conference as a step forward for the left (Foot, op. cit. pp. 267-9); and so did Palme Dutt — with some qualifications — in *Labour Monthly,* pp. 663-4.

31. See note 16 above.

32. G.D.H. Cole, *British Trade Unionism Today* (1939), p. 525. See also the volume by G.D.H. Cole and M.I. Cole, *The Condition of Britain* (1937), Ch. IX, where the same general point was made as in the text, although additional emphasis was placed upon the role of the trade unions in tne maintenance of democratic rights and liberties. The question of civil liberties is not discussed in this essay, but it was an issue of great importance to contemporaries, and certainly accounted for part of the processes of radicalisation. In August 1935 there was held a conference of university and school teachers and those working in scientific research to discuss the question of academic freedom. *The Report of the Conference on Academic Freedom, Oxford, August 1935* (published for the Academic Freedom Committee by W. Heffer & Sons Ltd., Cambridge) is a rare and little known document. For a general survey of civil liberties by the man who did more than anyone else to maintain individual liberties in these years, see Ronald Kidd, *British Liberty in Danger* (1940). Kidd was the founder of the National Council for Civil Liberties early in 1934.

33. Cole, *British Trade Unionism Today,* Pt. IV. Ch. XXIII. H.A. Clegg, *General Union* (1954), *passim;* H. Pelling, *A History of British Trade Unionism* (1963), Ch. X.

34. 'The occasions on which Bevin and I discussed policy outside the (TUC General) Council chamber might be counted on one hand, certainly two.' W. Citrine, *Men and Work* (1964), p. 239.

35. Cole, *British Trade Unionism Today,* pp. 540-1.

36. There is as yet no definite history of the ILP in the 1930s. See for parts of the story, A. Fenner Brockway, *Inside the Left* (1942); Cole, *History of the Labour Party from 1914, passim;* R.E. Dowse, *Left in the Centre* (1966), with a useful bibliography.

37. For the Socialist League, see the essay in this volume by Patrick Seyd.

38. Miliband, *Parliamentary Socialism,* p. 217.

39. J. Redman, *The Communist Party and the Labour Left, 1925-1929* (Reasoner Pamphlets, 1957), 31pp. L.J. MacFarlane, *The British Communist Party* (1966), *passim;* Miliband, op. cit., pp. 153-4.

40. *Economica* (November 1931), p. 394.

41. The J.T. Murphy episode is especially instructive. The story unfolded in the monthly journal, *Communist Review,* April and June 1932. In the June issue was republished the statement of the Political Bureau condemning Murphy's deviation. It first appeared in the *Daily Worker,* 10 May 1932.

42. See the statement by the Political Bureau in *Communist Review* (April

1931). There is a brief discussion of 'Hornerism' in R. Martin, *Communism and the British Trade Unions, 1924-1933* (Oxford, 1969), pp. 120-1.

43. The previous history of the CP was unknown to most of the new recruits who joined in the anti-Fascist years after 1933-4. There was no discussion at all inside the CP of the social-Fascist period. Allen Hutt's lively and influential *Post-War History of the British Working Class* (1937) which was the basic text for CP members had a remarkably muted account (pp. 192-3) of the 1928-32 years, in which the term 'social-Fascist' was not to be found.

44. Including, also, a high proportion of those killed. For a contemporary Communist account, W. Rust, *Britons in Spain* (1939). A list of the British Brigade who were killed will be found pp. 189-99. There is a useful regional analysis in H. Francis, 'Welsh Miners and the Spanish Civil War', *J. of Contemporary History*, Vol. 5, No. 3 (1970), pp. 177-91.

45. The social history of the intellectuals of the 1930s has still to be written, although the materials for its production are abundant. Far too much attention has been paid to the poets, especially the political poets, of the decade, and far too little to the radicalisation of the students, quite large numbers of scientists, sections of the Jewish community and the various social groups — mostly only partially identified so far — who made up the Left Book Club. Among the lesser-known writing that is relevant may be noted: F. Warburg, *An Occupation for a Gentleman* (1959); D.D. Egbert, *Social Radicalism and the Arts: Western Europe* (1970), an essential source book with excellent bibliographies; Malcolm Page, 'The Early Years at Unity Theatre', *Theatre Quarterly*, Vol. 1, No. 4 (October-December 1971). The volumes of *Left Review* have been reprinted by Cass and were the occasion for an illuminating commentary by Edward Thompson, *Times Literary Supplement*, 19 February 1971, pp. 203-4.

46. J. Hinton and R. Hyman, *Trade Unions and Politics: The Industrial Politics of the Early British Communist Party* (1975), 78pp.

47. J.F. Naylor's excellent book, *Labour's International Policy. The Labour Party in the 1930s* (1969) provides a brief survey of the twenties in his opening chapter. See also W.R. Tucker, *The Attitude of the British Labour Party towards European & Collective Security Problems, 1920-1939* (General, 1950) and H.R. Winkler, 'The Emergence of a Labor Foreign Policy in Great Britain, 1918-1929', *J. of Modern History*, Vol. 27 (September 1956). For the left inside and outside the Labour Party, R.E. Dowse, *Left in the Centre* (1966) has a short commentary on the foreign policy of the ILP, pp. 48-51, 96-9, 169-70; and for the Communist Party the most useful and detailed source are the 'Notes of the Month' in the *Labour Monthly*, which R. Palme Dutt wrote almost continuously. *Labour Monthly* was founded in 1921. See also S. Davis, 'The British Labour Party and British Foreign Policy, 1933-1939', (Ph.D., London, 1950).

48. E. Wertheimer, *Portrait of the Labour Party* (1929), pp. 188-9.

49. This is not to suggest that the years immediately following 1918 were empty of anti-war literature. One of the most powerful anti-war books ever published, C.E. Montague's *Disenchantment*, appeared in 1924.

50. There is an interesting discussion of the anti-war literature and its social and political effects in Corelli Barnett, *The Collapse of British Power* (1972), pp. 424ff. Mr Barnett misses the ineffable Beverley Nichols whose book, directed specifically towards a popular audience, had a striking response, but the other books listed in the text are taken from pp. 428-9.

51. Naylor, op. cit., p. 28. See also R. Bassett, *Democracy and Foreign Policy* (1952) for a more general analysis which is, however, by no means univer-

sally accepted.

52. H. Dalton, *The Fateful Years*, p. 45.

53. Quoted in R.F. Andrews, *The Labour Party and the Menace of War* (? 1934), p. 8.

54. Pseudonym for Andrew Rothstein, one of the foremost intellectuals of the Communist Party up to the present day, and especially noted as a specialist on Russia.

55. What makes the Andrews' quotation in the text so extraordinary is the evidence that was accumulating throughout 1933 and 1934 that the Soviet Union was moving slowly but steadily towards a major change in her foreign policy. Most diplomatic histories make the point; see, for example, W. Scott, *Alliance Against Hitler: The Origins of the Franco-Soviet Pact* (Durham, N.C., 1962).

56. D.C. Lukowitz, 'British Pacifists and Appeasement: The Peace Pledge Union', *J. Contemporary History*, Vol. 9, No. 1 (February 1974); L.R. Bisceglia, 'Norman Angell and the "Pacifist" Muddle', *Bulletin Institute of Historical Research*, XLV, No. 3 (May 1972).

57. See P.J. Noel-Baker, *The Private Manufacture of Armaments* (1936), *passim*.

58. The chairman of the Royal Commission on the Private Manufacture and Trading of Arms was the one-time judge, Sir John Eldon Bankes, aged 80 at the time of his appointment. Sir Philip Gibbs, the popular novelist, was a member, and his autobiography, *The Pageant of the Years* (1946), pp. 425-9, offers a few pages of rather superficial comment on the Commission's proceedings. Among the pamphlet literature, that published by the Union of Democratic Control was the most impressive. Dorothy Woodman, the secretary of the UDC, was indefatigable on this issue, as on so many others: see K. Martin, *Editor*, pp. 160-1 and C.H. Rolph, *Kingsley. The Life, Letters and Diaries of Kingsley Martin* (1973). The UDC's best-known pamphlets were *The Secret International* (1935) and *Patriotism Ltd* (1933). The CP published Harry Pollitt's evidence before the Commission in a penny pamphlet, *Dynamite in the Dock*.

59. Bullock, *Ernest Bevin*, Vol. 1, pp. 564-71. Kingsley Martin, *Editor*, p. 176, called it 'one of the most powerful speeches that I have heard'. Martin goes on to quote the often-repeated comment that Bevin is credited with having made after the debate: 'Lansbury has been going about dressed in saint's clothes for years waiting for martyrdom: I set fire to the faggots'.

60. Mowat, op. cit., pp. 542ff, esp. pp. 553-6; Miliband, op. cit., pp. 226-30. J.C. Robertson, 'The British General Election of 1935', *J. Contemporary History*, Vol. 9, No. 1 (February 1974). Mr Robertson's article clears up some problems, in particular the emphasis that leading Conservative Ministers gave to domestic rather than foreign affairs. He has some errors of facts (Cripps, for example, resigned from the EC of the Labour Party before, not after, the 1935 annual conference) but with Mr Robertson's conclusion I do not dissent: 'When the Government's treatment of the Ethiopian crisis in the election campaign is compared to the diplomatic situation, the official documents show beyond doubt that the electorate was misled. That such tactics robbed the Labour Party of victory, however, is very doubtful indeed.' (p. 164).

61. For a remarkably frank comment on the Hoare-Laval affair, see *Annual Register for 1935*, pp. 105-6.

62. Mowat, op. cit., pp. 475-6; see also below, note 72.

63. Dalton, *The Fateful Years*, p. 135.

64. Naylor, op. cit., Ch. 6 gives a detailed account; the Minutes of the Ad-

visory Committee on International Questions, Labour Party Archives, provide the necessary background information.

65. Labour Party Annual Report, 1937, pp. 196-7.

66. Ibid., p. 209.

67. The most powerful Marxist argument against the wrongheadedness of the left in the 1930s on this issue of rearmament is in Ralph Miliband, *Parliamentary Socialism* (1960), esp. pp. 220ff and Ch. 8. It is a book with which, apart from this important question of rearmament policy, I find myself in complete accord.

68. R.P. Dutt's speech is published in *For Peace and Plenty. Report of the Fifteenth Congress of the Communist Party of Great Britain . . .* 16-19 September 1938 (192pp.) pp. 88-92. Dutt's speech was headed 'The War Scare'.

69. The Labour Party abandoned non-intervention as an official policy in late October 1936; the TUC a year later.

70. Acceptance of a national campaign for Spain was one of the 'victories' with which the left comforted themselves at the 1937 Conference. A large meeting was organised in the Albert Hall, and then the campaign seems to have petered out: Foot, *Aneurin Bevan*, Vol. 1, p. 277.

71. *Manchester Guardian*, 23 March 1938.

72. The evidence is set out in the first chapter of A.S. Milward's *The German Economy at War* (1965).

73. An exaggeration that is, of course, understandable. It was much encouraged by pro-Fascist apologists such as Colonel Lindbergh.

74. This is a relative statement. The important issues in the 1920s were the Anglo-Russian treaties and the 1924 Labour government, the Zinoviev Letter campaign, and the Arcos Raid of 1927.

75. *Beatrice Webb's Diaries, 1924-1932* (Margaret Cole (ed.), 1956), pp. 307-8.

76. Employment, it must be reiterated, was never full employment. See above, Section III.

77. As the text goes on to note, the full list of pamphlets and books which gave a favourable view of Russia would be a very long one. One of the oddest, and a very special item for the collector of such pieces, is a 1933 pamphlet *The Drink Problem in Russia* by Thomas Murray, secretary of the Scottish Temperance Alliance and published by the United Kingdom Alliance. Its concluding sentence read: 'That astonishing things are happening in the Soviet Union no intelligent person will now deny, and not least astonishing is the undoubted success of the effort to wean the worker from the vodka bottle, that traditional curse of Russian manhood.'

78. There is an obituary notice of W.H. Chamberlin by D. von Mohrenschildt in *Russian Review*, Vol. 29, No. 1 (January 1970), pp. 1-5. There were, of course, many other critical comments on Russian policy available to contemporaries. Some, like the remarks on Sinkiang in Peter Fleming's *News from Tartary* (1936), in fairly unusual places.

79. *Plebs*, September 1936, pp. 211-12.

80. The classic statement on the acceptance of honours by members of the labour movement was R.H. Tawney's letter to the *New Statesman*, 22 June 1935.

81. The Stalin-Wells talk was published in *New Statesman*, 27 October 1934. It led to a famous exchange between Shaw and Wells.

82. *Inside Europe*, p. 443.

83. D. Watt, 'The Historiography of Appeasement', *Crisis and Controversy. Essays in Honour of A.J.P. Taylor* (1976), pp. 110-29.

84. H. Nicolson, *Diaries and Letters, 1931-39* (N. Nicholson (ed.)), p. 346.

85. As do most of the contributors to the symposium on the trials in *Survey*, No. 41 (April 1962).

86. The arrest of the employees of Metro-Vickers was on 12 March 1933; and their trial began a month later. The press coverage in Britain was enormous.

87. The literature on the Soviet Trials of the 1930s is immense. A selection of material would include: B. Nicolaevsky, *Power and the Soviet Elite* (1966), including the famous 'Letter of an old Bolshevik'; W. Lerner, *Karl Radek* (Stanford, 1970); R. Conquest, *The Great Terror* (Penguin ed., 1971); S.F. Cohen, *Bukharin and the Bolshevik Revolution* (1974), with an excellent bibliography. The three volumes by Isaac Deutscher which cover the life of Trotsky are indispensable.

88. See especially S.F. Cohen, *Bukharin*, Ch. 10, esp. pp. 372ff.

89. Voigt's discussion of the trials is in Ch. 9 esp. pp. 246ff, and his footnotes, pp. 341-8.

90. Conquest, op. cit., Ch. XI.

91. Lerner, in his biography of Radek, discusses briefly the Koestler thesis, and suggests other explanations: pp. 167ff.

92. The interview with Trotsky first appeared in *New Statesmen*, 10 April 1937; and Martin included extracts with additional commentary in *Editor*, Ch. XI.

93. I. Deutscher, *The Prophet Outcast. Trotsky: 1929-1940* (1963), p. 394.

94. The apologist literature of the Soviet trials was produced on a very large scale, and would be well worth serious evaluation. The standard Communist account, which went beyond the trials to an analysis of Trotskyism, was J.R. Campbell's *Soviet Policy and its Critics* (1939), published by the Left Book Club.

95. Davies, it should be noted, was in close daily touch with the American newspapermen who were covering the trials in 1937 and 1938. See his memorandum in *Mission to Moscow*, pp. 179ff.

96. F. Adler, *The Witchcraft Trials in Moscow* (1936).

97. In various places, including a well-known article in *Reynolds News*, 7 February 1937.

98. Emrys Hughes, throughout the period of the trials, conducted a principled editorial policy. He constantly criticised and refuted the apologists for the trials; reprinted articles by both Trotsky and Sedov, Trotsky's son; and at the same time opened his columns to advocates of the Soviet Union's position such as Zelda P. Coates and Peter Kerrigan.

99. R. Conquest, *The Great Terror*, pp. 670-1 is not wholly fair to the *New Statesman*, although his comment is only a brief one. The *New Statesman* did, in fact, publish a good deal of material that was sceptical and critical, and in the absence of hard evidence it could not have gone much further than it did. See the famous article of 30 January 1937, 'Will Stalin Explain'; and on May Day 1937, Kingsley Martin, under his own name, published a very long and favourable review of Andre Gide's *Back from the USSR*, a book that at the time was causing fury among Communist and pro-Soviet publicists. Martin's review was an important statement of the principles of socialism and liberty.

100. The correspondence on the trials in the *Manchester Guardian* would be worth evaluation. It included letters from Russian émigré's and leading members of Continental Social-Democracy, mostly from Paris addresses.

101. *Controversy* was an interesting journal, edited by C.A. Smith, at the time a leading figure inthe ILP and who later found a career in right-wing propagandist organisations. The journal was the first important literary 'breakthrough' of Trotskyist and 'Trotskysant' groups in the later thirties. See

also B. Pearce, 'The British Stalinists and the Moscow Trials', *Essays on the History of Communism in Britain* (M. Woodhouse and B. Pearce (eds.), 1975).

102. Isaac Deutscher, *The Prophet Outcast*, pp. 429ff, for a brief account of the emergence of a Trotskyist intellectual movement in America. In France it was rather more solidly based. See Victor Serge, *Mémoires d'un Révolutionnaire, 1901-1941* (Paris, 1951).

103. Reg Groves has begun to write his political recollections; see *The Balham Group. How British Trotskyism Began* (1974).

104. The history of Trotskyism in Britain is now (1976) slowly being written. The two main centres of documentation in public libraries, apart from the British Museum for printed literature, are the Library of the University of Hull and the Modern Records Centre, University of Warwick.

105. Deutscher, *The Prophet Outcast*, pp. 360ff. The names of the Commission of Inquiry are given on p. 371.

106. The secretary of the British Committee was Charles Sumner who for a time in 1938 was also secretary of the Revolutionary Socialist League, a unified Trotskyist organisation. I owe these facts to Mr Martin Upham. Mr Reg Groves has kindly sent me a Xerox of a leaflet advertising a meeting in the Memorial Hall, Farringdon Street, London, on 10 February 1937 calling for 'Justice for Leon Trotsky'. The speakers listed were Rowland Hill (President, Bradford Trades Council), Garry Allighan, Reg Groves, Harry Wicks, Henry Sara, Stewart Purkis and C.L.R. James.

107. L. Fischer, *Men and Politics* (1941), pp. 500-1.

108. R. Page Arnot, *The Miners in Crisis and War* (1961), pp. 236-40.

109. C.L. Mowat, *Britain Between the Wars*, p. 635.

110. A general point that Miliband in *Parliamentary Socialism* very properly emphasised. See, for example, his comments on p. 258.

111. *Labour Monthly*, November 1936, p. 671.

112. Miliband, op. cit., *passim*.

113. See the references above in note 3.

114. Bevin attended an unofficial Commonwealth Conference in the summer of 1938. He left Britain early in July and returned at the end of October. He came back full of high-minded, neo-imperialist ideas about the 'Commonwealth'.

115. Miliband, op. cit., pp. 249ff; Foot, *Aneurin Bevan*, pp. 243ff.

116. Foot, op. cit., pp. 276ff.

117. The most comprehensive statement of the case was by G.D.H. Cole, *The People's Front*, published in 1937 by the Left Book Club. For the last phase of the agitation, see Foot, op. cit., pp. 282ff.

118. Most of the Labour biographies and memoirs of this period make reference to the question of the leadership; see for example Dalton, *The Fateful Years*, Ch. XVI, and B. Donoughue and G.W. Jones, *Herbert Morrison* (1973), Ch. XVIII.

119. P. 55.

120. Dalton, op. cit., p. 213.

INDEX

Note: The operetta, *The Striker Stricken*, is not indexed. It will be found between pages 57-101.